The Discourses of Dispute Resolution

Linguistic Insights

Studies in Language and Communication

Edited by Maurizio Gotti,
University of Bergamo

Volume 123

PETER LANG
Bern · Berlin · Bruxelles · Frankfurt am Main · New York · Oxford · Wien

Vijay K. Bhatia, Christopher N. Candlin &
Maurizio Gotti (eds)

The Discourses of Dispute Resolution

PETER LANG
Bern · Berlin · Bruxelles · Frankfurt am Main · New York · Oxford · Wien

Bibliographic information published by Die Deutsche Nationalbibliothek
Die Deutsche Nationalbibliothek lists this publication in the Deutsche Nationalbibliografie; detailed bibliographic data is available on the Internet at ‹http://dnb.d-nb.de›.

British Library and Library of Congress Cataloguing-in-Publication Data:
A catalogue record for this book is available from *The British Library*, Great Britain.

Library of Congress Cataloging-in-Publication Data

The discourses of dispute resolution / Vijay K. Bhatia, Christopher N. Candlin & Maurizio Gotti (eds).
p. cm. – (Linguistic insights; studies in language and communication.)
ISBN 978-3-0343-0476-4 (alk. paper)
1. Dispute resolution (Law)–Language. I. Bhatia, V. K. (Vijay Kumar), 1942-
II. Candlin, Christopher. III. Gotti, Maurizio.
K2390.D57 2010
347'.09014–dc22

2010017560

This volume is part of a national research project on *Tension and Change in English Domain-Specific Genres* supported by the Italian Ministry of Education (COFIN Grant No. 2007JCY9Y9; for details see Website at <http://www.unibg.it/ cerlis/projects>) and is published under the auspices of the University of Bergamo, Dipartimento di Lingue, Letterature e Culture Comparate.
The work in this volume is also supported by an RGC CERG grant from The Government of Hong Kong SAR (Project No. CityU1051/06H) entitled, *International Arbitration Practice: A Discourse Analytical Study.* For details see Website at <http:/enweb.cityu.edu.hk/arbitrationpractice>.

ISSN 1424-8689
ISBN 978-3-0343-0476-4

Hochfeldstrasse 32, CH-3012 Bern, Switzerland
info@peterlang.com, www.peterlang.com, www.peterlang.net

Printed in Germany

Contents

Linguistic and discoursal features of dispute resolution

VIJAY K. BHATIA / CHRISTOPHER N. CANDLIN / MAURIZIO GOTTI

Introduction

1. The discourses of dispute resolution

Alternative dispute resolution (ADR) refers to all forms of dispute resolution mechanisms, either assisted by specialists in ADR or directly negotiated among the disputing parties, which fall outside of the jurisdictionally regulated process popularly known as litigation. Some of the major forms of ADR include conciliation, mediation and arbitration.

The parties at dispute may initially attempt to resolve the matter themselves, if they feel that the dispute is not too polarized, and where there exists some measure of trust and goodwill among the disputing parties. In such circumstances, the parties often try to arrive at direct conciliation with or without the help of a neutral internal or external facilitator. Conciliation thus primarily involves developing a suitable framework to encourage openness and a positive understanding between the parties at dispute. The job of a neutral conciliator is to facilitate such an understanding as a basis for the resolution of the dispute, by helping the parties to set up communicative channels, by means of these to clarify some of the main misunderstandings or issues, and to develop mutual trust among the parties. Conciliation may also be used in conjunction with other methods of ADR, particularly mediation. If conciliation fails to create an adequate environment of mutual trust and understanding, the parties may wish to explore other options of ADR, such as mediation, instead of going to the courts for litigation.

Mediation, once again, is a voluntary process, in which the disputing parties, with the help of a third party, who may or may not be a legal expert or a judge, seek to explore a mutually acceptable resolution of the dispute. This kind of assisted mediation process is generally evaluative, depending on the mutually acceptable procedures, and may be viewed as some kind of a litigative process with the aim of arriving at a preliminary evaluation of possible outcomes of the ADR.

Mediation may thus be viewed as an intervention by an impartial and neutral third party into a dispute in order to create conditions for a negotiated and acceptable resolution of the dispute, even though this third party often has no decision-making authority. The main objective of the mediator is to help the disputing parties by means of a voluntary alternative dispute resolution process to reach a mutually acceptable resolution of the dispute. Like conciliation, mediation is also voluntary and does not close off other options for dispute resolution, if the mediation fails. The mediation process may or may not result in a resolution of the dispute, but the process remains characteristically voluntary, private and confidential. A mediator, like a conciliator, makes procedural suggestions regarding how parties may reach agreement. A mediator may also propose some substantive options to encourage the parties to expand the range of possible resolutions under consideration. A mediator can work with the parties individually, or with both parties present, or a combination of both in a series, so as to generate interests and to explore options that address their interests.

Mediators differ widely in their degree of intervention. Often mediation does not only help the parties to resolve their present dispute, but may also create a constructive environment in which to develop mutual trust and improved relationship. The most important aspect of mediation is that the mediator does not intervene by directly suggesting a specific solution to the dispute, but only acts to assist the disputing parties to develop a suitable process that is acceptable to both, so that they can work towards a mutually agreeable resolution.

Mediators often draw on their expertise to involve the stakeholders to the dispute actively in the process, and hence may act as a neutral organizer of the interaction to help a diverse group of interested parties in resolving complex issues in mutually amicable and acceptable manner. However, if and when mediation fails to bring the disputing parties to an acceptable and amicable resolution of the dispute, the next option open to them is arbitration, which despite its increasingly interventionist character, nonetheless remains still private and confidential and remains inspired by a mutual agreement to resolve the dispute in question outside of the court.

In arbitration, parties or their representatives, often legal counsels, present a dispute to an impartial single arbitrator or an arbitration tribunal consisting of more than one member (often three or another odd number depending on the nature, extent and size of the dispute) so as to resolve the dispute and order a decision, which is similar to a legal judgment, but in ADR is conventionally known as an award. Unlike other forms of ADR, i.e., conciliation and mediation, which do not suggest or impose any specific decision to resolve the dispute, arbitration is explicitly intended to issue a decision or award which is often binding for the disputing parties. As such, an arbitral award is generally non-appealable in a court of law. In arbitration, the parties at dispute have considerable input in the selection of the members of the arbitration tribunal, and also in the choice of processes and procedures they would like the tribunal to follow, including the choice of language, the seat of arbitration, as well as the arbitration laws within which the resolution of the dispute is to be negotiated.

Arbitration is thus the most appropriate form of ADR when the disputing parties fail to reach any agreement to resolve their dispute, say by the processes of conciliation and mediation on their own, or with the help of a neutral mediator, and require in consequence a third party to determine the resolution of their dispute, while at the same time wishing to avoid the time and expense of litigation where they would have absolutely no influence or control over the decision-making process. As mentioned earlier, the decision of the arbitration tribunal is enforceable, and cannot be challenged in a court of law, except under a very restricted set of conditions. So, the main advantage of arbitration is that it is like litigation in effect, in that it is decided by a neutral third party, but unlike litigation, it is intended to be more informal, expedient, economical, private and confidential in nature, while at the same time giving sufficient voice and freedom to disputing parties in the way it is actually conducted. For some of these reasons, some specialists call it 'private litigation'.

Various forms of ADR have been increasingly gaining acceptance both from the point of view of the disputing parties as well as that of the legal community. Disputing parties feel, rightly or wrongly, that they can thereby save on precious time and money, and the legal community have found ADR a significant means of extending their professional calling and augmenting their business income. There is also a considerable support for ADR on the part of the judiciary because they find it a useful resource to cut down the excessive case-load prevalent in the courts of most jurisdictions, so much so that some courts have started instructing disputing parties to go for ADR before coming to courts for their dispute resolution.

Despite the recent popularity of ADR, its practices are not without problems. Although ADR is generally regarded as an economical and effective alternative to litigation for settling disputes, it has been commonly observed that ADR as non-legal practice is being increasingly influenced by the practices and procedures of litigation, a development which seems to be contrary to the spirit of ADR, and of arbitration in particular, to resolve disputes outside of the courts. Nariman (2000: 262) points out that "International Commercial Arbitration as practised has become almost indistinguishable from litigation, which it was at one time intended to supplant". In a similar manner, Marriott (2000: 354) writes:

> Although the 1996 Act gave arbitrators very considerable power over the running of an arbitration and greater confidence in their autonomy, my sense is that they are not really producing radically new procedures more efficient and prompt than hitherto. The English passive tradition dies hard and self-interest is a dominant factor. The practitioners dominate the arbitral processes.

In order to study the extent to which ADR and its various practices today are being dominated and even 'colonised' by litigative practices, an international initiative has been undertaken by a group of specialists in discourse analysis, law, and arbitration from more than twenty countries, who have been studying ADR practices, in particular, international commercial arbitration practice. The project in question[1] draws on discourse-based data (narrative, documentary, interactional)

---

1 The project in question is supported by an RGC CERG grant from the Government of Hong Kong SAR (Project No. CityU1051/06H) entitled *International Arbitration Practice: A Discourse Analytical Study*. For details see Website: <http://enweb.cityu.edu.hk/arbitrationpractice>.

to investigate the extent to which the 'integrity' of arbitration principles is maintained in international commercial arbitration practice, and to what extent there is an increasing level of influence from litigative processes and procedures over arbitration practice. The primary evidence for such practices comes from textual and discourse-based studies, ethnographic observations, and narratives of experience on the part of experts in the field, as well as on the part of some of the major corporate stakeholders drawn from commercial sectors.

The present volume presents some of the findings from this project on various aspects of ADR, including conciliation, mediation, and arbitration practices.

2. Contents of the volume

Many of the issues presented above are investigated in the various chapters of this volume. To facilitate a comparison of the perspectives taken by the authors, their contributions are grouped into two parts, each of which highlights specific aspects of the discourses of dispute resolution.

2.1. Dispute resolution across media and cultures

The first section of the volume deals with contributions concerning the realization of the discourses of dispute resolution across various media and among different cultures. GIULIANA GARZONE's chapter is based on a research conducted jointly with Paola Catenaccio (whose results are illustrated in the following chapter), and explores the communication practices of arbitral institutions as carried out through the modality of their websites. As the Internet has evolved to be one of the most important informative channels for such institutions, communication through the web has become of particular interest because of the role it plays in the discursive construction of arbitration and mediation in contemporary society. In particular, this chapter focuses on a comparative analysis of the communicative strategies enacted in the presentation of arbitration and mediation by four important European arbitration centres and aims at finding similarities and differences in the overall discursive profiles of their websites in terms of semiotic organization, strategies deployed, and intended recipients. As regards methodology, the study relies primarily on discourse analysis, also applying notions specifically developed within genre analysis, as well as principles drawn on in recent studies on multimodality. The analysis highlights a dynamic relationship existing between website construction and discursive practices deployed on the one hand, and the operational profile of each of the four institutions examined on the other, a relationship which is shown to result from a whole range of institutional, social, legal, and marketing variables as well as from the intended audience addressed in each case. These same variables also help account for the remarkable differences in terms of deployment of technological affordances.

PAOLA CATENACCIO's chapter is a companion study to the previous one by Garzone, and takes its lead from the findings of that research to delve deeper into the informative materials published online by major arbitration institutions, with a view to analysing the way in which arbitration and mediation are discursively constructed as alternatives to judicial adjudication. A starting point for the study is the recognition that over the last few years a marked increase in recourse to arbitration has been accompanied by a progressive institutionalisation (often with legal undertones) of arbitration procedures. These developments have been argued to be leading to a blurring of boundaries between the discourse of arbitration and the discourse of litigation, and to the progressive 'colonisation' of arbitration practices on the part of litigation procedures. The study sets out specifically to address this issue, investigating the way in which arbitration and other forms of alternative dispute resolution are framed *vis-à-vis* litigation. By analysing the discursive strategies adopted in each of the websites examined to deal with various forms of dispute resolution along the arbitration – mediation – ADR continuum, the investigation shows that, in spite of considerable variation, in the majority of the websites there is an obvious effort to differentiate arbitration from litigation, in some cases explicitly, through explanation and comparison, or through direct argumentation, or more implicitly simply describing the advantages of arbitration in operational terms. If arbitration is typically pitched against litigation, mediation is set against the background of arbitration – or, more often, of arbitration *and* litigation. While the perceived graduation in terms of formality between mediation and arbitration, and between arbitration and litigation, justifies the use of this comparative strategy, the close association between arbitration and litigation often entailed in the description of mediation has the effect of pushing arbitration towards the litigation end of the continuum, thus corroborating the hypothesis that the domain of arbitration is being colonised by litigation.

The relationship between litigation and arbitration is also investigated by STEFANIA M. MACI, who mainly concentrates on the Italian context. Relying on a textual analysis of some Italian awards, the investigation reveals that in these texts syntactic patterns typical of legal language are exploited to the full. The reason for this lies in the fact that such awards are compiled by legal experts who express their legal voice, despite their issuing awards for laymen wishing for clear resolutions in the matter of their disputes. This seems to suggest that international arbitration in Italy encourages the exploitation of litigation features particularly in the discourse of awards. Although the 2006 Italian Reform of Arbitration apparently aligns Italy with the UNCITRAL Model Law, which calls for harmonization of the arbitral practices within the international context, the Reform actually reflects the different legal culture underlying Italian arbitration.

ANNE WAGNER investigates International Commercial Arbitration procedures in France and shows how they provide fertile ground for the resolution of conflicts between the parties involved. The aim of her chapter is to better apprehend and comprehend the true ambit of French International Arbitration by taking into account not only the explicit cross-cultural environment but also the straightforward regulations set up for this practice. Her analysis shows that where arbitrators may arrive at a conclusion they have a wide range of remedies at their disposal. Nevertheless, owing to the flexibility of interpretation associated with the concept of equity, the task of devolving decision-making to the amicable context of dispute resolution is a precarious one because it requires the counterbalancing of many variables in order to achieve a fair arbitration award.

OLGA DENTI and MICHELA GIORDANO analyse premarital agreements, a type of document with which couples contemplating marriage prepare for possible future divergences in their married life, describing the rights and duties of the parties in the case of termination of marriage as a result of divorce. This study investigates premarital agreements in an intercultural perspective, comparing the linguistic features of American 'prenups' with Spanish *capitulaciones matrimoniales*. In American culture, prenuptial agreements represent a type of mediation within the framework of ADR meant to resolve disputes other than through litigation, and they include provisions regarding post-nuptial disagreements in order especially to handle the financial aspects arising in the case of any divorce. Instead, in Spanish culture, which is mainly Catholic, *capitulaciones matrimoniales* or *acuerdos prematrimoniales* have been traditionally intended as economic and patrimonial pacts with the purpose of adding a supplementary agreement to a marriage in order to determine its economic conditions distinctive to that of a legal arrangement. From a linguistic point of view, the chapter compares the textual organization and lexical choices adopted in the documents under scrutiny to illustrate examples of legal discourse in various cultures regulated by and through different legal systems.

LARISSA D'ANGELO's chapter analyses the Online Dispute Resolution (ODR) practice in Italy and compares it with traditional forms of arbitration, litigation and mediation. ODR is a fairly new and recent way of dealing with disputes, which is slowly making its appearance on the Italian commercial scene. Although it is considered a faster and cheaper tool and one which overcomes geographical barriers, parties still seem to prefer the traditional mediation and arbitration practice. Experts believe that this is due to cultural barriers and to the fact that in an ODR procedure it is more difficult to establish authority. Moreover, a certain familiarity with long distance communication media is necessary. In order to evaluate the cultural and linguistic characteristics of this phenomenon, the author compares a number of Italian ODR procedures to a corpus comprising arbitration, litigation and mediation cases in Italian.

2.2. Linguistic and discoursal features of dispute resolution

The second section of the volume comprises investigations of dispute resolution texts in order to identify their main linguistic and discoursal features. CELINA FRADE's chapter mainly focuses on arbitration clauses present in a number of multilingual ready-made model types of contracts designed to be used by the parties as a frame of reference. Frade's analysis shows that arbitration clauses are not as simple as heretofore in that they are becoming increasingly complex and multi-tiered due to the detailed specification of a series of interrelated steps the parties need to go through before finally indicating a choice for arbitration. On the legal level, drafters should therefore make their best efforts to avoid ill-suited, equivocal or unhappily drafted clauses – also called 'pathological clauses' – which may result in another dispute and/or litigation between the parties (and even invalidity of the arbitration agreement by the arbitral tribunal) arising out of poor drafting. Furthermore, linguistic 'pathologies' and inadequate and/or inaccurate translation from multilingual versions to English versions may increase the cost and duration of arbitration due to misunderstandings, errors and ambiguities. This chapter identifies some of these linguistic 'pathologies' in standard model clauses produced by international arbitral institutions. The claim is that such linguistically defective clauses may jeopardize some of the advantages of arbitration and should therefore be avoided by drafters and translators. Besides raising legal drafters/translators' awareness of these 'pathologies', the chapter also provides some guidelines to be followed in the process of drafting a clear and proper arbitration clause.

The importance of writing clear and convincing legal texts in an arbitration procedure is also emphasised by MICHELE SALA. According to him, legal experts should possess the linguistic competence not only to discuss concepts in ways that are appropriate to legal contexts but also to formulate decisions which have the impact and deontic force of normative acts by drawing on linguistic and rhetorical choices that are typical of this legal procedure. The author investigates to what extent, and through which discursive resources, arbitrators interpret and transform the conciliatory nature of arbitration. Based on a corpus of 20 commercial awards, the analysis examines the argumentative and interdiscursive strategies used by the drafters to express epistemic and interactive meanings in order to confer efficacy and definitiveness to their pronouncements, and to give deontic value to the whole text.

CHIARA DEGANO also focuses on arbitration awards to investigate, in particular, their use of indicators of argumentation. Starting from the assumption that recourse to argumentation is a distinguishing feature of litigative discourse – and in particular of judgments – as a consequence of the courts' need to justify their decisions, the author evaluates the presence of this feature in arbitration texts. The analysis relies on a corpus of international awards spanning over two decades, from which indicators of argumentation are retrieved with a view to verifying whether their use has increased over time. This quantitative analysis is then integrated with qualitative analysis, carried out through close reading of selected texts, in order to back up quantitative findings with insights at the lexico-grammatical and textual level. The analysis shows a marked increase in the recourse to argumentative strategies in arbitration awards over time and this provides evidence of the increasing influence of litigation in this field.

PATRIZIA ANESA's analysis explores Italian domestic arbitration in order to identify the principal linguistic and communicative strategies that are employed in the proceedings, mainly in the party examination phase. The data chosen for analysis are drawn from audio-recorded instances of authentic arbitration proceedings that took place in Italy in recent years. The chapter offers a description of the specific communicative events involved and their institutional nature, to comply with a clear set of conventions and to respect the professional communicative norms that characterize the field and its customary rhetorical features. From a linguistic perspective, the study focuses on turn-taking sequences and describes the partially pre-established nature of the allocation of such turns. Particular attention is devoted to the fundamental role played by the arbitrator in determining the selection of speakers and the structure of interactional sequences. The chapter identifies and explores some of the most significant linguistic dynamics present in the arbitrations under study and shows their complexity in the key area of party examination.

GIROLAMO TESSUTO's study investigates commercial arbitration rules and mediation procedures coded on the web by the American Arbitration Association. The qualitative and quantitative analysis in this study focuses on the main linguistic and discoursal features that shape the rhetorical actions of this 'regulatory' genre in a conventionalized professional setting. It does so by providing a description of the genre as it results from the use of macro and micro-level resources in the writing practice. The exploitation of generic resources in response to the social expectations, interests and values of genre producers and their intended audiences, leads the author to identify the degree of discursive features and identity shared by the current genre and legislative writing in general, whether or not dealing with similar topics of the law.

The aim of ALESSANDRA FAZIO's study is to verify whether the use of English as a lingua franca in sports arbitration influences the formal use of the specific terminology, which, it is assumed, has already been standardized and harmonized. Italian sports arbitrators using English in an international setting were observed in a preliminary study. Reiterated language patterns were noticed which differed from those used by their mother-tongue counterparts. Taking into account the language Italian sports arbitrators use in international settings as a starting point, similar language patterns are analysed with particular emphasis on socio-cultural factors. The analysis shows that it is possible to determine a specific linguistic code (even though informal) capable of affecting the formal patterns in use. Both complex strings and terms, as well as additional linguistic occurrences, are then analyzed in order to trace underlying connections that influence their use.

3. Concluding remarks

There are a number of perspectives from which the chapters in this edited collection have more general relevance than is indicated from an observation of their discourse analytical and genre-based studies in particular sites. These perspectives focus principally on the construct of *interdiscursivity* as an increasingly central theme, not only in the domain of legal discourse, but in applied linguistic and discourse analytic work more generally.

Firstly, the chapters evidence the extent to which the discourses of dispute resolution now constitute an intimate and reflexive network of discourses within, and among which there is considerable contestation and professional struggle. This *interdiscursivity* is marked not only by once distinctive but now increasingly blurred professional practices, but by a concomitant melding and creating of new discursive practices, generating what may now be properly called an overarching Discourse of Dispute Resolution (Candlin/Maley 1997, Gee 1999).

At the same time, and as a consequence of this blurring of boundaries, both professional and discursive, exploring this Discourse requires contributions from, and, desirably, cooperation among, the professional partners in our discourse analytic enterprise: lawyers, mediators, conciliators, arbitrators, legal counsel, as well as public and private stakeholders outside the broad legal community. This is itself an *interdiscursive* exercise of some significance but also of some challenge to researchers.

Thirdly, and now centrally from our perspective in this volume, exploring such professional *interdiscursivity* requires the engagement of discourse and genre analysts, themselves from distinctive disciplinary backgrounds, coming together in a common descriptive, interpretive and explanatory enterprise. As Sarangi and Candlin (2001) emphasise, accounting for the distinctive *motivational relevancies* (including here both those of the discourse analysts *and* of their professional 'partners') lies at the heart of what we see as a future guiding principle for applied linguistic and discourse analytical practice.

This, in turn, is at the base of a fourth, methodological, perspective on i*nterdiscursivity*. As the chapters amply signal, authors bring a range of different toolboxes to their analytic task, and, moreover, select distinctive and appropriate tools from them, relevant to their analytical purposes, but also in line with the legitimate interests and expectations of their professional collaborators, for whom the results of the research are paramount.

Finally, all that has been emphasised above in relation to *inter-discursivity* is by no means limited to the domains of law and legal practice. The relevance is quite general across the broad sweep of domains and sites, ensuring that the chapters in this volume extend in their significance, *beyond dispute*.

References

Candlin, Christopher N. / Maley, Yon 1997. Intertextuality and Interdiscursivity in the Discourse of Alternative Dispute Resolution. In Gunnarsson, Britt-Louise / Linell, Per / Nordberg, Bengt (eds) *The Construction of Professional Discourse*. London: Longman.

Gee, James P. 1999. *An Introduction to Discourse Analysis: Theory and Method*. London: Routledge.

Marriott, Arthur 2000. Less is More: Directing Arbitration Procedures. *Arbitration International* 16/3, 353-356.

Nariman, Fali S. 2000. The Spirit of Arbitration: The Tenth Annual Goff Lecture. *Arbitration International* 16/3, 261-278.

Sarangi, Srikant / Candlin, Christopher N. 2001. Motivational Relevancies: Some Methodological Reflections on Sociolinguistic Practice. In Coupland, Nikolas / Sarangi, Srikant / Candlin, Christopher N. (eds) *Sociolinguistics and Social Theory*. London. Pearson.

Dispute resolution across media and cultures

GIULIANA GARZONE

Promoting Arbitration and Mediation on the Web

1. Introduction

In the last few years, as recourse to arbitration to settle disputes has become ever more frequent, there has been an increase in the amount of informative material about arbitration and other forms of ADR made available by arbitral institutions around the world to inform/ persuade potential clients of the advantages of these kinds of dispute resolution over litigation. This form of communication was originally effected by means of brochures, with very limited circulation, reaching only those who were already interested and aware of the options. Only relatively recently, thanks to the increasing importance of the Web as a medium, has it taken the form of a real information effort addressed to an ever wider audience.

The different semiotic configuration of the institutions' informative materials due to the shift to a web-based Hypermedia Computer Mediated Environment (HCME: Hoffman/Novak 1996) and to the extension of the audience addressed has involved the revision of the materials used for communication (texts and graphics), if not the drafting of totally new materials to meet the requirements of Web design. Through their websites, arbitration institutions present themselves and the services they offer to a potentially global audience, although of course their target addressees belong to limited interest groups, essentially businesses – from the sole trader to multinational corporations – and public and private organizations. In consequence, the analysis of the discourses they deploy on their websites can help shed light not only on the particular audience (cf. Perelman/Olbrechts-Tyteca 1969: 19-20) they are aimed at, but also on how they operate and how they represent themselves and their activities.

Starting from these considerations, the research presented in this chapter, which links up with that carried out by Paola Catenaccio in her chapter in this volume, explores some specific areas which are deemed to be of particular interest because of the role they play in the discursive construction of arbitration and mediation in the contemporary world. In particular, this study focuses on a comparative analysis of the communicative strategies enacted in the presentation of arbitration and mediation by some important European arbitration centres with a view to finding similarities and differences in their overall discursive profiles in terms of semiotic organization, strategies deployed, and intended recipients, identifying the possible factors that determine such variations, with special attention given to the interplay between the HCME and the communicative strategies enacted.

1.1. Study design

This chapter explores the discourses of arbitration/mediation as they are realised in the websites of arbitration institutions and on the use of multimodal affordances, looking not only at communication aimed at insiders but also on the strategies deployed by such institutions in communication to the public at large. It is based on a research conducted by the author in collaboration with Paola Catenaccio (cf. her chapter in this volume) as part of the National Research Programme *Tension and Change in Domain-specific Genres* funded by the Italian Ministry of University.[1] It also brings together two other strands of research in which Garzone and Catenaccio are involved, one concerning arbitration/ADR, within the general framework of an international project on international commercial arbitration, the other focusing on institutional communication to the general public as part of a project on public and institutional communication.[2]

---

1 *Programma di Rilevante Interesse Nazionale* nr. 2007JCY9Y9 – 2007, directed by Maurizio Gotti.

2 The arbitration project is sponsored by the RGC (HKSAR) and the City University of Hong Kong and is directed by Vijay K. Bhatia (<http://www.english.cityu.edu.hk/ arbitration/>). The research programme on public com-

The starting point is the analysis of the websites[3] of four European arbitral institutions operating internationally. In selecting such sites, care was taken to include organizations based in different countries, with different histories and traditions, so as to offer a snapshot of the various types of websites found in the extensive arbitral institution landscape. Besides meeting this requirement of international-status, the criteria adopted for the selection were: 1) that the institution deals with international *commercial* arbitration, and 2) that it operates with private interlocutors (and not, or not only, with governments and institutions).

Among the various websites that met these criteria, four major European centres were identified, including the two leading and oldest institutions (ICC and LCIA), both established as global actors, and two smaller centres also acting internationally but on a more 'regional' basis, which seemed to be particularly representative:

- the International Court of Arbitration of the International Chamber of Commerce (ICC) (<http://www.iccwbo.org/>);
- the London Court of International Arbitration (LCIA) (<http://www.lcia-arbitration.com/>);
- the SCC Institute – Arbitration Institute of the Stockholm Chamber (<http://www.sccinstitute.com/uk/Home/>);
- the Milan National and International Arbitration Chamber (Camera Arbitrale nazionale e internazionale di Milano) (<http://www.camera-arbitrale.it>).

Although on the surface these four websites do belong to the same (macro-)genre, the profound and immediately perceptible differences among them lead us to believe that they actually have divergent communicative aims, albeit slightly, and do not address exactly the same audiences.

---

munication, directed by Giuliana Garzone, is entitled *Lingua e discorso nella comunicazione pubblica* [Language and Discourse in Public Communication], and was funded in 2008 by Università degli Studi di Milano.

3 All websites were last accessed on December 20, 2009.

1.2. Aims and method

As its aim is to identify shared features and diverging characteristics of the websites analysed, this chapter combines a descriptive approach – used initially to provide a brief overview of the communicative and discursive coordinates of the various sites – with a more strictly analytical one. From a methodological point of view, the analysis relies primarily on discourse analysis, also applying notions specifically developed within genre analysis (Swales 1990; Bhatia 1993, 2004), as well as on principles drawn from recent studies on multimodality (Kress/van Leeuwen 2001, 2006; Garzone 2007). Wherever useful, this is supported by recourse to data obtained by means of automatic text interrogation routines (Scott 2004: *WordSmith Tools 4.0*).

While all websites offer a set of 'basic' authentic documents and texts concerning their activities, i.e. Arbitration Rules and Mediation Rules or Procedures, together with the relative schedules of costs and recommended clauses, etc. (mostly in pdf format), attention is focused here on the main sections of the websites illustrating the institutions, the way they function, and the arbitration/ADR services they offer, all of which are organized differently by each single institution and vary greatly from case to case, as will be illustrated below. These materials have also been collected and organized into four small corpora, to make computer analysis possible.

Based on the above, the study essentially aims at (i) providing a semiotic evaluation of each website by means of multimodal analysis; (ii) examining the communicative practices deployed, especially in relation to the way in which they exploit the affordances of the web-mediated environment (Agre 1995), in light of the websites' intended audience; (iii) evaluating their effectiveness in terms of the two main purposes arbitral institutions' websites are intended to serve, i.e. provide preliminary information for anyone who intends to take advantage of arbitration/mediation or considers the possibility of doing so, or of inserting an arbitration clause in a contract, and inform the public at large about the advantages of arbitration/mediation, promoting an awareness of the availability of these forms of dispute resolution.

The chapter is organised as follows. First, a brief overview of the general characteristics of the four websites under investigation will be given and their generic structure outlined, discussing the way it is realised in each of them in terms of web design and multimodal affordances (Sections 2 and 2.1). Secondly, the materials available on the sites will be analysed from a discourse-analytical perspective, with a view to identifying the core features of the promotional discourse about ADR, identifying commonalities and differences among the various institutions (Section 3). Finally, in light of the results of the general analysis conducted in the first three sections, in Section 4 attention will focus more specifically on the first two moves of the website's structure (*Establishing credentials of the arbitration institution* and *Describing the structure of the institution and how it works*) in order to offer a complete account of the self presentation strategies enacted by the institutions in their communication to the public. Some closing considerations will follow in Section 5.

2. Web-mediated communication about arbitration and mediation: an overview

In this section, which is essentially aimed at exploring the communicative approach characterizing each website, as well as the use it makes of the affordances of the web environment, I rely essentially on notions developed within the framework of multimodal analysis (Kress/van Leeuwen 2001).

Among the websites considered, the ICC Court is unique in that, although it is accessible also directly, it is part of the much larger website of its parent institution, the Paris International Chamber of Commerce (ICC) (<http://www.iccwbo.org/>) – 'the world business organization' as it presents itself in the caption accompanying its logo. The other institutions have a self-standing website, even if the Milan National and International Arbitration Chamber (<http://www.camera-arbitrale.it>) is part of the Milan Chamber of Commerce (<www.mi.

camcom.it>), and the Arbitration Institute of the Stockholm Chamber of Commerce is a separate entity within the Stockholm Chamber of Commerce (<http://www.chamber.se>). Despite being embedded in a larger hypertextual structure, however, the ICC website is perfectly comparable to the websites of the other institutions, being self-contained as the communication tool of a separate arbitration body (although, as we shall see, its embeddedness is in some respects meaningful).

The contents of the four websites vary greatly, although all of them do offer access to the basic authentic documents and texts concerning their activities, as already described above (cf. §2.1). If in addition to these documents the SCC website features only two concise texts to present briefly the Institute (231 words) and the Mediation Institute (126 words), all the other institutions devote some words to introducing arbitration and mediation in general and/or arbitration and mediation as conducted by the institution itself, either with brief texts (e.g. respectively 226 and 157 words in the case of the Milan Arbitration Chamber) or with longer texts (LCIA), sometimes made accessible in more than one version through distinct navigation paths and links, also comparing arbitration with litigation (ICC). Furthermore, each website illustrates some additional aspects specific to the institution, e.g. ICC has a section devoted to its own Dispute Board, Expertise and DOCDEX (Credit Dispute Resolution Expertise)[4] services, LCIA also presents its Fundholding Service and its joint venture with the new Dubai International Financial Centre (DIFC), the Milan Chamber also has sections devoted to its Online Mediation Service (RisolviOnline), its Studies Centre on ADR (a documentation service) and its ICBMC (Italy-China Business Mediation Centre), a Chamber of Mediation for the resolution of commercial disputes among Italian and Chinese companies, while SCC has in the central column of its homepage an update on the main events – conferences, seminars, courses, etc. – regarding arbitration and ADR.

---

4 ICC's DOCDEX (Credit Dispute Resolution Expertise) is a service taking care of settling letter of credit disputes.

From a genre-theory perspective, the materials featured in the websites appear to realise four distinct rhetorical moves, which can be summed up as follows:

- *Establishing credentials of the arbitration institution.*
- *Describing the structure of the institution and how it works.*
- *Introducing arbitration.*
- *Introducing ADR/mediation.*

Three of these moves appear in all four sites, while – as will be seen in Paola Catenaccio's chapter – the fourth constitutive move, *Introducing arbitration*, does not occur in the SCC website, which presents itself as a "leading arbitration institution" and refers to its Arbitration Rules, but does not devote any textual attention to presenting arbitration itself, presumably considering it unnecessary.

2.1. Website construction

In this section, the technical aspects of the construction of the four websites are investigated in terms of web design. Broadly speaking, the results of this analysis are in line with the more superficial macroscopic differences identified in the general overview outlined in Section 2. In particular, they reveal substantial variation in terms of Web design and 'granularity', i.e. in the way materials are 'parcelled out' into pages and the texts are displayed. These aspects of text structuring have a strong impact on the conditions of fruition on the part of users, influencing their choice between the two modes available, i.e. the navigation mode and the reading mode (Sosnoski 1999: 135; Askehave/Ellerup Nielsen 2004, 2005).

The LCIA website is characterized by an overwhelming prevalence of the reading mode. It consists only of five main 'scrolling' pages each containing a very large quantity of text (e.g. in the 'Alternative Dispute Resolution' page there are 814 words, and as many as 5,202 words in the 'About LCIA' page), divided into titled sections, although the site offers the possibility of accessing the various sections without reading the whole text through, simply by clicking on links displayed in the left column of the screen with a hypertext-like effect. Hotwords in the text lead to new shorter pages illustrating a specific aspect (e.g. the Institution's history) or giving access to basic resources, and in particular Arbitration Rules (including model clauses and costs) with a choice between the html or the pdf formats (languages: English, French, Italian, Spanish, German, Russian, Arabic, Chinese, Portuguese). Similarly, access is given also to Mediation Procedure Rules and their relative recommended clauses together with a schedule of costs. Although this organization is obviously not conceived for Web publication, there is an evident effort to adapt text to the basic rules of Web writing by not displaying it across the full width of the screen, but only in a narrow central column, and in breaking it down into short titled sections, and each section into short spaced paragraphs. However, for the visitor to this website there is hardly any option apart from the reading mode. This is confirmed by the scant recourse to visual resources, which are virtually absent: apart from the picture of a planisphere featuring on the homepage, the pages are totally taken up by text in black print displayed on a blue-gray background.

A similarly austere graphic organization, made only slightly more colourful by the red-brown links but much more streamlined, is presented by the Milan Arbitration Chamber website, which is characterized by a relatively simple overall construction. Each single topic (arbitration, mediation, etc.) is dealt with on one page, in a limited amount of text, and in each case a series of links are given to all the documents relating to the topic itself, with the materials arranged in orderly sequences. The interface – while making adequate use of the affordances of the hypertext format – is rather straightforward, with information being presented in suitably short 'lexias'[5] that can be expanded on demand.

---

5 The term 'lexia' refers to the alphabetic-text units in Internet communication, i.e. the graphically separated blocks, often coinciding with paragraphs and usually connected to each other in a network, into which text is divided on webpages. As the word was originally introduced in French by Barthes (1970/1974) as *lexie*, it is sometimes borrowed as it is into English, but here preference is given to *lexia,* the translation used by Landow in his seminal book (1997), because through his work this term has become established as a technical term in the specialized literature.

As far as the SCC website is concerned, as noted earlier, this is even more streamlined, with only two pages, one devoted to arbitration and one to mediation, and with all basic documents branching off from each of them. The simplicity of the SCC site is so extreme that it verges on scantiness, with only essential information being provided besides the 'basic' documents common to all the websites.

This simplified structure stands in sharp contrast to the constructive complexity of the website of the ICC Court, which features a well-designed homepage, with five iconic pictures illustrating its main branches (International Court of Arbitration, ADR, Dispute Boards, Expertise, DOCDEX) each accompanied by an introductory text alternating with the relevant links. The text relative to every single branch is broken down into pages, each devoted to a single topic and accessible through an index. This organization is highly hypertextual, and consultation of the website requires the user to navigate his way through a range of actions.

Another meaningful aspect is the way the 'short texts' and the 'very short texts'[6] in each website are formulated. In the ICC website, in addition to links consisting of noun phrases, e.g. *Arbitration today*, *More advantages of arbitration*, etc., there are many links introducing crucial elements that are formulated more interpersonally, for instance by means of a direct question (*What is ICC arbitration? What is ICC ADR?* and *Who can benefit?*) or an indirect one (*How it works*) or an imperative (*Tailor arbitration to your needs*). These features indicate a clear intention to activate the interpersonal function, with a phatic or conative/directive approach realised respectively by questions and (by) imperatives.

This intention to engage with the user is not found in the other three websites: in the case of the SCC Institute all short texts are purely nominal (*About the SSC*, *Mediation Institute*, *Rules,* etc.) with the exception of the text of the link leading to the cost calculator, which is clearly directive: *Calculate the cost.*

---

6 Here the expression 'very short texts' is used as a term referring to the so called 'microcontent' of websites (e.g. page titles, sub-titles, links, etc.) and in particular to links (cf. Nielsen 2000).

The texts of links in the LCIA website consist exclusively of noun phrases, sometimes also including non-finite verb forms, e.g. *Managing costs and delay*, *Commencing the mediation*, etc., while all links in the Milan Chamber website consist essentially of noun phrases, with the exception of two full interrogative sentences embodying two of the main questions that may arise when someone considers the possibility of making recourse to arbitration or mediation: respectively, *Which kind of disputes* [can arbitration be applied to]? *Who can benefit from mediation?*

2.2. Discursive approaches: general considerations

These different linguistic/pragmatic choices are consistent with the variation in the overall discursive approach adopted by each of the websites, as confirmed by a close analysis of the texts featured in each of them. The ICC site is the only one where there is some substantial use of the pronoun *you* and its associated possessive adjective *your*, which are obvious indicators of interpersonality and interactivity, with respectively 20 and 15 entries. There are four occurrences of *you* and three of *your* in the Milan Chamber website, while these words do not appear at all in the other two websites.

It is also interesting to see the contexts where these pronouns and adjectives appear in the two relevant websites. In the ICC website the second person pronoun is used when the advantages of arbitration and of ADR are discussed (e.g. to answer such questions as *Who can benefit? Why ICC arbitration?*), or when the procedures and conditions of their application are considered (e.g. to explain how you can *Tailor arbitration to your needs*), and this is obviously the result of the choice of illustrating the advantages of arbitration not in general or abstract terms, but by referring them to the personal/existential dimension of the virtual addressee. By contrast, the LCIA and the SCC websites opt for a much more impersonal approach – more noticeable in the case of the LCIA, as the conciseness of SCC makes this choice less meaningful and less amenable to extensive analysis – with the Milan site featuring both impersonal and interpersonal elements.

The rationale underlying the discursive strategy deployed by ICC stands out when the texts appearing on its website are compared with those of LCIA, where – as observed above – all information and arguments are presented in exclusively impersonal terms, e.g. by making consistent recourse to passives or nominalizations, or by using the 'impersonal' subject *the parties*. Compare the way each of the two websites introduces the idea of the greater cost-effectiveness of arbitration as compared to litigation in court. ICC states:

(1) **Cost-effective**

The relative speed of arbitration compared with litigation keeps lawyers' costs down. Parties generally pay less in the long run for arbitration than if they take their case to national courts.

If you are worried about arbitrators dragging out proceedings to pad their fees, forget it. The Court sets ICC fees according to a fixed scale, primarily based on the amount in dispute. Wasting time is not in the arbitrators' financial interest.

You can get a rough idea of what you will have to spend by using the cost calculator on the Court website. Simply enter the amount in dispute to receive an estimate of administrative and arbitrator fees, which are set by the Court.

Factors like the place of arbitration and the number of arbitrators influence expenses and may affect the final bill. So your own choices can also keep costs down.

The first obvious principle inspiring this text is the effort made to involve and engage the recipient. After the first introductory paragraph which is formulated impersonally, starting from the second sentence the interlocutor is addressed directly, using the second person pronoun and even making recourse to an imperative (*forget it*), and the language used is obviously aimed at involving him/her as an interlocutor and at dealing with problems from the client's point of view, a strategy reinforced by the final sentence, which emphasises the sense of the individual's control over the whole process. This is a distinctive feature of the ICC website, which – as already pointed out – is the only one where the pronoun *you* appears consistently.

In general, this text gives the impression that an effort is being made to use language that is accessible also to those who are not versed in the legal sciences, with a few colloquialisms including various phrasal verbs (e.g. *to keep costs down, to drag out, to pad fees, forget it, get a rough idea, to take the case in court*). Quite interestingly, the concept expressed in the first sentence, regarding the cost-effectiveness of arbitration ("The relative speed compared with litigation keeps lawyers' costs down"), is immediately rephrased in the second into an even more down-to-earth formulation ("Parties generally pay less in the long run for arbitration than if they take their case to national courts"). This really qualifies as a popularization effort, 'rephrasing' being one of the popularizing strategies described by Calsamiglia/van Dijk (2004) in their study of popular science articles. Incidentally, I may note that there is a strong argumentative component here: the text insists on the fact that the costs of any arbitration case entrusted to ICC are certain, given that the amount of the fees does not depend on the time the procedure takes. The ICC system is silently contrasted with LCIA's policy of calculating charges (both arbitrators' and tribunal's fees) on the time actually spent on it.[7] Quite interestingly, the same issue is also raised on the LCIA website, but with opposite arguments, arguing that fees calculated on the basis of hourly rates are more convenient for clients.

Another typical feature of this passage which confirms its character as non-specialised discourse is the avoidance of the use of nominalizations and, more in general, of a nominal style. This stands out clearly when this passage is compared with the section dealing with the same topic in LCIA's presentation of the Basics of Arbitration and Mediation:

(2) **Cost-Effectiveness and Speed**
There is a strong case for international arbitration as the cost-effective alternative to litigation across different jurisdictions. It may be easier to get parties of different nationalities into a neutral arbitration venue in the first place than into the national courts of one of them. So, the costs of initiating proceedings and of preparing the case are less likely to be wasted than in court litigation. Also, and crucially, at the end of the proceedings (assuming no settlement), an award may be more likely to be complied with, or to be enforced, than would be the judgment of the courts of one jurisdiction in the courts of another. So, the successful party to an arbitration is less likely to experience the hollow victory that often besets international litigation.

7 It is to be noted that LCIA is the only institution amongst those considered here adopting this policy; all the others calculate charges on the basis of the amount in dispute.

> Time is money (though undue haste may be more costly in the long run) and the inherent flexibility and party control of arbitration enable parties and tribunals to adopt as tight a procedural timetable as they wish, with potentially substantial cost savings. (LCIA)

The preference for a nominal style characterising this excerpt becomes all the more evident if one compares the initial sentence with the first two sentences of the ICC text quoted above (Example 1). Here the concept that in the ICC text was formulated as "Parties generally pay less" becomes "the cost-effective alternative", and "parties take their case to national courts" becomes "litigation across different jurisdictions".

Frequent recourse to nominalization engenders great textual density and a high level of complexity at noun-phrase level. This is a constant characteristic of texts on the LCIA website, which is also the most exhaustive in dealing with all possible aspects (Casework, Seat of the Arbitration, Arbitrators, Charges, UNCITRAL Arbitration, Enforcement of Awards, Procedural Flexibility, Party-nominated Arbitrators, Neutrality, Privacy and Confidentiality, The Case for Administered Arbitration, etc….). In some cases the clauses have the real feel of English legalese; see for instance the following example, taken from a section dealing with the commencement of the mediation process:

(3) Mediation is an entirely consensual process. There must be agreement to mediate, and agreement to continue to mediate once the process has begun. Parties will either have agreed to mediation in their contract, or they may agree to attempt a mediated settlement once a dispute has arisen, even when they have provided in their contract for some other form of dispute resolution, and even when they are in the course of litigation or arbitration.

This paragraph is characterized by a typically casuistic approach, considering two propositions, one as an alternative to the other, connected by *or,* and two possible 'extreme' conditions or circumstances which may prevent their application, but in actual fact do not. This phrasing is obviously influenced by the common law drafting style where the notion prevails that the text should contain all indications for its interpretation in the widest possible range of cases, taking into consideration different alternatives in order to make each provision all-inclusive

(Bhatia 1994: 140ff). This confirms the findings of previous studies which pointed out the inability of LCIA drafters to forsake the discursive conventions of the legal system in force in the country where the institution has its seat (cf. Garzone 2003: 211-215),

The SCC Institute does not deal at all with issues of cost-effectiveness and delay, nor does it address any other aspects of the arbitration process, but simply presents itself as an organization and establishes its own credentials. The Milan Chamber provides only a very short introduction to arbitration and its advantages, with speed and cost-effectiveness being simply included in this general introduction:

(4) Though arbitration administered by the Chamber of Arbitration of Milan cannot be certainly considered suitable for all kinds of disputes, it has become increasingly popular because of its advantages like *speed*, competent and impartial arbitrators, confidentiality of the proceedings. *Costs of the proceedings are fixed, controlled and proportionate to the service rendered.* (MILAN; my emphasis)

The approach is very synthetic and practical, totally free of 'technical' or legal considerations, with the focus on practicality. It is also interesting that the tone adopted should be so subdued, with the strong hedging statement at the beginning that deliberately excludes all kinds of promotional connotation. There is an obvious effort to make the text accessible to people with a practical business mentality, but not necessarily competent in the technicalities of dispute resolution.

Overall, the analysis of the discursive strategies enacted in the four websites under investigation highlights a high degree of variability, even though there are a number of common features shared by all of them.

3. Self presentation

A confirmation of these findings can be sought through the analysis of the sections of their websites specifically devoted to presenting themselves as organizations, which may contribute to drawing a more complete discursive profile of each of the institutions investigated here. Self presentation is part of the opening sections of each website, being a necessary component in the establishment of the institution's credentials and thus figures in the first two of the four main basic moves that are constitutive of the arbitration institution's website genre (cf. §3), i.e. *Establishing credentials of the arbitration institution* and *Describing the structure of the institution and how it works*. This section will focus on institution self-presentation as it is realized in these two moves, while the other two moves (*Introducing Arbitration* and *Introducing Mediation*) are dealt with in Catenaccio's chapter in this book.

The analysis of how the various moves are realized requires some navigation within each website, as moves are not completely realized on one single page, but rather in 'instalments' on different pages, recursively, usually featuring general statements at the higher levels and becoming ever more specific as one navigates deeper into the website, in conformity with the inverted pyramid principle in information distribution characterizing websites (cf. Nielsen 2000). This applies even to the SCC website, in spite of the limited amount of 'optional' text it deploys. On the 'About us' page, directly accessible though a link from the homepage, the Arbitration Institute is presented, first by establishing its credentials, and then by describing how it is organised and how it works:

(5) **'About us' Page**

The SCC Institute The Arbitration Institute of the Stockholm Chamber of Commerce (SCC Institute) was established in 1917 and is a separate entity within the Stockholm Chamber of Commerce. Recognised in the 1970's by the United States and the Soviet Union as a neutral center for the resolution of the East-West trade disputes, the SCC Institute has since expanded its services in international arbitration to over 40 countries. Over the past few decades the SCC Institute has emerged as one of the leading arbitration institutions in the world.	Establishing credentials
The SCC Institute has a Board of 12 Members and a Secretariat. Chairman of the Board is Mr. Johan	

Gernandt, Partner, Gernandt & Danielsson Law firm, and the Secretary General is Mr Ulf Franke who is also President of the International Federation of Commercial Arbitration Institutions and former Secretary General of the International Council for Commercial Arbitration (ICCA). The Secretariat consists of, apart from Mr Franke, an Assistant Secretary General, three Lawyers (of which one is Russian speaking) and three Assistants. The current Arbitration Rules of the Arbitration Institute of the Stockholm Chamber of Commerce (SCC Rules) entered into force 1 January 2007. Most arbitrations administered by the SCC Institute are conducted in accordance with the SCC Rules. Apart from the SCC Rules the SCC Institute has adopted Rules for Expedited Arbitrations, Insurance Arbitration Rules, Procedures and Services under the UNCITRAL Arbitration Rules and Mediation Rules.	Describing the structure of the institution and how it works.

The other page, on the same rank, realizes the same moves with regard to the Mediation Institute:

(6) **'Mediation Institute' Page**

THE SCC MEDIATION INSTITUTE The SCC Mediation Institute was established in 1999 to assist in the settlement of domestic and International disputes in accordance with the SCC Mediation Rules.	Establishing credentials
The SCC Mediation Rules offers [sic] an efficient dispute resolution to parties not wishing to engage in formal arbitral proceedings. The salient features of the Rules are the following: • A sole Mediator is appointed, unless otherwise agreed by the parties. The Mediator may be appointed by the parties jointly, or by the SCC Mediation Institute. • The time limit for the Mediation is two months, unless otherwise agreed by the parties. After having reached a settlement agreement, the parties may agree to appoint the Mediator as arbitrator in order to enable him to confirm the settlement agreement in an arbitral award.	Introducing Mediation

The way in which the *Establishing credentials* move is realized is particularly meaningful as it typically involves the illustration of the strengths of an organization and by necessity entails at least a degree of evaluative language. Therefore, its analysis can provide useful elements on the approach to the promotion of the institution's reputation and its services, thus shedding light on its aims and the target audience it addresses.

In the SCC text quoted above (Example 6), credentials are essentially established through the short historical sequence at the beginning, expounding the centre's experience in international dispute resolution, with the paragraph ending with a clearly evaluative statement concerning its reputation ("Over the past few decades the SCC Institute *has emerged as one of the leading arbitration institutions in the world"*). A similar function is performed by the use of the adjective *efficient* in the section concerning mediation ("The SCC Mediation Rules *offers an efficient dispute resolution….*").

Also streamlined – although not as concise – is the website of the Milan Arbitration Chamber, which introduces itself and establishes its credentials only in the 'About us' page, so credentials (highlighted in italics in the text here below) are intertwined with brief information about the structure of the Chamber and the services it provides:

(7) *The Chamber of National and International Arbitration of Milan (created by the Chamber of Commerce of Milan) provides alternative dispute resolution services for businesses and consumers at reasonable costs.*
Services provided:
Arbitration
Mediation
Online mediation (RisolviOnline)
Studies centre for ADR
Moreover, the Chamber of Arbitration advises businesses on drafting ADR clauses to insert in contracts.
The proceedings are administered by a professional staff responding to neutrality, confidentiality and flexibility criteria. Working languages are Italian, English and French.
We are located in the very centre of Milan, 5 minutes walk from Duomo's square [sic]: [details follow]. (MILAN; my emphasis)

The presentation is very synthetic and features a minimum of evaluative elements (*reasonable costs, professional staff responding to neutrality, confidentiality and flexibility criteria*).

The two cases examined so far stand in sharp contrast to the websites of the other two institutions, where the *Establishing credentials* move is realized extensively, and on multiple pages. In the case of ICC, credentials are first established on the *Arbitration today* page:

(8) The ICC International Court of Arbitration is the world's leading institution for resolving international commercial and business disputes.
The total number of cases handled by the Court since it was founded is more than 15,000. In 2006 alone, 593 cases were filed, involving 1,613 parties from 125 countries. (ICC)

While the expression 'leading institution' provides a comparative evaluation, the figures given support this evaluation, and the use of the adjective 'alone' after '2006' conveys the idea that these figures are substantial. This same move appears again on the *Why ICC arbitration?* page, as follows:

(9) **Why ICC Arbitration?**
Reputable
ICC arbitration is respected worldwide. It is supervised by the ICC Court and administered by the Court's Secretariat. The Court – which numbers business specialists as well as international lawyers – was created in 1923 and tracks the progress of each case and reviews the awards in order to facilitate their enforcement ever since.
Global
Every part of the world is represented in the ICC Court and Secretariat. No other arbitration institution can match ICC's global reach.

- In the year 2006, ICC arbitration took place in 52 countries and involved arbitrators of 71 different nationalities.
- The Court's membership is drawn from 88 countries. *Click here* to view the *list of the members.*
- The Court and Secretariat can call upon *ICC national committees* in some 90 countries for assistance in finding the best arbitrators.
- The Secretariat has a staff of more than 50 of over 20 different nationalities, speaking all the world's main languages. (ICC)

In this case, the title of the page itself, while engaging directly the interlocutor by phatically activating the interpersonal meta-function, makes it clear that what is being given is a value judgement; subsequently, all the elements of judgement provided are synthesized in the titles – *Reputable, Global* – which serve as pragmatic indicators for the reader on how to interpret the statements that follow. The text itself is rich in openly evaluative elements (underlined in the excerpt above).

In the case of LCIA, the first link on the home page leads to a lengthy 'About LCIA' page which is opened by a section significantly entitled 'International credentials':

(10) **International credentials**
The LCIA is one of the longest-established international institutions for commercial dispute resolution. It is also one of the most modern and forward-looking.
Although based in London, the LCIA is a thoroughly international institution, providing efficient, flexible and impartial administration of dispute resolution proceedings for all parties, regardless of their location, and under any system of law.
Its operation and outlook are geared to ensuring that the parties may have complete confidence in its international credentials and in its impartiality.
A brief history of the LCIA may be found *here*. (LCIA)

Here evaluative language is used both to qualify the institution in itself (*longest established, most modern and forward looking, thoroughly international, efficient, flexible and impartial administration*) and to reassure the parties of its trustworthiness. In a subsequent section its credentials are completed by describing the total confidence it receives from "major international businesses":

(11) **Casework**
Many major international businesses entrust their disputes to the LCIA. Many cases are technically and legally complex and sums in issue can run into US$ billions. Parties come from a very large number of jurisdictions, of both civil law and common law traditions.
The subject matter of contracts in dispute is wide and varied, and includes all aspects of international commerce, including telecommunications, insurance, oil and gas exploration, construction, shipping, aviation, pharmaceuticals, shareholders agreements, IT, finance and banking. (LCIA)

Hard information about LCIA's casework is used here as a credential for the institution, letting facts speak for themselves, simply highlighting the quantity and importance of the cases handled.

3.1. Self-mention

Finally, to complete this picture about self-representation, one last word should be said about self-mention, as one of the strategies through which each organization constructs itself in the text. The analysis of the concordance lines for the names of the institutions reveals some interesting patterns. A particularly noteworthy element which sets aside the Paris court from the other institutions is that in as many as 29 of the 41 entries of *ICC*, this acronym is used as a pre-modifier (frequency 1.08%), prevalently (16 times) in combination with *arbitration* (e.g. 'ICC arbitration'). In the LCIA website this happens only 18 times (frequency 0.29%), out of a total of 82 entries and only once does LCIA collocate with *arbitration* and once with *mediation* to produce a self-standing noun group ('LCIA arbitration', 'LCIA mediation').[8] In the SCC website out of the 15 entries of the institution's name eight occur as pre-modifiers (frequency 2.21%), while this never happens in the case of the Milan Chamber. A hypothesis to explain this pattern is that in the case of ICC and SCC the name of the institution is used as a brand name to 'sell' arbitration as a quality product, banking on their solid international reputation. This use of the institution's name does not certainly occur in the LCIA website, whose denomination – as pointed out above – occurs only twice as a premodifier of 'arbitration'/'litigation'. Rather, attention is more consistently focused on the Chamber itself, on its status and on the services it offers, although it is certainly not less internationally renowned. In fact, in LCIA's case, the function of self-mention is often part of the rheto-

8 In actual fact, LCIA collocates other four times with 'arbitration' and five times with 'mediation', but inside two larger noun groups, 'LCIA Arbitration Rules' and 'LCIA Mediation Procedures', where it is certainly not used as a brand name.

rical strategy called dissociation,[9] as it distinguishes arbitration as administered by the London Chamber – and by few other first-class arbitration institutions – as different from the procedures administered by the myriad of minor institutions operating in the sector or by teams of professionals practising *ad hoc* arbitration. Thus LCIA describes and promotes its services as a case of best practice in an arbitration scenario which is subject to mounting criticism. The following example is a case in point:

(12) The most vociferous and sustained criticism of commercial arbitration is levelled at cost and delay. However, many of the leading institutions, including the LCIA, seek actively to moderate their costs and the fees charged by the tribunals they appoint. It is, therefore, frequently the case that these costs are better controlled and contained under the supervision of the leading institutions than in ad hoc proceedings.

As far as the Milan centre is concerned, it also adopts an approach focusing more on the institution and its services than on its name, illustrating its main points of strength and its efficiency, a strategy which in this case is more easily justified on account of its more local reputation. The analysis conducted on the way in which credentials are established shows that there is considerable variation in the realization of this move.

4. Closing considerations and possible implications

The analysis presented in this chapter makes it possible to draw together a number of elements concerning the general semiotic organi-

---

9 The term 'dissociation' is used here in a pragma-dialectical framework with the meaning attributed to it by van Rees (2002), who defines it as an "argumentative technique that serves to resolve the contradictions that a notion that originally was covered by a single term and that was considered a unity, gives rise to" (van Rees 2002: 1). Pragma-dialectics is an argumentation theory used to analyze and evaluate argumentation in its entirety in actual practice, combining a dialectical dimension inspired by formal dialectics with a pragmatic dimension (cf. among others van Eemeren/Grootendorst 2004).

zation of the websites under investigation, their intended audience and communicative purposes. In terms of mere discursive effort and commitment, LCIA's and ICC's websites show a much higher profile than those of the other two institutions – if only in terms of sheer size. This could be partly accounted for by the great prestige of both institutions, who seem to attribute themselves also the role of depositories of wisdom, expertise and resources concerning arbitration and other ADR systems. It could also partly be seen as resulting from the evident intention of reaching an ever wider audience and providing it with a substantial amount of information, for the possible ultimate aim of maintaining or enlarging their volume of casework.

From the web design point of view, the LCIA website stands out as the most conservative one, featuring large quantities of text on each page and obliging the user to access it chiefly through the reading mode. The traditional approach to communication is accompanied by a very low degree of interpersonality and interactivity, while its syntactic and discursive organization is obviously influenced by the syntactic and discursive conventions of common law legal drafting, thus providing evidence of a more marked interference on the part of the local legal culture. Furthermore, it indicates that the audience addressed is mainly one of lawyers or at least of legally-minded corporate or institutional executives.

The other three websites are more obviously designed for a HCME, with a smaller grain (i.e. a fragmentation of text into smaller lexias and into multiple pages: cf. Garzone 2007: 24-26) and a more genuinely hypertextual organization. The Milan Chamber website is relatively streamlined and seems to be addressed to an audience of practically-oriented businessmen, as it provides basic and concise matter-of-fact information. The SCC website is little more than a portal offering access to the 'basic' authentic texts (Rules, Laws and Conventions, Arbitrators' guidelines, etc.) and an update on events and conferences, which suggests that it is addressed to an audience that is already sufficiently competent and aware of how arbitration works and what its advantages are.

The ICC website stands out for its complexity and its evident hypertextual construction, which requires users to opt for the navigation mode. This interactive approach to communication is matched by the strong interpersonal component activated in the texts. The language used is often more evaluative, while in many cases it incurporates colloquial features, resulting in an overall promotional tone, which seeks to address the business community on its own terms. This is also in keeping with its being part of the website of the Paris Chamber of Commerce, an organization that depicts itself on its homepage as the "voice of world business championing the global economy as a force for economic growth, job creation and prosperity".

The organization of information – and more specifically the communicative strategies deployed and the way in which the affordances of the medium are exploited in the website analysed – also offers valuable insights as to the envisaged readership. The marked interpersonal focus of ICC, combined with its expert use of multimodal technologies, suggests a typically business-oriented focus. On the other hand, the structure of the LCIA site, where the affordances of the hypertextual environment are only limitedly put to use with a very low degree of interactivity and the deployment of long and more complex texts, provides evidence of a more conservative and legally-oriented approach, meeting the tastes and needs of a particular audience mainly consisting of corporate legal consultants rather than to managers or businessmen. The Milan Arbitration Chamber has a simple, but well articulated site, much more streamlined than the previous two as is appropriate for a much smaller regionally-oriented institution, and adopts an essentially practical, operational attitude, which befits an organization operating in an area with a predominance of small and medium-sized enterprises. Albeit well-constructed in terms of web design, the SCC website is even more compact; its slenderness matches the scantiness of general information provided, showing little desire to attract any addressees other than those that are familiar with arbitration.

Overall, the analysis highlights a dynamic relationship between website construction and discursive practices deployed, and the operational profile of each of the four institutions examined, a relationship which I have shown to be resulting from a whole range of institutional, social, legal, and marketing variables as well as the intended audience addressed in each case. These same variables also help account for the remarkable differences in terms of deployment of technological affordances.

References

Agre, Phil 1995. Designing Genres for the New Media. *The Network Observer* 2/2. Available online at <http://communication.ucsd.edu/pagre/tno/november-1995.html #designing>.

Askehave, Inger / Ellerup Nielsen, Anne 2004. Web-mediated Genres: A Challenge to Traditional Genre Theory. *Working Paper no. 6.* Aarhus: Center for Virksomhedskommunication.

Askehave, Inger / Ellerup Nielsen, Anne 2005. What are the Characteristics of Digital Genres? Genre Theory from a Multi-modal Perspective. *Proceedings of the 38th Hawaii International Conference on System Sciences*. Online at <http://www. computer. org/plugins/dl/pdf/proceedings/hicss/2005>.

Barthes, Roland 1970/1974. *S/Z* (transl. by R. Miller). New York: Hill and Wang (*S/Z*, Paris: Éditions du Seuil).

Bhatia, Vijay K. 1993. *Analysing Genre: Language in Professional Settings*. London: Longman.

Bhatia, Vijay. 1994. Cognitive Structuring in Legislative Provisions. In Gibbons, John (ed.) *Language and the Law*. New York: Longman, 136-155.

Bhatia, Vijay K. 2004. *Worlds of Written Discourse*. London: Continuum.

Calsamiglia, Helena / van Dijk, Teun A. 2004. Popularization Discourse and Knowledge about the Genome. *Discourse and Society* 15/4, 369-389.

Garzone, Giuliana 2003. Arbitration Rules across Legal Cultures: An Intercultural Approach. In Bhatia, Vijay / Candlin, Christopher / Gotti, Maurizio (eds) *Legal Discourse in Multilingual and Multicultural Contexts: Arbitration Texts in Europe*. Bern: Peter Lang, 177-220.

Garzone, Giuliana 2007. Genres, Multimodality and the World Wide Web: Theoretical Issues. In Garzone, Giuliana / Poncini, Gina / Catenaccio, Paola (eds) *Multimodality in Corporate Communication. Web Genres and Discursive Identity*. Milano: Franco Angeli, 15-30.

Hoffman Donna L. / Novak Thomas P., 1996. Marketing in the Hypermedia Computer-Mediated Environment, Conceptual Foundations. *Journal of Marketing* 60/3, 50-68.

Kress Gunther / van Leeuwen, Theo 2001. *Multimodal Discourse*. London: Arnold.

Kress, Gunther / van Leeuwen, Theo 2006. *Reading Images. The Grammar of Visual Design*. London: Routledge.

Landow, George 1997. *Hypertext 2.0. The Convergence of Contemporary Critical Theory and Technology*. Baltimore: Johns Hopkins University Press.

Nielsen, Jakob 2000. *Designing Web Usability*. Indianapolis: New Writers Publishing.

Perelman, Chaïm / Olbrechts-Tyteca, Lucie 1969. *The New Rhetoric: A Treatise on Argumentation* (*Traité de l'Argumentation, La Nouvelle Rhétorique* 1958, trans. Wilkinson, John / Weaver, Purcell). Notre Dame: University of Notre Dame Press.

Scott, Mike 2004. *WordSmith Tools Version 4*, Oxford: Oxford University Press.

Sosnoski, James J. 1999. Configuring as a Mode of Rhetorical Analysis. In Jones, Steve (ed.) *Doing Internet Research*. London: Sage, 127-144.

Swales, John M. 1990. *Genre Analysis – English in Academic and Research Settings*. Cambridge: Cambridge University Press.

Van Eemeren, Frans H. / Grootendorst, Rob 2004. *A Systematic Theory of Argumentation: The Pragma-dialectical Approach*. Cambridge: Cambridge University Press.

Van Rees, M. Agnes 2002. Indicators of Dissociation. In van Eemeren, Frans H. / Houtlosser, Peter (eds) *Argumentation in Practice*. Amsterdam: John Benjamins, 53-67.

PAOLA CATENACCIO

Framing the Discourses of Arbitration and Mediation: A Comparative Analysis

1. Introduction and study design

This chapter analyses the discursive representations of arbitration and mediation on the web, and is a companion study to the chapter by Garzone in this volume, which focused on the communicative strategies deployed in the web-based promotion of ADR.[1] It is based on the same corpus, collecting materials published on the websites of four important arbitration institutions – the International Court of Arbitration of the International Chamber of Commerce (ICC) (<http://www.iccwbo.org>), the London Court of International Arbitration (LCIA) (<http://www.lcia-arbitration.com>), the SCC Institute – Arbitration Institute of the Stockholm Chamber of Commerce (<http://www.scc institute.com>), and the Milan National and International Arbitration Chamber (Camera Arbitrale Nazionale e Internazionale di Milano) (<http://www.camera-arbitrale.it>) – organized into four small corpora amenable to computer-assisted analysis. The corpus was used in combination with discourse- and text-analysis from a genre-based perspective. In particular, the analysis presented here is grounded in research on interdiscursivity (Fairclough 2003; Bhatia 2004: esp. 48ff and 87ff., 2007; Candlin 2006), focusing on the relationship and interference between the discursive formations associated with different forms of ADR.

---

1 The research on which this chapter is based was conducted jointly by Paola Catenaccio and Giuliana Garzone (cf. previous chapter) within the framework of the National Research Programme *Tension and Change in Domain-specific Genres* directed by Maurizio Gotti, funded by the Italian Ministry of University, no. 2007JCY9Y9 – 2007.

This study builds upon the insights provided by the results of the analysis presented in the previous chapter, which identified both commonalities and differences in the website communication of the arbitration institutions investigated. Considerable variation was also found in the realization of the first two moves of the websites' structure – *Establishing credentials of the arbitration institution* and *Describing the structure of the institution and how it works.* I now intend to delve deeper into the textual and discursive articulation of the informative and promotional materials posted on the websites, focusing in particular on the two more specific moves in the websites' structure – *Introducing arbitration* and *Introducing ADR/mediation* – with a view to investigating the way in which arbitration and mediation are discursively constructed.

In doing so, my main purpose is to identify the strategies deployed to depict arbitration and mediation as alternatives to judicial adjudication. My research starts from the recognition that in the last few decades, recourse to arbitration as a means of international dispute resolution has become increasingly popular (Hunter/Marriot/Veder 1995; Mattli 2001). This can be attributed to the flexibility, confidentiality and rapidity of arbitration procedures, combined with the technical expertise of arbitrators, which compare positively with the much more cumbersome, lengthy and uncertain nature of litigation. However, as international commercial relations become more complex and the legal framework within which they take place fuzzier (Reiner 1998), a tendency has emerged for parties to select arbitrators on the basis of their legal, rather than technical, expertise (Miles 2003). In addition, in many countries the rise of arbitration has prompted a progressive institutionalisation (often with legal undertones) of arbitration procedures (Bernardini 2000; Nabatchi 2007), as international arbitration bodies establish protocols and publish documents aimed at regulating and promoting ADR and arbitration, often in cooperation with the judicial system. This blurring of boundaries between the discourse of arbitration and the discourse of litigation has been argued to have led to the progressive 'colonisation' (Bhatia 2004) of arbitration practices on the part of litigation procedures, especially insofar as lawyers rely on discourses and practices typical of their profession when acting as arbitrators or counsel in arbitration proceedings. The progressive narrowing of the gap between litigation and arbitration has given rise to a scenario characterised by the co-existence and mutual influence of various discourses, ranging from litigation to arbitration and other ADR methods such as mediation and conciliation, as the procedural and discursive space previously occupied by arbitration vis-à-vis litigation is also taken up by other forms of non-judicial conflict resolution (Candlin/Maley 1994, 1997; cf. also Tang 1996 and Sanders 1999). In turn, this complex discursive scenario is reflected in the texts generated within the field of arbitration and ADR, which encode features that can be traced to the multiple discursive domains referred to above.

From this perspective the first issue I explore concerns therefore the contention that the integrity of arbitration is increasingly being threatened as a result of its 'colonization' by litigation and 'judicialization' (Nariman 2000: 262; Marriott 2004: 354) in terms of techniques, procedures, shared expertise and discursive practices, and, in consequence, is losing its original essence as a non-legal practice.

Some further issues are discussed which are connected with another important development in this domain, i.e. the spread of other less 'structured' forms of ADR – mediation, conciliation, mini-trial, ODR – which are also being offered by the same institutions and are certainly much less litigative and legalized. In this context, I start from the assumption that the exploration of the discourses used to present options for dispute resolution along the litigation / arbitration / mediation continuum can yield useful constructs by which to assess on the one hand the actual degree of colonization of arbitration by litigative practices, and on the other, the distinctive discursive features drawn on when dealing with each different form of dispute resolution procedure.

In light of the foregoing, this chapter aims therefore to (i) provide an overview of the way in which arbitration and mediation are framed within the more general framework of institutional self-presentation; (ii) identify and describe contrastively the discursive strategies deployed in the dissemination of information about arbitration vs other forms of ADR and (iii) find discursive evidence in favour/against the hypothesis that arbitration is being colonized by litigation.

2. Core discursive traits

2.1. Arbitration vs. mediation

The analysis of the moves *Introducing arbitration* (present in only three of the four websites) and *Introducing mediation* will provide elements to explore the way in which the institutions under consideration present mediation and, more in general, ADR services other than arbitration, *vis-à-vis* arbitration and/or litigation. The respective positioning of arbitration and mediation and the way in which they are contrasted with each other and with litigation, are of particular interest here because they may provide some insights into the discursive structuring of these domains within the overarching discourse order of dispute resolution/adjudication, as well as evidence of the (possible) erosion and/or redefinition of the discursive territory of arbitration as a result of the recent expansion of mediation.

In this respect, some preliminary considerations can be made using quantitative data as a starting point. Table 1 details the statistics, obtained by means of the WordList Tool of Wordsmith 4.0 (Scott 2004), concerning the occurrences of the lexical items *arbitration* and *mediation* in the four websites considered:

		arbitration	mediation	ADR	*Neutral*
ICC	rank	7	**149**	26	17
	no. occ	48	**3**	17	23
	%	1.77	**0.11**	0.63	0.85
LCIA	rank	10	17	51	
	no. occ	83	50	15	
	%	1.37	0.83	0.25	
SCC	rank	8	11	–	
	no. occ	9	7	–	
	%	2.44	1.90	–	
Milan	rank	13	6	48	
	no. occ	23	57	8	
	%	0.85	**2.10**	0.29	

Table 1. Frequency of arbitration/mediation/ADR in the websites considered.

The data confirm that – as could be expected – *arbitration* occurs very frequently in all the websites analysed (ranking 7 to 13 in the respective frequency lists, and with frequencies ranging from 0.85 to 2.44%). On the contrary, the frequency of the lexical item *mediation* is much more uneven: it is as low as 0.11% in ICC (rank: 149), while in the website of the Milan Arbitration Chamber it ranks higher than *arbitration* at 2.10%. *ADR* does not occur in SCC at all, and appears remarkably less frequently in ICC compared to LCIA and Milan.

The extremely low statistical value registered for *mediation* in the ICC corpus is partially compensated for by the much higher frequency of the superordinate *ADR*, as well as by a fairly high occurrence of the item *neutral*, often used as a noun with a capital N to refer to a third neutral party participating in dispute resolution procedures other then arbitration, as shown in the excerpt below:

(1) **ICC ADR - The role of the Neutral**

The success of ADR hinges largely on the wisdom, tact, common sense and expertise of an individual known as a Neutral. His or her task is to create trust and assist the parties in their quest for a settlement. The Neutral is a facilitator, not a judge or arbitrator.

Practical and potentially difficult decisions that the Neutral may have to make include which language should be used and where meetings should be held.

The Neutral's opinion does not itself bind the parties, but opens the way for them freely to agree a settlement that they are legally bound to carry out. Or they may simply act in line with the Neutral's findings, without formal agreement.

The exceptionally limited number of occurrences of *mediation* in ICC and the proportionally more frequent use of *ADR* suggests that this institution has deliberately opted for *ADR* over *mediation* as the favoured label for all alternative dispute resolution methods. At the other end of the scale, the unusually high frequency of *mediation* in the website of the Milan Arbitration Chamber points to a choice not only to favour this term when talking about ADR, but in fact to favour the promotion of mediation alongside – and possibly over – that of arbitration. Yet another case is represented by SCC, which only refers to arbitration and mediation, with no recourse anywhere in the website to the more general umbrella term ADR.

These preliminary quantitative observations lead to a number of considerations. To begin with, it is apparent that ICC and LCIA, as major institutions traditionally devoted to arbitration, maintain a firm focus on this form of dispute resolution, with other forms being treated as secondary modes. By contrast, the Milan Arbitration Chamber appears to give priority to the presentation of mediation, presumably as a result of its intended readership, which is likely to be made up primarily of small and medium-sized enterprises, more inclined to opt for the least costly form of dispute resolution available. Still different is the position of SCC, which has very little recourse to the mention of arbitration, at the same time citing mediation as a kind of novelty among the services provided.

Secondly, if lexical choices provide an indication of the kind of conceptual consolidation a particular practice has achieved, the variation in the terminology used to refer to various forms of alternative dispute resolution other than arbitration suggests that mediation, as a practice, is still far from being standardised.

In the next sections the way in which arbitration and mediation are introduced in the websites will be analysed, with a view to qualifying qualitatively the discursive variation in the presentation of these two practices following the indications emerging from the preliminary quantitative results discussed above.

2.2. Introducing arbitration

An especially interesting fact is that not all websites define what arbitration is. If LCIA and the Milan Arbitration Chamber provide definitions, ICC and SCC do not. The LCIA definition of arbitration reads as follows:

(2) Arbitration is now the first-choice method of binding dispute resolution in the widest range of international commercial contracts. It is a private process requiring the agreement of the parties, which is usually given by way of an arbitration clause in the contract. If there is no contractual provision to arbitrate, a separate arbitration agreement may be entered into once a dispute has arisen.

> Arbitration offers parties the freedom to choose a method of dispute resolution tailored to their precise needs. That freedom extends to the choice of applicable law, the venue, the language, and the choice of arbitration procedures, whether under institutional rules, stand-alone procedures, like the UNCITRAL rules, or entirely ad hoc.
> Parties may also choose their arbitrators, thus ensuring the constitution of a tribunal with precisely the right qualifications and experience.
> It is this freedom of choice that reinforces the key elements of international arbitration: enforceability, procedural flexibility, party-control, neutrality, privacy and confidentiality, cost-effectiveness and speed. (LCIA)

The main definition, formulated in a typically conceptual form (i.e. stating specifically *what arbitration is*), is given exhaustively in the first paragraph, while the following two paragraphs have a more evaluative tone and add a number of elements which illustrate the convenience and advantages of the procedure, focusing in particular on flexibility ('freedom of choice') in the evident effort to counteract accusations of rigidity and unmanageability sometimes raised against arbitration.

The Milan Chamber of Commerce website also provides some kind of definition, but it formulates it phenomenologically, in operational terms (i.e. describing how arbitration works in a practically-oriented manner, with special regard for its effects):

(3) Through arbitration, companies can decide to settle their commercial disputes without the need to resort to the jurisdiction of the Courts, by submitting them to arbitrators chosen by the parties.
National and foreign companies may avoid being bound by one legal system; thereby promoting constructive relationship between the parties.
The parties can submit their disputes to an arbitration if they have included an arbitration clause in their contract or, if they did not, by stipulating a submission agreement. Particular attention must be given to the drafting of the clause. (Milan)

Also here we have some considerations added to the basic information about arbitration as a dispute-resolution option, this time focusing more on the problem of jurisdiction and on the relationship between the parties.

It is worth noting that both in (13) and (14) the definition, while positioning arbitration as an alternative to litigation, does not overtly contrast it with litigation. This comparison is made by LCIA further down in the text. It is also made by ICC, despite the fact that it does not provide a full-fledged definition of arbitration:

(4) Today's business and operating conditions underscore arbitration's advantages over litigation, especially in cross-border disputes. (ICC)

If ICC does not provide a definition of arbitration, it does, however, give a long and articulated list of reasons for choosing arbitration. Often these reasons contrast the advantages of arbitration with the disadvantages of litigation, a strategy which, as pointed out above, is common to both ICC and LCIA, as can easily be inferred from a reading of the concordances for the lexical item *litigation* in the two corpora.

nderscore arbitration's advantages over	*litigation,*	especially in cross-border
legal backgrounds. They want to avoid	*litigation*	because they fear bias by
me-consuming and less expensive than	*litigation.*	Who can benefit? You
of Foreign Arbitral Awards. Unlike	*litigation,*	arbitration is flexible.
speed of arbitration compared with	*litigation*	keeps lawyers' costs

Concordance 1. *Litigation* in the ICC corpus.

attempt to avoid, or during the course of	*litigation*	or arbitration. As with
the courts. Privacy and Confidentiality.	*litigation*	in national courts is
as the cost-effective alternative to	*litigation*	across different
less likely to be wasted than in court	*litigation.*	Also, and crucially, at
victory that often besets international	*litigation.*	Time is money (though
of the time that would be spent on	*litigation.*	And the issue of a final

Concordance 2. *Litigation* in the LCIA corpus.

These examples are compounded by others – especially in the ICC corpus – which, although they do not use explicitly the term *litigation*, continue to build on the contrast between arbitration and litigation:

(5) *Arbitral tribunals usually take less time than national courts to reach a final decision*, against which recourses are restricted.
The Court monitors deadlines from start to finish. The Court has the power to step in and replace arbitrators on the rare occasions that they fail to fulfill their obligations. If the parties agree on a fast-track arbitration, cases can be decided within a few months.
National courts are often congested. They may need between three and five years to resolve a dispute, sometimes even longer. (ICC)

(6) The Court respects your privacy. *In contrast with ordinary courtroom proceedings under public and media gaze*, ICC does not divulge details of an arbitration case and keeps the identities of the parties completely confidential. (ICC)

In these cases the juxtaposition of arbitration and litigation is reformulated in terms of opposition between (national) court(room)s and arbitral tribunals.

2.3. Litigation and arbitration vs mediation

The concordances for *litigation* in the LCIA corpus also show that in some cases litigation and arbitration are grouped together and contrasted, either explicitly or implicitly, with *mediation:*

likely to be a shorter process than either	*litigation*	or arbitration, there
and even when they are in the course of	*litigation*	or arbitration. The
for the purposes of any arbitration or	*litigation.*	Concluding the

Concordance 3. *Litigation* and *arbitration* in the LCIA corpus.

This pattern can also be found, albeit on a smaller scale, in the website of the Milan Arbitration Chamber:

has a number of advantages over	*litigation*	and arbitration processes
transactions by means that don't invoke	*litigation*	and arbitration. The

Concordance 4. *Litigation and arbitration* in the Milan corpus.

In both cases mediation is described in opposition to litigation *and* arbitration and in this context the latter two sound almost like components of a binomial expression (*arbitration* is in fact the most frequent collocate of *litigation*, which suggests that the two are often mentioned in close connection). This usage has important implications if the degree of the encroaching of the discourse of litigation on the discourse of arbitration is to be assessed, as it has the effect of lumping together arbitration and litigation, thus suggesting, by implication, that they may be similar.

That arbitration may increasingly be perceived as being little different from litigation (especially in terms of costs and time) is clear also from a passage included in the extended description of the advantages of arbitration as provided by LCIA in the section *The case for administered arbitration* under the heading *Costs and delays*, which is quoted in full below:

(7) The most vociferous and sustained criticism of commercial arbitration is levelled at cost and delay. However, many of the leading institutions, including the LCIA, seek actively to moderate their costs and the fees charged by the tribunals they appoint. It is, therefore, frequently the case that these costs are better controlled and contained under the supervision of the leading institutions than in ad hoc proceedings.
The LCIA is of the view that a very substantial monetary claim (and/or counterclaim) does not necessarily mean a technically or legally complex case and that arbitration costs should be based on time actually spent by administrator and arbitrators alike. The LCIA's charges, and the fees charged by the tribunals it appoints, are not, therefore, based on the sums in issue.
Ad hoc arbitrations do not run themselves and important administrative tasks can only be allocated to a member of the arbitrator's own staff; to members of the parties' legal teams; or to the parties themselves, at considerable opportunity and financial cost. The counterpoint to the concern that the institution's costs are costs which would not otherwise be incurred, therefore, is that the administration will be more efficiently, and more cost-effectively, done by an institution whose speciality it is.
The major institutions also act as secure and independent fundholders of sums deposited by the parties, disbursing these funds as required and, at all times, accounting to the parties for sums held and disbursed. The LCIA provides this service not only in cases conducted under the LCIA rules, but also in UNCITRAL-rules and ad hoc arbitrations.

> The parties' own legal costs, are, however beyond the control of the institution and, if these are to be reduced, the parties and their attorneys must work together to avail themselves of the leaner and more expeditious procedures that are inherent in good arbitration practice.
> Closely related to the costs issue, then, is the issue of delay. Whilst it is not the role of an institution to interfere with the conduct of the proceedings, as agreed between the parties, directed by the tribunal or prescribed by the rules, institutions do have an important role in monitoring the process, in lending support to parties, counsel and arbitrators, and in keeping the process moving at as lively a pace as due process will allow.
> And if the parties wish to adopt 'fast track' procedures, these are readily available from the LCIA and from a number of other institutions.
> The cure for the costs and delay complaint is, therefore, largely in the hands of the parties and their Counsel, which will certainly have the support of the institution in any effort to effect that cure.

The passage makes the case for *administered* arbitration – i.e. for an arbitration procedure in which the institution plays a key role, and which has been criticised for its costs, lengthy duration and structural rigidity. The defence of administered arbitration put forth by LCIA justifies the strongly argumentative nature of the passage, in which a standpoint made up of two propositions (1. administered arbitration is not cost-effective; 2. administered arbitration is not fast) is refuted by addressing each of the propositions in turn, and ultimately laying the blame for the cost and delay issue on the parties themselves. The argumentative nature of the passage is confirmed by recourse to the technique of dissociation (van Rees 2002) which – as pointed out in Garzone's chapter in this book (§3.1 and note 9) – is used here to distinguish LCIA's practices from those of minor institutions, and from *ad hoc* arbitration.

The LCIA website is unique in its explicit addressing of arguments against administered arbitration. There are indications, however, that institutions are aware that some of the claims typically made about arbitration – most notably its speed and cost-effectiveness – may be difficult to uphold. A close reading of the section of the ICC website detailing the advantages of arbitration suggests as much, with a strategic use of hedges aimed at reducing the epistemic strength of the propositions, thereby making them easier to defend:

(8) ICC arbitration is an attractive alternative because it is international and confidential. *Usually*, it is less time-consuming and less expensive than litigation. (ICC)

(9) Arbitral tribunals *usually* take less time than national courts to reach a final decision, against which recourses are restricted. (ICC)

(10) Parties *generally* pay less in the long run for arbitration than if they take their case to national courts. (ICC)

(11) *In the great majority of cases,* parties accept the award spontaneously and there the matter ends. (ICC)

The discursive strategies deployed by LCIA and ICC for the purpose of justifying the validity of their claims (and, in fact, legitimising the usefulness of their activity) do not appear at all in the websites of the other two institutions under consideration. This tendency to pre-empt criticism of arbitration by engaging in overt defensive strategies, or by making qualified generalisations, may therefore be seen as a salient feature of these two institutions, and is not necessarily shared by all arbitration-related bodies. The discursive impact of this comparative approach is greatest in the LCIA text, where the materials are organised in a full-fledged argumentative structure.

2.4. Mediation

If the websites of arbitration institutions do not necessarily offer an explicit definition of this practice, more flexible forms of ADR such as mediation are generally defined even by those institutions such as ICC and SCC which take a basic knowledge of what arbitration is for granted. Definitions of ADR and/or mediation can take different shapes, and can be embedded in textual forms which make them not necessarily recognizable as such. This is the case of ICC, which – as already pointed out above – is also the only institution which does not define mediation separately. Although it actually features a short section entitled 'Mediation', this is in one of the secondary branches of the hypertext, and does not really talk about mediation nor does it define it, but rather illustrates the role that the Neutral plays in the process:

(12) **Mediation**
The Neutral may meet each of the parties separately to help them find common ground for resolving the dispute amicably. The meetings are confidential and clear the way for negotiations. The Neutral is not called upon to pronounce on the merits of the dispute.

Otherwise, in the main section where ADR is introduced, mediation is not even mentioned as a method of dispute resolution in its own right:

(13) **What is ICC ADR?**
ICC ADR – A wise precaution
When business partners conclude a deal, they make every reasonable effort to ensure that they can deliver as agreed. Product quality, specifications, delivery times, spare parts, servicing, payment – these are some of the considerations. But sometimes things go wrong. External circumstances like a national financial crisis cannot always be foreseen. Prudence demands that parties to contracts make due provision for all types of dispute, including those that mutual goodwill and informed outside help can settle.
The choice is yours
The International Chamber of Commerce offers a full spread of dispute resolution services so that you and your business partner can make the best choice. The problem may perhaps be a disagreement on the interpretation of a contractual provision that is no more than a difference of opinion.
ADR, which covers all techniques of amicable dispute resolution, can be the solution for this and many other issues confronting business partners that are open to settlement on the basis of consensus and trust. (ICC)

It is interesting to note that the heading of the section is formulated as a question, suggesting that a definition should be forthcoming. In tune with ICC's eminently customer-oriented approach, however, the definition (underlined in the text) only comes at the end of a paragraph which begins with a general statement about business practices and then narrows the focus on possible problems that may arise, finally putting forth a suggestion for a suitable solution. It is also worth noting that ADR is not contrasted with arbitration, but rather described as a self-standing constellation of methods whose defining features are their amicable nature, consensus, and trust.

A different approach is taken by LCIA, which splits the description of mediation into two different texts, not directly linked to one another. The first one appears in a section entitled 'Arbitration and mediation – the basics', which seems to put the two services on the same level, and reads as follows:

(14) **LCIA MEDIATION**

The LCIA mediation procedure may be used both by parties who are already committed to mediate, by virtue of contractual dispute resolution provisions, and by parties who have not provided for mediation, but who wish to mediate their dispute, either in an attempt to avoid, or during the course of, litigation or arbitration.

As with its arbitrators, the LCIA has access to a large number of experienced and highly-qualified mediators from many jurisdictions.

And, as with the arbitrations it administers, the LCIA aims to make its mediations cost-effective. To this end, mediation costs are also based on the hourly rates of the mediators and of the LCIA's administrative staff, without reference to the sums in issue. (LCIA)

Two aspects are worth noting here: first of all, mediation is defined against (although not contrasted with) litigation and arbitration, an aspect which has already been discussed in Section §2.2; secondly, LCIA insists on its ability to deliver effective services also in mediation, as it does with arbitration for which it is most renowned for. Despite this initial introduction, a proper definition of mediation (underlined in the text) only comes at a deeper level, and is preceded by a more general definition of ADR:

(15) **MEDIATION**

Introduction

In most jurisdictions, ADR is taken to mean only the non-adjudicative dispute resolution options, of which mediation is the most frequently used. In essence, mediation is a negotiated settlement, conducted and concluded with the assistance of a neutral third-party. The process is voluntary and does not lead to a binding decision, enforceable in its own right.

Most commercial disputes, in which it is not imperative that there should be a binding and enforceable decision, are amenable to mediation. Mediation may be particularly suitable where the parties in dispute hope to preserve, or to renew, their commercial relationships. As mediation is likely to be a shorter process than either litigation or arbitration, there may also be economic arguments for attempting a mediated settlement. (LCIA)

In this case as well, mediation is described evaluatively as a speedier and more economical option than litigation and arbitration. Presumably on account of the non-enforceable nature of mediation, the statement is accompanied by epistemic modulation ("is likely to be"; "there may be"), a feature that fits well with the typically legalistic discursive approach of LCIA. Once again the association of arbitration with litigation, while functional to the promotion of mediation, encourages an interpretation of arbitration as a not-so-convenient option.

A similar impression is also conveyed by the description of mediation included in the SCC site. SCC does not provide a definition of arbitration, and its presentation of mediation is only slightly more explanatory, embedded as it is in a text whose focal point is clearly procedural:

(16) SCC Mediation Institute was established in 1999 to assist in the settlement of domestic and international disputes in accordance with the SCC Mediation Rules.
The SCC Mediation Rules offers [sic] an <u>efficient dispute resolution to parties not wishing to engage in formal arbitral proceedings</u>.
The salient features of the Rules are the following:

- A sole Mediator is appointed, unless otherwise agreed by the parties. The Mediator may be appointed by the parties jointly, or by the SCC Mediation Institute.
- The time limit for the Mediation is two months, unless otherwise agreed by the parties.
- After having reached a settlement agreement, the parties may agree to appoint the Mediator as arbitrator in order to enable him to confirm the settlement agreement in an arbitral award.

Mediation is defined against arbitration ("parties … not wishing to engage in *formal* arbitral proceeding"), but the definition in turn qualifies arbitration – which the SCC website does not define – as a *formal* procedure, thereby conveying an impression of lack of freedom, and evoking litigation.

The last case is represented by the Milan Arbitration Chamber. As with arbitration, the Milan Chamber provides a full definition of mediation (underlined in the text), which it contrasts – as pointed out in Section §2.3 – with *both* litigation and arbitration:

(17) Business Mediation is the intervention of a neutral third party in a dispute or negotiation with the purpose of assisting the parties to reach a mutual satisfactory agreement.
Mediation is voluntary and confidential.
Any settlement reached becomes binding once put into writing and signed by the parties.
If parties cannot find a settlement through the mediation, they are free to arbitrate or litigate.
Mediation has a number of advantages over litigation and arbitration processes:
- **Informal and flexible** - the process suits companies' needs.
- **Successful** - 90 per cent of cases are settled during Mediation.
- **Quick** - Mediation meeting lasts 4 to 8 hours, the entire process usually takes place within 35 days.
- **Low cost** - Mediation is a less expensive way to resolve disputes.
- **Mediation can maintain business relationships.**

Once again, mediation is defined against the background of the better known option of arbitration, which is used as a benchmark against which the advantages of mediation are measured.

3. Closing considerations

The analysis of the discursive strategies adopted in each of the websites examined to deal with different forms of dispute resolution along the arbitration / mediation / ADR continuum shows that, in spite of considerable variation, in three out of four websites there is an obvious effort to differentiate arbitration from litigation, in some cases explicitly, through explanation and comparison as in ICC, or through direct argumentation, as in LCIA, or more implicitly, as in the Milan Chamber website, which simply describes the advantages of arbitration in operational terms. SCC stands out as the only site which does not argue in favour of arbitration, a fact which is in line with the

Swedish tradition of verbal concision in legislative drafting,[2] but could also be seen as the result of SCC's status as the arbitration institution of choice in East-West relations and in investment treaty arbitration.

Particularly interesting is LCIA's defence of the advantages of arbitration vis-à-vis the "vociferous and sustained criticism" (cf. example 7 above) levelled against it attributing to arbitration the same expensiveness and delay characterising court litigation, as it presupposes that what has come under criticism is not the spirit of arbitration itself, but rather arbitration as conducted by the major arbitral institutions. In this context it is highly meaningful that evidence of the discursive encroachment of judicial discourse should be found mainly, and most evidently, in the texts of LCIA: in them litigative discourse clearly intrudes into the discourse of non-judicial dispute resolution.

If arbitration is typically pitched against litigation, mediation is set against the background of arbitration – or, more often, of arbitration *and* litigation. This comparative approach to the description/ definition of mediation is also shared by SCC, and can therefore be seen as a discursive trait that is common to all websites, despite the persistence of considerable variation at other levels, not least that of terminology, with *mediation* alternating with *ADR* and other expressions like *conciliation, ODR,* etc. While the perceived graduation in terms of formality between mediation and arbitration, and between arbitration and litigation along the litigation / arbitration / mediation cline justifies the use of this comparative strategy, the close association between arbitration and litigation often entailed in the description of mediation has the effect of pushing arbitration towards the litigation end of the continuum, thus corroborating the allegations of increasing judicialization to which it is subject.

2 The Stockholm Rules, issued in 1999, were by far the shortest amongst those of major arbitration institutions (4,055 words, against 6,026 in UNCITRAL Rules, 6,277 in ICC Rules and 8,266 in LCIA) and had the lowest number of words per sentence. The new Rules, issued in 2007, have just over 5,900 words. Cf. Garzone (2003: 186-187).

References

Bernardini, Piero 2000. *L'arbitrato commerciale internazionale*. Milano: Giuffrè.

Bhatia, Vijay K. 2004. *Worlds of Written Discourse. A Genre-Based Approach*. London: Continuum.

Bhatia, Vijay K. 2007. Interdiscursivity in Critical Genre Analysis. *Simpósio Internacional de Géneros Yextuais. Anais Proceedings*. Tubarão SC (Brazil): UNISUL, 391-400 (online at <http://www3.unisul.br/paginas/ensino/pos/linguagem/cd/English/36i.pdf>).

Candlin, Chistopher N. / Maley, Yon 1994. Framing the dispute. *International Journal for the Semiotics of Law/Revue Internationale de Semiotique Juridique* 7/19, 75-98.

Candlin, Christopher N. / Maley, Yon 1997. Intertextuality and Interdiscursivity in the Discourse of Alternative Dispute Resolution. In Gunnarsson, Britt-Louise / Linell, Per / Nordberg, Bengt (eds) *The Construction of Professional Discourse*. London: Longman, 201-222.

Candlin, Christopher N. 2006. Accounting for Interdiscursivity: Challenges to Professional Expertise. In Gotti, Maurizio / Giannoni, Davide (eds) *New Trends in Specialized Discourse Analysis*. Bern: Peter Lang, 21-45.

Fairclough, Norman 2003. *Analysing Discourse – Textual Research for Social Research*. New York: Routledge.

Garzone, Giuliana 2003. Arbitration Rules across Legal Cultures: An Intercultural Approach. In Bhatia, Vijay / Candlin, Christopher / Gotti, Maurizio (eds) *Legal Discourse in Multilingual and Multicultural Contexts: Arbitration Texts in Europe*. Bern: Peter Lang, 177-220.

Hunter, Martin / Marriott, Arthur / Veder, V. V. 1995. *The Internationalisation of Arbitration*. London: Graham and Trotman.

Marriott, Arthur 2004. Less is More: Directing Arbitration Procedures. *Arbitration International* 16/3: 353-356.

Mattli, Walter 2001. Private Justice in a Global Economy: From Litigation to Arbitration. *International Organization* 554/4, 919-947.

Miles, Wendy 2003. Practical Issues for Appointment of Arbitrators: Lawyer vs. Non-Lawyer and Sole Arbitrator vs. Panel of Three or More. *Journal of International Arbitration* 20/3: 219–232.

Nabatchi, Tina 2007. The Institutionalization of Alternative Dispute Resolution in the Federal Government. *Public Administration Review* 67:4, 646-661.

Nariman, Fali S. 2000. The Spirit of Arbitration: The Tenth Annual Goff Lecture. *Arbitration International* 16/3: 261-278.

Reiner, Andreas 1998 Les mesures provisoires et conservatoires et l'arbitrage international, notamment l'Arbitrage CCI. *Journal du Droit International* 4, 853- 904.

Sanders, Pieter 1999. *Quo Vadis Arbitration*? Sixty Years of *Arbitration Practice, A Comparative Study*. The Hague: Kluwer Law International.

Scott, Mike 2004. *WordSmith Tools Version 4*. Oxford: Oxford University Press.

Tang, Houzhi. 1996. Is There an Expanding Culture that Favors Combining Arbitration with Conciliation or Other ADR Procedures? In van den Berg, Albert (ed.) *International Dispute Resolution: Towards an International Arbitration Culture. ICCA Congress Series* 8/47, 101-120.

Van Rees, M. Agnes 2002. Indicators of Dissociation. In van Eemeren, Frans H. / Houtlosser, Peter (eds) *Argumentation in Practice*. Amsterdam: John Benjamins, 53-67.

STEFANIA M. MACI*

The Modus Operandi of Litigation in Arbitration

1. Introduction

Due to the rapid expansion and growth of international trade, the institution of arbitration has been largely and consistently incorporated into the commercial systems of most countries. Arbitration is, therefore, a method of amicable settlement of disputes in international trade settings, particularly when parties belong to different legal traditions. Parties are free to choose the way in which they want their dispute resolved. The choice of whether to resolve international commercial disputes through legal jurisdiction or arbitration depends on the type of agreements the parties have signed in the contract, which is generally expressed through the arbitral clause, i.e., an agreement within an international agreement (Seriki 2006). Indeed, as indicated by the Italian Code of Civil Procedure (Article 808), "The parties may establish in their contract or in a separate document that disputes arising out of the contract may be decided by arbitrators, provided such disputes are made subject to an arbitration agreement".[1] Although the agreement is essentially commercial, the resolution of the dispute has a legal effect: "Except in those cases covered by Article 825, as from the date of its

---

* The research on which this chapter is based is part of an international research project entitled *International Commercial Arbitration Practices: A Discourse Analytical Study* (http://www.english.cityu.edu.hk/arbitration/), headed by prof. Vijay Bhatia of the City University of Hong Kong. It also contributes to the National Research Programme *Tension and Change in Domain-specific Genres* directed by prof. Maurizio Gotti of the University of Bergamo, funded by the Italian Ministry of University (COFIN Grant No. 2007JCY9Y9).

1 Available at <http://www.codicisimone.it/codici/index0.htm> (my translation).

last signature the award shall have the same effects as a judgment rendered by the judicial authority" (Article 824 bis).

Despite the fact that arbitration is an alternative to litigation, just like other modes of Alternative Dispute Resolution (ADR) such as mediation and conciliation, it is quite different from these because in the latter the parties are effectively involved in the process. In arbitration, the parties agree that an independent third party, the Arbitrator or the Arbitral Tribunal, should pronounce the final decision after considering the evidence and submissions in exactly the same way as a judge would do in a court of law. In other words, arbitration seems to be a sort of private litigation (Rutherford 2004). Indeed, the webpages of the International Bar Association (IBA), the Chartered Institute of Arbitrators (CIArb), the International Chamber of Commerce and Court of Arbitration-Italy (ICC) and the Italian Association for Arbitration (AIA), while promoting international arbitration as an alternative to litigation, offer legal expertise for such a process. The arbitral clause inserted in (inter)national commercial transactions has a legal nature which foreshadows the jurisdictional process of arbitration. It is, therefore, evident that there is a lack of integrity in international arbitration practices: the type of language employed in arbitral awards is legal.

Studies in arbitration have been extensively carried out from the viewpoint of law, focussing on such issues as the role of international arbitration (Brower 2008), the drafting and enforcement of arbitration awards (Zaiwalla 2003; Marriott 2004; Debattista 2005; Webster 2006), the appointment and number of arbitrators (Miles 2003; Kurkela *et al.* 2007) and their international function (Aksen 2007), challenging arbitrators and awards (Nicholas/Partasides 2007) and several other issues dealt with in the many specialised journals on arbitration which were founded in the last few decades. In Italy, arbitration law has been the object of in-depth legal interpretation (Ferronato/Rebecca 1998; Bocchini 2006) and training courses (e.g. those of the International Arbitration Chamber of Milan); particular attention has also been devoted to those aspects connected with the challenge of arbitral awards (Consolo 2006; Lino 2006; Santi Di Paola 2006). Yet there has been little research about the relationship between arbitration and litigation despite the fact that "ICA [International Commercial Arbitration] has become almost indistinguishable from litigation" (Nariman 2000: 262). This relationship is, however, the main focus of a recent linguistic research project whose results have been published in Bhatia *et al.* (2003a, 2003b), and of a current project on *International Commercial Arbitration Practices: A Discourse Analytical Study.*[2] More recently, the analysis of Italian arbitration *in action* has revealed instances of arbitration colonized by litigation (Gotti/Anesa forth.; Maci forth.).

It is the purpose of this chapter to reveal the extent to which arbitration processes follow litigation procedures in (inter)national contexts. To attain this goal, this study will investigate those legal aspects in arbitral awards which have caused a modification of Italian arbitration practices in terms of intentions, purposes, and processes. The results will demonstrate that linguistic integrity in international arbitration is far from being adopted: arbitration encourages the exploitation of litigation features particularly in the discourse of awards.

2. The Background

2.1. Arbitration in Italy

The 1994 reform of the Italian Civil Procedure Code (hence CPC) officially promulgated arbitration as a mode of Alternative Dispute Resolution and aligned Italy with both European and international legislation. Yet, while in most European countries the adoption of the UNCITRAL Model Law on International Commercial Arbitration favoured the development of international arbitration into a flexible procedure free from the constrictions of national laws, in Italy the provision of separate regulations for national and international arbitration (Article 832 of the CPC) made international arbitration a subcategory of national arbitration. The recognition of the potential conflicts existing between the Italian Arbitration Law as stated in the CPC and inter-

2 For further information, see <http://www.english.cityu.edu.hk/arbitration/>.

national conventions led to the drafting of Law 80/2005 which delegated the reform of arbitration legislation to the Government in order to resolve such issues (Cutolo/Esposito 2007: 53). The reform drafted by the government legislators took place in 2006 with Legislative Decree 40.[3] Since then, the local Chambers of Commerce, within which Arbitral Courts have been constituted, have strongly invited the parties not only to adopt a standard arbitration procedure according to the guidelines of its institutional body (the Arbitral Chamber of the local Chamber of Commerce), but also to allow the Arbitral Chamber to appoint legal experts as arbitrators.[4] The reason for that lies in the fact that the majority of awards delivered up to 2006 have been challenged in front of the Court of Appeal on legal grounds. Therefore, if the parties are strongly recommended to have recourse to standard arbitration under the control of an institutional body with legal experts as arbitrators, then arbitration practices are likely to develop as litigation proceedings.

3. Corpus and methodological approach

Despite the fact that the original concept of international arbitration meant having an expert to settle a commercial dispute, lawyers are commonly regarded as the best people with enough arbitral competence and expertise to deal with this matter (Aksen 2007: 257). In order to understand the extent to which arbitration has been hybridised by legal language in Italy, I collected six awards written in Italian and

3 See the link at <http://www.parlamento.it/leggi/deleghe/06040dl.htm>.

4 In theory, any professional can be a member of the Board of Arbitrators of the local Arbitration Chamber. This is possible provided that the would-be arbitrator complies with certain requirements as established by the law, such as, for example, having at least three-years' experience in legal and financial matters and having been appointed as an arbitrator at least three times. In practice, only legal specialists are appointed as *arbitrators* in an arbitration procedure, whereas all the other experts are appointed as *consultants*.

pronounced in Italy.[5] Although the issue of confidentiality, which is the main prerogative of international arbitration, might have resulted in corpus paucity, I nevertheless was able to create a corpus of 30,512 words. All awards were scanned and digitalized in text format in order to allow a quantitative computation, which was then followed by a qualitative analysis.

If on the one hand the unprecedented increase in global trade and commerce has created zones of mixed jurisdiction (Bhatia 2003: 353), on the other the fact that the arbitral award has a legal effect on commercial disputes forces the arbitral tribunal to follow the language of the legal system within which the award is issued. As sentence construction seems to be the main trait of the legal language pertaining to the Italian legal system, I concentrated my research on this linguistic feature, which is particularly evident in my corpus.

4. Results and discussion

4.1. The Italian corpus: sentence length.

In a previous analysis (Maci forthcoming), I illustrated how the cognitive structuring and the type of register used in awards strongly resembles the language used in judicial discourse. Indeed, both awards and verdicts have elements that can be itemized in the moves and steps classified by Bhatia (1993) for legal cases. These are: identification of the case; facts; *ratio decidendi*; pronouncing judgement. Furthermore, the lexical items found in awards are those pertaining to legal language and can be summarized in the use of archaic and Latin

---

5 One award (issued in 2006) was obtained from the Arbitral Chamber of Venice; one (issued in 2005) from a lawyer's office in Milan; one (2004) was obtained from the International Arbitration Chamber of the Milan Chamber of Commerce; one (2001) was retrieved from the link <http://lavoropubblico.formez.it/sections/focus/arbitrato/giurisprudenza/camera-arbitrale> and one (2000) downloaded from <www.giust.amm.it>.

forms, specialized terms, nominalizations, pre-modifications, passives and impersonal constructions, fragmentation of the syntactic structure characterized also by continuous cross-referencing to laws, regulations, and provisions. Amongst the characteristics of legal language in Italy, there is a high frequency of lengthy and complex sentences (Belotti/Facchinetti/Giannoni 2003: 215). Statutory language is indeed characterized by such a feature which arises from the fact that legislators tend to include all possible information in a single sentence in order to avoid ambiguity and vagueness, and to such an extent that they increase the extent of information density (Belotti 2002: 131). Although in countries where civil law is applied, legal statements express general principles in order to allow flexibility while giving the impression of lack of vagueness (Bhatia 2003: 338), judgements have to be detailed and specific because of their performative function.[6] The Italian corpus of arbitral awards is characterized by a frequent occurrence of long propositions (Table 1):

	IAA no.1	IAA no.2	IAA no.3	IAA no.4	IAA no.5	IAA no. 6	*Total*
sentences separated by full stop	59	19	56	127	113	185	*559*
number of words	3,687	1,687	2,418	5,525	6,778	10,417	*30,512*
average sentence length	62.49	88.78	43.17	43.50	59.98	56.30	*54.58*
sentences separated by semi-colon	24	17	7	21	25	13	*243*
average sentence length	4.42	46.86	38.38	37.33	49.11	52.61	*45.81*

Table 1. Average sentence length.

The data in Table 1 reveal that the average sentence length is longer than the traditional legal sentence, which, as Belotti points out (2002: 115), was measured in 37.06 words per sentence in the 1990s. Recently,

6 Maley (1994: 13) states that verbosity and prolixity in legal language date back to the eighteenth century: at that time, the longer the document, the more expensive the drafting fee.

Hiltunen (2001: 56) claimed that an average was about 45.04 words per sentence. Although these rates have been calculated for the English legal system, we can apply them to the Italian one since there the relatively recent reform concerning the simplification of administrative and legal language, which has been in force since 1993,[7] suggests that sentences in legal and administrative texts should contain no more than 25 words. Table 1 above shows an average of 54.58 words per sentence, as illustrated in the fourth row. Nevertheless, those Italian arbitral awards taken into consideration have revealed peculiar punctuation usage. Indeed, any sentence ending with a full stop usually corresponds to a legal topic expressed in a paragraph which contains more than one sentence separated by a series of semi-colons. If we take into consideration such an atypical orthographic device, we may add the numbers of sentences separated by a semicolon to the general figures given in row four. In this case, the average number of words contained in a sentence would be reduced to 45.81, in line with Hiltunen's (2001) research yet still disregarding the suggestions provided by the Italian Government concerning the simplification of legal language.

4.2. Sentence type

Sentence length, obviously, has a great impact on readability: the longer the sentence, the more difficult it is to understand. The first analytical step involving sentence length has therefore been the classification of sentence types. Simple sentences, i.e. sentences containing one predicate, are generally easier to understand because of the simplicity of their syntactic construction. Complex sentences, on the contrary, are sentences consisting of one main clause and one or more subordinates. They are, indeed, difficult to understand, not only because of their length but also because of the presence of embedded and left- and right-dislocated clauses. Indeed, the presence of subordinates, present participles or gerunds that interrupt or even invert the typical Italian structure S + V + O + Adjunct, causes problems of accessibili-

7 See <http://www.funzionepubblica.it/chiaro/direttiva.pdf>.

ty, as we can see in the Italian arbitral award (IAA) excerpted below (my translation):

(1) Che, in concreto, l'esecuzione dei lavori possa aver comportato per l'Impresa costi non preventivati è argomento che non merita approfondimento istruttorio, essendo noto che nei contratti di appalto il 'rischio economico' (art. 1655: "con organizzazione dei mezzi necessari e con gestione a proprio rischio") è a carico, per definizione, dell' appaltatore.
[In practice, the fact that carrying out the work could have obliged the company to bear unforeseen costs is a topic which does not deserve further in-depth analysis from a pre-trial perspective, as it is a well-known fact that in a contract 'the economic risk' (art 1655: "with organization of the necessary tools and with at-own-risk management") is, by definition, to be borne by the contractor] (IAA no. 5)

Here, we have a main sentence which is introduced by a *that*-clause and followed by: (i) a rclativc, (ii) an implicit causal sentence expressed by means of a gerund, (iii) another *that*-clause which has (iv) an embedded reference to a provision of the CPC.

As we can see from Table 2 below, there is a great occurrence of complex sentences in IAAs:

	SIMPLE	*COMPLEX*	*TOTAL*
IAA no. 1	17 (23%)	58 (77%)	75
IAA no. 2	5 (16%)	26 (84%)	31
IAA no. 3	14 (20%)	55 (80%)	69
IAA no. 4	38 (27%)	101 (73%)	139
IAA no. 5	84 (43%)	112 (57%)	196
IAA no. 6	44 (25%)	171 (75%)	215
TOTAL	202 (28%)	523 (72%)	725

Table 2. Breakdown of simple and complex sentences in Italian awards.

The figures in Table 2 reveal that IAAs display a syntax in which complex sentences play an important role, as they account for 72% of all clauses, whereas simple sentences seem to have a more marginal role. An in-depth analysis makes it clear that 39.28% of complex sentences appears in the *ratio decidendi* section of the IAAs, whereas the rest (61.72%) is spread over the other three remaining sections (which roughly indicates an average of 20%). The fact that complex sentences are concentrated in the award *motivation* is vital for IAAs. Indeed, since the main aim of the arbitral tribunal is to pronounce awards on the basis of the objective and impartial interpretation of the documents presented by the parties, the resulting interpretation will be constructed *contra proferentem*, i.e., against the interests of the party responsible for drafting the award (McMeel 2005). This implies that in order to be as specific as possible, awards have to be compiled with a detailed and unambiguous description of all legally relevant facts, and a precise account of the arbitrators' reasoning, which in turn are responsible for lengthy sentences. Only after stating the Arbitral Tribunal's (argumentative) reasoning is the decision pronounced by means of a simple sentence, with a more linear structure and the use of the present simple indicative, the latter implicitly indicating the performative meaning of the decision (Garzone 2003: 206) because of its directness and unconditionality.

4.3. Frequency of secondary clauses

In my corpus, the figures of main clauses (559) and secondary clauses (872) show a difference of about 36%. Secondary clauses have been classified according to their distribution, as Table 3 shows. As Hiltunen (2001: 61) illustrates, *that*- and relative clauses are the most commonly used sentences in legal language. This, too, seems to be a feature of awards. Indeed, *that*-clauses and relative sentences respectively cover 26% and 39% of the total sentences. *That*-clauses mainly appear in the detailed representation of when and where the plaintiff's and the defendant's *memoriae* are reported (76%) and in the *ratio decidendi* part (24%), where the arbitrators' reasoning is developed. Indeed, they are introduced by such verbs as *chiedere* [to ask], *aggiungere* [to add], *convenire* [to agree], *ritenere* [to deem], *rammentare* [to remember/remind] *affermare* [to claim] and occur in reported speech structures, as we can see in examples (2) and (3).

	that clause	*relative clause*	*Infinitive clause*	*causal clause*	*concessive clause*	*purpose clause*	*if clause*	*Total*
IAA no.1	47 (29%)	63 (38%)	8 (5%)	25 (15%)	6 (4%)	13 (8%)	2 (1%)	164
IAA no.2	13 (24%)	10 (19%)	12 (23%)	13 (24%)	4 (8%)	1 (2%)	0	53
IAA no.3	19 (17%)	54 (49%)	0	23 (21%)	9 (8%)	5 (5%)	0	110
IAA no.4	30 (22%)	55 (41%)	14 (11%)	20 (15%)	10 (8%)	5 (4%)	0	133
IAA no.5	56 (46%)	24 (29%)	23 (19%)	17 (14%)	0	1 (1%)	0	122
IAA no.6	63 (22%)	137 (47%)	13 (4%)	53 (18%)	15 (5%)	9 (3%)	0	290
TOT	228 (26%)	343 (39%)	70 (8%)	151 (17%	44 (5%)	34 (4%)	2 (0.2%)	872

Table 3. Distribution of secondary sentences.

(2) Rileva ancora la resistente che le parole 'cyber' e 'search' sono oggi termini [...]
[the defendant claims that nowadays the words 'cyber' and 'search' are terms [...] (IAA no. 4)

(3) [...] ritiene il Collegio che ci si trovi di fronte ad argomento radicalmente nuovo [...]
[the arbitral tribunal believes that a completely new topic is being dealt with] (IAA no. 5)

All relative clauses in my corpus are defining, and occur whenever there is a need to unambiguously limit and define facts, people and norms. This clearly makes for clarity. Yet the tendency to render relative clauses more concise, paradoxically results in such a great information density that readability seems to be compromised: almost 50% of the relative clauses are formed with the omission of the relative pronoun and the auxiliary. Thus, the main verb of the relative clause becomes a past participle which can render the clause more pedantic semantically, especially when embedded in a secondary clause, or as a right-branching clause of a secondary sentence, as excerpt (4) below shows:

(4) Il Collegio, precisato l'acconto che gli Arbitri ritenevano di chiedere in via solidale alle parti, disponeva C.T.D. – nominando l'Ing. M.B. – con riserva di formulare il quesito alla successiva udienza, precisando che allo stesso C.T. le parti, in solido, avrebbero dovuto preventivamente versare il fondo spese – poi indicato in € 4.000 + accessori.
[The Arbitral tribunal, after defining the refund the Arbitrators decided to award to the parties jointly, requested the consultant – appointing Ing. M. B. – to conditionally formulate the question at the following hearing, and emphasized that the parties should have already paid the expenses to the consultant, later indicated as € 4,000 plus extra charges] (IAA no.5)

As to causal sentences, in Italian they can be expressed with such connectives as *poiché*, *dato che* [as, since], *perché* [because]. In this case they are explicit. They can also be implicitly expressed by means of non-finite clauses realized with the gerund. In my corpus, 45% of the causal sentences are conveyed in such an implicit way. This increases conciseness because the use of non-finite forms in the gerund avoids the use of causal connectives. These forms compact information, but since they are used also when the subject of the secondary clause is different from the subject of the main clause, they augment semantic complexity, as example (5) shows:

(5) Non è rilevante stabilire in questa sede che conseguenze si abbiano nel caso di pluralità di parti necessaria: nella presente controversia indubbiamente siamo in presenza di un litisconsorzio facoltativo semplice, trattandosi di domande volte ad ottenere l'adempimento di obbligazioni che o sono solidali (secondo la prospettazione dell'attore) o sono del tutto autonome e diverse (secondo la prospettazione dei convenuti).
[Here, deciding what consequences may result where there has been a plurality of parties is not relevant. In the present dispute, we undoubtedly have to deal with an optional simple case of litigation, since it concerns requests aimed at obtaining the fulfilment of obligations which are either joint (according to the plaintiff) or completely autonomous and different (according to the defendant)] (IAA no. 1).

5. Concluding remarks

The analysis of some Italian awards has shown that they are conceived as judicial sentences. While the UNCITRAL MODEL LAW[8] calls for international arbitral alignment and harmonization, the 2006 Italian Reform seems to act as the national response to a global request, reflecting the different legal cultures underlying arbitration in those countries. Indeed, arbitral awards seem to be pronounced according to the legal system of the nation in which they have been issued. Therefore, not only do awards take a legal form but also the legal language typical of their legal cultures. Such an adaptation of international arbitration to national legal procedures seems to be particularly evident in the realization of Italian awards, which are characterized by lengthy sentences.

IAAs contain long sentences with dense information packaging because of the necessity placed on the Arbitrator to unambiguously identify the discourse referents and to explain the Arbitral Tribunal's reasoning in pronouncing the final decision in detail. Despite the fact that arbitration is essentially commercial, the Italian award is treated as if it were a legal sentence. Although sentences and awards are issued for laymen wishing for clear resolutions to resolve their disputes, the documents are compiled by legal experts who express their legal voice. Hence, syntactic patterns typical of legal language are exploited to the full: complex sentences are mainly used, with left, right-dislocated and embedded sentences and exophoric and endophoric references. This is an attempt to reflect precision and map the text, to augment semantic density, which may result in non-comprehension. Lengthy sentences are used to unambiguously identify the discourse referents *and* the Arbitral Tribunal's reasoning. Since, however, simple sentences are usually found whenever the decision or one point in argumentation is made clear, IAAs appear less complicated for businessmen.

As the Milan Chamber of National and International Arbitration states, "arbitration is an extra-judicial method of dispute resolution"

8 Available at <http://www.uncitral.org/>.

(<www.camera-arbitrale.it/show.jsp?page=118303>). This means that arbitration is a *private* (= confidential) *judicial process* and an alternative to the *public judicial process* held in the court of law. It is therefore evident that Italian (inter)national arbitration follows the litigation *modus operandi* of Italian legal culture – as does arbitration language.

References

Aksen, Gerald 2007. Reflection on International Arbitrator. *Arbitration International* 23/2, 255-259.

Belotti, Ulisse 2002. The Language of Italian Arbitration Rules in English: Some Measurable Aspects. *Linguistica e Filologia* 15, 113-141.

Belotti, Ulisse / Facchinetti, Roberta / Giannoni, Davide, Simone. 2003. An Introduction to the Legal System in Italy. In Bhatia/Candlin/Engberg/Trosborg (eds), 193-224.

Bhatia, Vijay 1993. *Analyzing Genre Language Use in Professional Settings*. London: Longman.

Bhatia, Vijay 2003. Specificity and Generality in Legislative Expression. In Bhatia/Candlin/Gotti (eds), 337-356.

Bhatia, Vijay / Candlin, Christopher, N. / Engberg, Jan / Trosborg, Ann (eds) 2003. *Multilingual and Multicultural Contexts of Legislation. An International Perspective*. Frankfurt a.M.: Peter Lang.

Bhatia, Vijay / Candlin, Christopher, N. / Gotti, Maurizio (eds) 2003. *Legal Discourse in Multilingual and Multicultural Contexts. Arbitration Texts in Europe*. Bern: Peter Lang.

Bocchini, Ermanno (ed.) 2006. *L'Arbitrato*. Padova: CEDAM.

Brower, Charles N. 2008. W(h)ither International Arbitration?. *Arbitration International* 24/2, 181-197.

Camera Arbitrale di Milano. *L'Arbitrato*. At <www.camera-arbitrale.it/show.jsp?page=118303>.

Consolo, Claudio. 2006. *Le impugnazioni delle sentenze e dei lodi.* Padova: CEDAM.

Cutolo, Daniele / Esposito, Antonio 2007. The Reform of the Italian Arbitration Law. The Challenging of Arbitrators and the Setting of Time Limits. *Journal of International Arbitration* 24/1, 49-62.

Decreto Legislativo 40/2006. At <http://www.parlamento.it/leggi/deleghe/06040dl.htm>.

Debattista, Charles 2005. Drafting Enforceable Arbitration Clauses. *Arbitration International* 21/2, 233-240.

Dipartimento per la Funzione Pubblica. 1993. *Direttiva sulla semplificazione del linguaggio dei testi amministrativi.* At <http://www.funzionepubblica.it/chiaro/direttiva.pdf>.

Ferronato, Francesco / Rebecca, Giuseppe1998. *L'Arbitrato*. Lavis (TN): Il Sole 24Ore.

Garzone, Giuliana. 2003. Arbitration Rules across Legal Cultures: an Intercultural Approach. In Bhatia/Candlin/Gotti (eds), 177-220.

Gotti, Maurizio / Anesa, Patrizia. (forthcoming). Professional Identities in Italian Arbitral Awards: The Spread of Lawyers' Language. In Bhatia, Vijay K. / Evangelisti Allori, Paola (eds) *Issues of Identity in and across Cultures and Professional Worlds*. Bern: Peter Lang.

Hiltunen, Risto. 2001. Some Syntactic Properties of English Law Language. In Hiltunen, Risto / Battarbee, Keith / Peikola, Matti / Tanskanen, Sanna-Kaisa (eds) *English in Zigs and Zags: A Festschrift for Marita Gustafsson*, Anglicana Turkuensia, 23: 53-66.

Kurkela, Matti S. / Levin, Richard C. / Liebscher, Christoph / Sommer, Patrick 2007. Certain Procedural Issues in Arbitrating Competition Cases. *Journal of International Arbitration* 24/2, 18-210.

Lino, Vincenzo 2006. *Cassazione e Arbitrato.* Cercola (NA): Edizioni Giuridiche Simone.

Maci, Stefania Maria (forthcoming). Arbitration in Italy. Litigation Procedures in Arbitral Practice. In Bhatia, Vijay K. / Evangelisti Allori, Paola (eds) *Issues of Identity in and across Cultures and Professional Worlds.* Bern: Peter Lang.

Maley, Yon 1994. The Language of the Law. In Gibbons, John (ed.) *Language and the Law*. London: Longman, 11-50.

Marriott, Arthur. 2004. Less is More: Directing Arbitration Procedures. *Arbitration International* 16/3, 261-278.

McMeel, Gerard 2005. Language and the Law Revisited: An Intellectual History of Contractual Interpretation. *Common Law World Review* 34/3, 256-286.

Miles, Wendy 2003. Practical Issues for Appointment of Arbitrators: Lawyer vs. Non-Lawyer and Sole Arbitrator vs. Panel of Three (or More). *Journal of International Arbitration* 20/3, 219-232.

Nariman, Fali S. 2000. The Spirit of Arbitration. *Arbitration International* 16/3, 261-278.

Nicholas, Geoff / Partasides, Constantine 2007. LCIA Court Decisions on Challenges to Arbitrators: A Proposal to Publish. *Arbitration International* 23/1, 1-41.

Rutherford, Marcus 2004. Legal Know-How? Arbitration in the UK. At <http://www.reedsmith.com/library/search_library.cfm?Fa Area1 =CustomWidgets.content_view_1&cit_id=3776> [19.08. 2008].

Santi Di Paola, Nunzio 2006. *Il Nuovo Processo di Cassazione e Arbitrato*. Repubblica di San Marino: Maggioli Editore.

Seriki, Hakeem 2006. Anti-Suit Injunctions and Abitration: A Final Nail in the Coffin? *Journal of International Arbitration* 23/1, 25-38.

UNCITRAL MODEL LAW at <http://www.uncitral.org/> [07.09. 2008].

Webster, Thomas H. 2006. Evolving Principles in Enforcing Awards Subject to Annulment Proceedings. *Journal of International Arbitration* 23/3, 201-226.

Zaiwalla, Sarosh 2003. Challenging Arbitral Awards: Finality is Good but Justice is Better. *Journal of International Arbitration* 20/2, 199-204.

ANNE WAGNER

Acquiring Knowledge in the International Commercial Arbitration Space in France

His judgments suited neither side,
Forsooth, in either party's view,
He never held the balance true
But Swerved in every cause he tried.
(The Arbiter, the Almoner and the Hermit, *Fables of Jean de La Fontaine*, Book XII)

Equity and the ideal of justice it conveys
Exactly correspond to the noble-mindedness of people.
(Henry Motulsky)

Justice has always been in the hands of not only traditional courts but also arbitration jurisdictions. French procedures, with their traditional courts, are very well organized but sometimes far too complex and rigid. Time is one of the constraints leading to the emergence of an alternative mode of resolution. The 'amicable' or alternative dispute resolution is considered faster and more flexible in case treatments.

The emergence of commercial arbitration in France has a very long history dating back to the 13th century. The interest raised by arbitration processes led in 1999 the *Chambre Arbitrale de Paris (CAP)* to ask for wider powers over rules, regulating arbitration processes in France. This method of dispute resolution, as an alternative to litigation in courts, was supported not only by the Government but very definitively by the French courts for the simple pragmatic reasons that (1) it was considered a speedier, less expensive process and that (2) it relieved the court of much valued time constraints.

International arbitration, which happens to be a site of contention for cross-cultural as well as cross-jurisdictional concerns, raises interesting conceptual, practical, technical and legal issues regarding its scope, its basis, its proceedings, the choice of procedural and substantive rules. But, how do we capture the complexity of the cross-cultural environment we are to look at and how is it going to be a challenge to acquire a valid and communicative discourse in the French arbitration discourse?

1. Mapping French arbitration law

1.1. The evolution of French arbitration practice

Arbitration was conceived from the very start as a more flexible, adaptable, fair mode of justice and as a 'derivation circuit'.[1] With the various meanings of equity in history, this concept has always evolved to form a consensus in international commercial arbitration. Aristotle (1984) was the first one to give a definition of equity:

> What creates the problem is that the equitable is just, but not the legally just, but a correction of legal justice. The reason is that all law is universal, but about some things it is not possible to make a universal statement which will be correct. In those cases, then, in which it is necessary to speak universally, but not possible to do so correctly, the law takes the usual case, though it is not ignorant of the possibility of error [...]. When the law speaks universally, then, a case arises on it which is not covered by the universal statement, then it is right, when the legislator fails us and has erred by over-simplicity to correct the omission – to say what the legislator himself would have said had he been present, and would have put into his law if he had known. Hence, the equitable is just, and better than one kind of justice – not better than absolute justice but better than the error that arises from the absoluteness of the

---

1 This 'derivation circuit' was initiated to decrease the workload in ordinary state jurisdictions. From an interview of R. Badinter to the newspaper *Le Monde* (19 March 1996: 14): "Je pense que toutes les forces de médiation sont utiles. Certains types de conflits appellent ce que je dénommerai des circuits de dérivations". [My translation "I think that all forces of mediation are useful. Some kinds of conflicts need what I would call derivation circuits."]

> statement. And this is the nature of the equitable, a correction of law where it is defective owing to its universality.

The principle of equity is highly visible in several domestic laws. For arbitration, the best meaning to consider would be the notion of *aequitas* which means 'common sense and justice' so as to avoid the confusion with its *common law* sense. This notion of *aequitas* is the one presently used in civil law.

There were, and there still are multifarious ways of solving disputes in a social space (Belley 1994: 15),[2] in a living reality (Gény 1922: 75). Thus, the arbitrator's prime interest is 'equity' and "arbitration was invented so that equity could be used" (Aristote 1991: 14, my translation). Arbitration is an 'institution of peace' (Gouiffès *et al.* 1997: 12) where all powers of mediation are to be considered. But the use of this 'derivation circuit' took time.

Under the Revolutionary period, arbitration could be sought as a constitutional principle (Constitution of 3 September 1791):

> The right of citizens to terminate definitively their protests with an appeal to arbitration cannot be threatened by acts of the Legislature. (Art. 5, Chapitre V du Pouvoir Judiciaire)

It was its heyday but also the start of its decline (Clère 1981: 3). Abuses and unfair justice were frequent. One of the first regulations imposed resulted from the *Code de Procédure Civile* promulgated by Napoleon in 1806 from articles 1003 to 1028. However, as manifest injustices still prevailed, the *Cour de Cassation* (equivalent to the Supreme Court) decided, in an unprecedented case of 10 July 1843,[3] to declare null and void the arbitration clause.

The hostility to the arbitration clause, especially on commercial issues, was still very important until the end of the 19th century. Several bills were submitted for consideration to the Parliament, but

---

2 "La justice s'exprime de multiples façons dans une grande diversité d'espaces sociaux où l'influence de la légalité étatique s'avère éminemment variable" [My translation: "Justice has several ways of expressing itself in a wide diversity of social spaces where the influence of State legality is extremely variable."]

3 Cass. civ., 10 July 1843: S. 1843, 1, 561; D. 1843, 1, 343.

none of them was conclusive until France ratified the Geneva Protocol of 24 September 1923 and the Geneva Convention of 26 September 1927 relating to international arbitration. This was the beginning of a slow change.

Although the French Law of 31 December 1925[4] was passed stating that the arbitration clause was valid relating to future commercial transactions, its scope was quite unsatisfactory. Only commercial transactions were concerned within the ambit of this Act. The prohibition of 1843 still remained for any mixed transaction, involving both civil and commercial activities.

On 1 February 1926, a congress was organized under the presidency of Louis Dreyfus to discuss the bases for the constitution of several arbitration chambers. A month later, on 25 March 1926, the *Chambre Arbitrale de Paris* (CAP) was officially set up.

On the international level, France signed the New York Convention on the Recognition and Enforcement of Foreign Awards (1958), the European Geneva Convention on International Commercial Arbitration (1961) and the Washington Convention (International Convention for Settlement of Investment Dispute – ICSID) of 18 March 1965. However, France remained ambivalent as to the 'commercial reservations' when it signed the Washington Convention.

In the same period, some high court judges in the *Cour de Cassation* and Court of Appeal of Paris made new rules in law – in their respective jurisdictions – and adopted a more favorable and flexible approach as to the arbitration process when international public policy was at stake.[5]

Consequently, it became necessary to clarify and modernize French Arbitration Law. This was carried out by a series of reforms, of pro-action bias from 1980 to 1981: Decree no. 81-500 of 12 May 1981, articles 1492 to 1497 Part V (International Arbitration), Book IV of the NCPC and articles 1498 to 1507 Part VI (Recognition, en-

---

4 This law was initiated by Louis Dreyfus, French deputy.

5 See 'Matter' in Civ. 17 May 1927, D.P. 1928 I. p.25, note H. Capitant: "To define international payments, it was stated that: A contract should lead to movement of flux and reflux across their borders" [My translation]. Refer also to the 'Messageries maritimes' case, Civ. 21 June 1950.

forcement of, & challenge procedures in the French courts relating to arbitral awards made abroad or in international arbitration). The ambivalent position towards arbitration was waived with the Decree of 16 February 1990.

French jurisprudence slowly evolved with a judgment delivered on 14 November 1991 where it stated that the arbitration clause was legal because of the general principle of autonomy of the arbitration convention:

> The arbitration clause is legal *per se* in the international order, on the basis of the general principle of autonomy of the arbitration convention, the material rule which secures its own efficacy. (Gaudemet-Tallon 1994: 116, my translation)

1.2. Specificities of French international arbitration law

France has not adopted and incorporated in its legislations the provisions of UNCITRAL Model Law of 1985 as it could restrict the powers of control exercised by French domestic courts. Nevertheless, French courts have a strong tradition of judicial non-interference in the arbitral process which is highlighted by a series of particularities enshrined in French administration of justice and law.

Both the *Cour de Cassation* and the Court of Appeal of Paris have a chamber specialized in cases involving arbitration within their territorial jurisdictions. For similar reasons, the President of the High Court jurisdiction in civil matter (*Tribunal de Grande Instance – TGI*) provides support to the arbitral process. This is enshrined in art. L 311-11 of the Code of Judicial Organization, as amended by Law no. 99-957 of 22 November 1999, article 3(2).[6]

For international arbitration, the High Court jurisdiction (*TGI*) is exclusive (art. 1493 para.2 NCPC) and extends to matters of arbitral award enforcement:

---

6 All enforceable titles or decisions can be the subject of compulsory enforcement measures. As provided by Section 3(2) of Law no. 99-957: "Foreign measures and judgments and arbitral awards declared enforceable by a ruling not subject to an appeal suspending enforcement".

> An arbitration agreement may, directly or by reference to arbitration rules, appoint the arbitrator or arbitrators or provide for the method of their appointment. If in an arbitration taking place in France or subjected by the parties to French procedural law difficulties arise in the constitution of the arbitral tribunal, the interested party may bring the matter before the President of the Tribunal de Grande Instance of Paris as provided in Art. 1457, unless the parties agree otherwise.

As provided in Article L311-11 of the New Code of Civil Procedure (NCPC), the president of the *TGI* sits as a single judge and has jurisdiction to grant or refuse an order of *exequatur* of an arbitral award. The judge of the *exequatur* may also decide to sit with three judges.

France enforced a series of rules to regulate arbitration law. The main sources being now applied in France are the Civil Code from articles 2059 to 2061 as well as the New Code of Civil Procedure (NCPC) from articles 1492 to 1507. Article 1492 NCPC provides that "an arbitration is international when it involves interests of international commerce". This rule is established as independent from any State or party's will. Article 1492 was the most problematic one in its interpretation as two concepts were obscure, fuzzy in their meanings – (1) 'international arbitration' and (2) 'international commerce'. Both concepts were clarified in two leading judgments:

(1) The meaning of 'international arbitration' was clearly defined in a leading judgment where the Court of Appeal of Paris[7] stated that:

> the international character of an arbitration must be determined on the basis of the economic reality of the transaction out of which it arises; in this connection, it suffices that the economic transaction in question gives rise to the transfer of goods, services or funds across borders, irrespective of the nationality of parties, the law applicable to the contracts or to the arbitration, and also the place to the arbitration. (Delvolvé *et al.* 2003: 29)

(2) In its judgment of 13 June 1996,[8] the Court of Appeal of Paris defined the second unclear concept provided in 1492 NCPC and stipulated that:

---

7 14 March 1989, *Murgue Seigle v. Coflexip*, Rev. Arb. 1991, p.355.

8 Paris, 13 June 1996, KFTCIC c/Icori Estero et a., Rev. Arb. 1997, p.251, note E. Gaillard.

> In international arbitration, the notion of 'commerciability' must not be confused with that of 'commercial act' in its narrow and technical sense under national laws [...]; the commercial character in question does not depend upon the status of the parties, or the subject-matter of the contract, or the law applicable thereto; it is sufficient for an arbitration to be characterized as both commercial and international, that it involves an economic transaction which entails the movement of goods or services or a payment across borders. And it is irrelevant, in this respect, whether one of the parties to such arbitration is a state, or an entity of a state, and the other a foreign private enterprise and the arbitration concerns the performance of works which are eventually destined to become public. (Delvolvé *et al.* 2003: 32)

Articles 1493 to 1500 of NCPC relate to the recognition and enforcement of awards made in France in international arbitration whereas articles 1501 to 1507 deal with challenge procedures in French courts for these awards. The Civil Code also provided grounds for the use of arbitration procedures under articles 2059 to 2061 but with some very restrictive aspects.

> Article 2059 of the Civil Code: All persons may agree to arbitration in relation to rights which they are free to dispose of.[9]
> Article 2060 of the Civil Code: "It is not permissible to submit to arbitration matters of civil status and capacity of individuals, or relating to divorce or judicial separation of spouses or disputes concerning public communities and public establishments and more generally all matters which concern public policy. Nevertheless, some categories of public establishments of industrial and commercial characters may be authorized by decree to submit to arbitration."[10]

The ambivalent element, within these articles, was that the arbitrator could not declare a dispute null and void, especially if the dispute concerned was of public policy. The arbitrator had to declare himself

9 "Toutes personnes peuvent compromettre sur des droits dont elles ont la libre disposition."

10 "On ne peut compromettre sur des questions d'état et de capacité des personnes, sur celles relatives au divorce et à la séparation de corps ou sur les contestations intéressant les collectivités publiques et les établissements publics, et plus généralement dans toutes les matières qui intéressent l'ordre public. Toutefois, des catégories d'établissements publics à caractère industriel et commercial peuvent être autorisées par décret à compromettre."

incompetent and only traditional court jurisdictions could sanction the illegality and consider a contract null and void. This element was set aside thanks to a reversal of jurisprudence, the *Ganz* case.[11] Indeed, in view of international arbitration, the arbitrator has a dual role; he has – firstly – to appreciate his competence and verify if the case can be submitted to arbitration when considering the applicable international public order rules, and – secondly – if the case is submitted to arbitration, the arbitrator applies the public order rules and may have to exercise civil sanctions which are not compatible with the nature of his role but depend on the judiciary power.

Owing to the growing complexity of defining the field of expertise of arbitrators, the access to arbitration was then more difficult. It then became necessary to prepare reforms to the Civil Code. From this perspective, the *Chambre Arbitrale de Paris* asked the Minister of Justice to modify article 2061 of the Civil Code. This was the start of the reform of 15 May 2001 known as the New Economic Regulations:

> Article 2061 of the Civil code is drafted as follows: "Unless provided otherwise in special statutory provisions, an arbitration clause is valid in contracts which are concluded in relation to professional activities. (Law no. 2001-420 of 15 May 2001 relative to New Economic Regulations; former article 2061, Law no. 72-626 of July 1972: "An arbitration clause is null and void unless an enacted law provides otherwise.")[12]

The 'Dalico' case of 1993 also insisted on the fact that the concept of autonomy was subordinated both to French Law and to international

11 Paris, 29 March 1991, Ganz, Rev. Arb. 1991, 478 note I. Idot: "in international arbitration, the arbitrator evaluates his own expertise as to the arbitrability of a dispute in line with the applicable international public order rules. He has the power to apply the subsequent principles and rules and the power to exercise civil sanction, under the supervision of a judge granting the annulment of the arbitral award". [My translation]

12 Article 2061 du Code Civil – art. 126 Loi n°2001 – 420 du 15 mai 2001): "Sous réserve des dispositions législatives particulières, la clause compromissoire est valable dans les contrats conclus à raison d'une activité professionnelle". Ancien article 2061: loi n°72 – 625 du 5 juillet 1972 : "La clause compromissoire est nulle s'il n'est disposé autrement par la loi. "

public order.[13] With the 'Zanzi' case in 1999, a principle of validity of international arbitration clauses as a rule of French substantive law was established. In the Gosset Case (25 November 2008), the Court de Cassation prioritized the arbitral tribunal on the basis of two main reasons: (1) the autonomy of the arbitration agreement and (2) the 'competence-competence' principle whereby arbitrators are empowered to rule on their own jurisdiction.

2. The key actor

2.1. Arbiter, arbitrator, amicabilis compositor – The key actor

Under the provisions of the *Corpus Juris Civilis*, in arbitration practice (esp. ecclesiastical arbitration) two types of arbiters were distinguished:

> There are, in fact, two kinds of arbitrators. The first we are obliged to obey whether he is fair or unfair; this principle applies in cases where people go to an arbitrator having made a mutual promise to abide by his decisions. The other is one whose decision must be made to conform with the judgment of a good man, even if the person by whose decision the matter is to go forward is expressly identified.[14]

This quotation makes it clear that arbiters were free in their decisions and were not bound by any rules of substantive law. Arbiters were "not there to judge according to rules, they were there to get the parties off the hook. They represented wisdom, the alternative virtue to

13 Cass. Civ. 1ère 'Dalico', 20 December 1993.

14 The Digest of Justinian (translation edited by Alan Watson), Vol. 1. Philadelphia: University of Pennsylvania Press, 1985, Book seventeen, 2 Partnership, 76. Originally; Proculus; letters, book 5): "Arbitratum erim genera sunt duo, unum eiusmodi, ut sive aequum sit sive iniquum, parere debeamus [quod observatur, cum ex compromisso ad arbitrum itum est], alterum eiusmodi, ut ad boni viri arbitrium redigi debeat, etsi nominatim persona sit comprehensa, cuius arbitratu fiat" (from *The Epistulae of Proculus*).

overly combative prowess" (Cheyette 1996: 175). Their awards were binding – whether equitable or inequitable. The second type of arbiter was assimilated to the *amicabilis* compositor, the 'amicable compounder' in English[15] or *amiable compositeur* in French: "a bishop, to whom the parties under certain circumstances had to refer their dispute and who acted as a kind of conciliator" (Zimmermann 1991: 527-528).

From the Middle Ages, *amicable* referred to a role of reconciliation, that is, of conciliation. This concept characterizing mediation or conciliation was also used for arbitration settlement:

> An arbitrator, for his part, is an amicable compounder, and he is not taken into a matter under dispute, e.g., to consider it but to conciliate [between the parties] and, when the matter is settled, to make the division [of the property]. And he is not obliged to obey [the rules of] the legal order, and his decision is not observed if it is unjust but the matter is forwarded to the discretion of a good man.[16]

International conciliation consists in "examining a dispute by an entity, commonly agreed by both parties and given the authority to propose a solution in view of a settlement" (Fortier 1998: 330). Contrary to arbitration, the suggested solution is not compulsory at all. In commercial trade, the word *composition* conveys the meaning of settlement commonly agreed by both parties (Pommier 1992: 11), its 'way of being' (Loquin 1985: 207). International arbitration practice conveys hidden meanings supported by the power of *ex aequo et bono* and leads "the discretionary authority jointly granted by the parties to a court or arbitrator to mitigate the effects of the application of strict law, when the latter would, in given circumstances, produce unjust result" (Rubino-Sammartano 1992: 9) whereas the amicable composition should be linked to 'settlement' or 'transaction' (Rubino-Sam-

15 Garner (2001) defined him as an "arbitrator with extensive equitable powers".

16 "Arbitrator vero est amicabilis compositor, nect sumitur super re litigiosa, vel ut cognoscat: sed ut pacificet, et quod certum est, dividat .../... Nec tenetur iuris ordinem servare: nec statur eius sententiae, si sit iniqua: sed reducitur ad arbitrium boni viri" (*Speculum Iudiciale*, Pars. I, Lib. I, Partic. I, Rubrica de Arbitro et Arbitratore, §1.3).

martano 1992: 14). Kühn (1997: 148) gives an additional value where "the *amiable compositeur* is in fact both a judge, but one who enjoys greater flexibility in adopting the solution which he regards as best".

2.2. The present role of arbitrators in France

In French domestic arbitration, the arbitrator's appointment is defined under Art. 1444 NCPC which provides that:

> If a dispute has arisen and problems occur with regard to the constitution of the arbitral tribunal due to the behavior of a party or to the implementation of the appointment method, the arbitrator or arbitrators shall be appointed by the President of the *Tribunal de Grande Instance*.
> The appointment shall be made by the President of the *Tribunal de Commerce* if the parties expressly so agree.
> If the arbitration clause is manifestly null and void or insufficient to constitute an arbitral tribunal, the President shall so determine and declare that there is no basis for appointment.

Art. 1453 requires that "an arbitral tribunal shall consist of one or an uneven number of arbitrators", while Art. 1454 stipulates that

> if the parties provided for an even number of arbitrators, an additional arbitrator shall be chosen either in accordance with the agreement of the parties or, in the absence thereof, by the appointed arbitrators or, if they fail to agree, by the President of the *Tribunal de Grande Instance*.

This provision of appointing an additional arbitrator by the President of the *Tribunal de Grande Instance* is also rooted in practice.[17] In the light of article 1493 (International arbitration), the interpretation is rather distinctive and allows the parties to agree upon an even number of arbitrators, with or without an additional one.[18]

---

17 Civ. II, 23 March 1999, RTD Com. 1999.370, obs. Dubarry & Loquin.

18 Art. 1493 of NCPC provides that: "An arbitration agreement may, directly or by reference to arbitration rules, appoint the arbitrator or arbitrators or provide for the method of their appointment". If in an arbitration process taking place in France or subjected by the parties to French procedural law difficulties arise

When an arbitrator accepts a mandate, he/she enters into a contractual relationship and this leads to the compliance and fulfillment of several obligations due to his/her role as an appointed arbitrator. These obligations can be identified with reference to four keywords, i.e. Independence – Impartiality, Availability – Diligence, Confidentiality, and Equality of treatment.

Arbitrators are chosen for their expertise in some specific fields, which is clearly posted on the *Chambre Arbitrale de Paris* website.[19] Their arbitral awards are binding on[20] the interested parties. In a judgment of 1973, the *Cour de Cassation* held that "intellectual independence is essential for the exercise of jurisdictional powers and is one of the essential attributes of arbitrators".[21] It is an "absolute requirement of the arbitral process".[22] France is in line with international arbitration and complies with Art. 12 of UNCITRAL Model Law,[23] Art. 7.1 of the ICC Rules[24] and Article 5.2 of LCIA Rules.[25] Indeed, ami-

---

in the constitution of the arbitral tribunal, *the interested party may bring the matter before the President of the Tribunal de Grande Instance of Paris as provided in Art. 1457, unless the parties agree otherwise*. [My emphasis]

19 <http://www.arbitrage.org/fr/liste_arbitres/index.htm>.

20 They constitute *res judicata* between the interested parties.

21 Civ. II 13 April 1972, JCP 1972 II 17.189, note P. Level.

22 Paris 6 April 1990, *Philipp Brothers*, Rev. Arb. 1990.880, note M. de Boisséson.

23 (1) When a person is approached in connection with his possible appointment as an arbitrator, he shall disclose any circumstances likely to give rise to justifiable doubts as to his impartiality or independence. An arbitrator, from the time of his appointment and throughout the arbitral proceedings, shall without delay disclose any such circumstances to the parties unless they have already been informed of them by him.

(2) An arbitrator may be challenged only if circumstances exist that give rise to justifiable doubts as to his impartiality or independence, or if he does not possess qualifications agreed to by the parties. A party may challenge an arbitrator appointed by him, or in whose appointment he has participated, only for reasons of which he becomes aware after the appointment has been made.

24 Every arbitrator must be and remain independent of the parties involved in the arbitration.

25 All arbitrators conducting an arbitration under these Rules shall be and remain at all times impartial and independent of the parties; and none shall act in the arbitration as advocates for any party. No arbitrator, whether before or after appointment, shall advise any party on the merits or outcome of the dispute.

cable compositors are bound by an obligation of confidentiality[26] in arbitral processes and have to remain free from outside influence (Bredin 1991: 171). Any breach of the rules of professional secrecy is considered as an offence under French criminal law.[27]

3. Conclusion

Arbitration may be considered as one remedy to unfairness in the legal context and provides fertile ground for the resolution of conflicts between the parties involved. It is an approach that makes it possible to better apprehend and comprehend the true ambit of French International Arbitration by taking into account explicitly not only the cross-cultural environment but also the straightforward regulations set up for this practice. Owing to the flexibility of interpretation associated with the concept of equity – *aequitas* – the task of devolving decision-making to the amicable context of dispute resolution is a precarious one because it requires the counterbalancing of many variables in order to achieve a fair arbitration award. However it is far from being a 'fragile instrument' of resolution. Some adjustments may be needed, but its foundation is solid (Motulsky 2007).[28]

Acknowledgment

I offer special thanks to Professor Heikki Mattila and his close collaborator with competence in Latin so as to better understand Justinian's *Corpus Juris Civilis*.

---

26 Article 1469 of NCPC provides that: "Arbitrators' deliberations shall be confidential."

27 Article 226-3 of the French Criminal Code.

28 See also <http://cfcj-fcjc.org/clearinghouse/drpapers/mcgill.htm>.

References

Aristote 1991. *Rhétorique* (trad. M. Dufour). Paris: Les Belles Lettres.

Aristotle 1984. *The Revised Oxford Translation*, vol. II. Princeton: Oxford University Press.

Belley, Jean-Guy 1994. Vous qui êtes un client juste et honnête. *Série Morales* 24, 25-45.

Bredin, Jean-Denis 1991. Le secret du délibéré arbitral. Collectif Litec (eds) *Etudes offertes à Pierre Bellet*. Paris: Litec, 71-82.

Cheyette, Fredric L. 1996. Giving Each His Due. In Rosenwein, Barbara H. / Little, Lester K. (eds) *Debating the Middle Ages: Issue and Reading*. London: Blackwell, 148-169.

Clère, Jean-Jacques 1981. L'arbitrage révolutionnaire – Apogée et déclin d'une institution (1790-1806*). Revue de l'arbitrage* Janvier-Mars, 3-14.

Delvolvé, Jean Louis / Rouche, Jean / Pointon, Gérald 2003. *French Arbitration Law and Practice*. The Hague: Kluwer Law International.

The Digest of Justinian (translation edited by Alan Watson) 1985. Vol. 1. Philadelphia: University of Pennsylvania Press.

Fortier, Yves 1998. La diplomatie et l'arbitrage. *Revue Québécoise de Droit International* 11/1, 327-336.

Garner, Bryan A. 2001. *A Dictionary of Modern Legal Usage*. Oxford: Oxford University Press.

Gaudemet-Tallon, Hélène 1994. Note sous l'arrêt 'Dalico'. *Revue de l'arbitrage* 3, 116.

Gény, François 1922. *Le Droit Positif Privé*. Recueil Sirey. Paris: Dalloz.

Gouiffès, Louis / Girard, Pascal / Taivalkoski, Petri / Mecarelli, Gabrièle 1997. *Recherche sur l'arbitrage en droit international et comparé*. Paris: Librairie Générale de Droit et de Jurisprudence.

Kühn, Wolfgang 1997. Choice of Substantive Law in the Practice of International Arbitration. *International Business Lawyer* 4, 148-179.

Loquin, Eric 1985. Pouvoir et devoirs de l'amiable compositeur. A propos de trois arrêts de la cour d'appel de Paris. *Revue de l'arbitrage* 3, 199.

Motulsky, Henri 2007. *Etudes et notes sur l'arbitrage.* Paris: Dalloz.

Pommier, Jean-Christophe 1992. La résolution du conflit de lois en matière contractuelle en présence d'une élection de droit: le rôle de l'arbitre. *Journal de Droit International* 119, 5-11.

Rubino-Sammartano, Mauro 1992. Amiable compositeur (Joint Mandate to Settle) and Ex bono et aequo (Discretional Authority to Mitigate Strict Law). *Journal of International Arbitration* 9/1, 5-27.

Zimmermann, Reinhard 1996. *The Law of Obligations: Roman Foundations of Civil Tradition.* New-York: Clarendon Press.

Olga Denti / Michela Giordano[1]

Till Money (and Divorce) Do us Part: Premarital Agreements in American and Spanish Legal Discourse

1. Introduction

The phenomenon of a steadily increasing number of divorces in many cultures calls for a growing need for couples contemplating marriage to foresee future divergences in their married life and to try to prevent them through *premarital agreements*. Premarital, prenuptial, or antenuptial agreements (commonly abbreviated to 'prenups' or 'prenupts') "describe the rights, duties and obligations of prospective spouses during and upon termination of marriage through death or divorce" (Greenstein 1992). They are a type of mediation within the framework of Alternative Dispute Resolution (ADR), aiming at resolving disputes other than through litigation, and taking the form of contracts used by individuals who want to precisely define the disposition of their assets.

The present study aims at investigating premarital agreements in an intercultural perspective. The investigation will focus on a comparison between some linguistic features in two examples of American prenuptial agreements and two Spanish *modelos de capitulaciones matrimoniales*, chosen for the purpose of this study and selected among a wider corpus which is currently being built up.

As Bix (2001: 232) aptly remarks, "The 'folk wisdom' regarding premarital agreements is that most such agreements (though far

1 The present chapter has been jointly planned. Both authors wrote the Introduction and the Conclusions. Olga Denti wrote sections 2, 4, 5, 6.1 and 7.1. Michela Giordano wrote sections 3, 6, 6.2 and 7.2.

from all of them) are entered by rich men to protect their assets from less well off women". Nowadays, more and more couples in the United States, including mixed-nationality couples, are increasingly signing *prenuptial agreements in contemplation of divorce* for protection against post-nuptial disagreements and especially to handle the financial aspects of their marriage. At the same time, due to recent legal reforms and amendments, and to some important changes in Spanish society, the traditional *capitulaciones matrimoniales,* through which Spanish couples were entitled to choose the financial marital regime, are currently experiencing some change.

Prenups can be classified as "operative legal documents, in that they create or modify legal relations" (Tiersma 1999: 139). Moreover, they "tend to have not only very formal and formulaic legal language, but they traditionally adhere to a very rigid structure" (Tiersma 1999: 139). They are prescriptive legal texts whose priority is to set up rules to regulate the matter of property division after divorce or death, "in such a way as to ensure that there is no room for misinterpretation" (Williams 2005: 122). This entails their compliance with specific rules or norms and certain linguistic choices typical of their specific text genre. As Gotti (2005: 112) puts it, "there is usually a close link between the type of specialized text and its structure, which in turn implies a number of correlations between the conceptual, rhetorical and linguistic features that characterize the text itself".

After a brief overview of the legal aspects of prenups in the USA and in Spain, we will frame them as the ADR method of mediation and investigate them as texts belonging to the specific genre of contracts. The linguistic analysis will focus on:

1) the textual organization of the agreements, the organization of their several parts and their contribution to the overall pattern;
2) the lexical items referring to participants or human actors in the agreements.

2. Prenuptial agreements in the USA

Historically, a wife had few property rights: she was absorbed within the legal person of her husband and, in case of divorce, she had no rights on the family property, even losing her own. Until 1970, prenups were mainly used to predetermine property rights and were not enforceable in all states as they were deemed to violate "public policy by increasing the likelihood of divorce" (Greenstein 1992). Nowadays, these agreements are recognized in all fifty states, though sometimes they may not be enforced, and there seems to be a lack of uniformity among the states. Starting from the assertion that "marriage is not just an emotional and physical union; it is also a financial union" (Al Mureden 2005: 3) the USA offers a particular domain of application of prenups since the states are divided into two groups:

1) community property states (nine states: Arizona, California, Idaho, Louisiana, Nevada, New Mexico, Texas, Washington and Wisconsin);
2) equitable distribution states (41 states).

In the former, if no agreement has been signed, those assets accumulated during marriage, and which therefore belong to the couple, are divided into equal parts; in the latter, those assets are divided between the partners by the courts, according to more discretional criteria such as income power, contribution to the common and own asset accumulation, age, health, duration of marriage (Al Mureden 2005). This framework further varies within both community property states and equitable distribution states, but this is not the topic of the present study. These differentiations influence both the patrimonial consequences of a divorce when a premarital agreement is missing, and its draft and enforcement when foreseen.

In general, in the USA, premarital agreements have the main purpose to modify or exclude community of property in community property states and to limit judicial discretion in equitable distribution states (Al Mureden 2005: 8). There have been some efforts on the part of the National Conference of Commissioners on Uniform State Laws

(NCCUSL) to give the American states uniform guidelines through the 1970 Uniform Marriage and Divorce Act and the 1983 Uniform Premarital Agreement Act (UPAA). Additionally, the American Bar Association (ABA) and the American Law Institute have also tried to make the premarital agreements work in a homogeneous manner through the 2002 Principles of the Law of Family Dissolution.

Nevertheless, the lack of uniformity still today is the consequence of each state's own rules for prenups as well as of their normative context. Some, especially in the No-UPAA jurisdictions, consider those prenuptial agreements regulating alimony as not valid. In any case, restrictions on spousal support cannot leave one of the parties unable to support him/herself.

The Principles of the Law of Family Dissolution, drawn up by a Commission of the American Law Institute in 2002, represent an intermediary position between the system where prenups cannot limit the judges' wide discretion and those states which consider them as 'business contracts' (Al Mureden 2005: 19). Therefore, prenups, in order to be enforceable, must be valid contracts under general contract principles. Al Mureden (2005: 20) underlines that most jurisdictions require some elements in order for the prenup to be valid:

- it must be in writing and signed by both parties;
- it must be voluntarily executed;
- it cannot be unconscionable, or 'morally abhorrent' (*Collins Dictionary of Law* 2007: 440) and unequal in terms of bargaining power; in other words, it cannot be the product of fraud, duress, coercion, or overreaching;
- it must be executed and acknowledged before a notary public;
- the other party must have had at least seven days to deal with it (30 before marriage);
- the disclosure of the property and/or financial obligations must be fair, reasonable and full.

In addition, a premarital agreement becomes effective upon marriage of the parties, and after marriage it may be amended, revoked, or abandoned only by a written agreement signed by the parties. Sometimes, if a certain amount of time has gone by and the underlying conditions have changed, the agreement may lapse or the parties may privately contract so. In order to fully understand the text and for the agreement to be enforceable, a party should be able to seek independent legal counsel. The agreement should be 'reasonably understandable' (Al Mureden 2005: 17) even by a non-legal expert adult, who must comprehend whether and to what extent his/her own rights or interests are damaged, especially if restrictions on spousal support and marital property are foreseen.

Despite the great diffusion of prenups in the USA, there are still many myths and misconceptions which, on the one hand create concern for ordinary less wealthy people and, on the other hand, contribute to further spreading the tendency to stipulate premarital contracts, especially among wealthy individuals worried to leave their fiscal and financial assets in the hands of state regulations. However, the agreements do help avoiding fears and uncertainties about how a court could divide property in case of divorce, thus protecting assets, income and family businesses. It is widely believed that agreements are just for wealthy and famous people, that discussing money and property issues is not romantic and might kill love, and finally, that the wealthier spouse (generally the man) might use it to deny his wife's rights, such as spousal support, pension and even the custody of children.

3. *Capitulaciones matrimoniales* in Spain

Capitulaciones matrimoniales [articles of marriage] identify the agreement between the spouses who are willing to establish, modify or substitute their matrimonial property regime. According to art. 1325 of the *Código Civil*, through *capitulaciones matrimoniales* "podrán los otorgantes estipular, modificar o sustituir el régimen económico de su matrimonio o cualesquiera otras disposiciones por razón del mismo [the parties may stipulate, modify or change the economic regime of their marriage or any other provisions related to it [the marriage]]" in which the last phrase clearly indicates that other provisions could be included in the contract which are not directly pertaining to economic or financial matters. Spouses are not obliged to establish the articles of marriage in Spain, but if they decide to do so, *capitulaciones matrimoniales* have to fulfil some conditions; they:

- must be agreed on before a notary;
- must be registered with the Spanish Civil Registry;
- must establish the regime of matrimonial properties;
- may be changed as many times as the spouses jointly decide to change them.

Not all Spanish regions apply the same regulations or procedures when dealing with *capitulaciones matrimoniales*. More precisely, if nothing is agreed on by the spouses, according to the *Derecho Común,* the Community Property regime will be applied by default, except in the Autonomous Communities of Catalonia, the Balearic Islands, Aragon, Pais Vasco, and Navarra where, in case of no agreement between the spouses, the Separate Property regime is applied according to the *Derecho Foral* (regional law applied in some areas of the country and co-existing with the *Código Civil de España*).Since a third type of regime exists, in addition, a brief explanation of the three will help understanding:

- The *régimen de gananciales,* Community Property Matrimonial Regime, is the most common, especially if no prenuptial agreement is signed. Under it, all properties and rights acquired by a husband and wife during their marriage are jointly owned, and in the case of divorce, each one of them is entitled to his/her half.
- The *régimen de separación de bienes,* Separate Property Matrimonial Regime, is based on a full independence of the spouses within the economic or financial sphere. Each spouse continues to own the assets or properties acquired before, and in the course of marriage, through work, gifts, inheritance or legacies.
- The *régimen de participación de bienes*, Profit Sharing Matrimonial Regime, the least used throughout Spain, implies that both spouses jointly participate in, manage, or share the profits obtained by the other spouse.

The chosen regime must be agreed upon in the articles of marriage before or during marriage. According to the *Código Civil, las capitulaciones matrimoniales* must be stipulated before the celebration of marriage (art. 1315); in contrast, according to the *Derecho Foral,* they can be stipulated even after, or during, the marriage. In addition, the articles of marriage cannot be modified after the marriage has been celebrated (art. 1320 in the *Código Civil).* In the regions where the *legislación foral* exists, they can be modified at any time. According to art. 1326 of the *Código Civil* the articles of marriage are void, or do not have any effect, in the event that the marriage is not celebrated and, even if the civil code does not explicitly state that, the matrimonial economic regime ceases to exist if marriage is dissolved following the death of one of the spouses.

Lamarca *et al.* (2003) observe an exponential 600% increase of marital contracts stipulated in Catalonia from about 1999 to 2003, and a significant but milder rise also in the rest of Spain. Considering that Spain is a plurilegislative state where the two marital property regimes coexist, these scholars offer some hypotheses in order to explain this phenomenon, some of which are strongly connected to recent modifications in the legal regime and in the social and economic context.

The increase in population together with different social and economic traditions in Catalonia and the rest of Spain, have brought about a change in the married couples' decisions to enter into marital contracts. Furthermore, the increase of Alternative Dispute Resolution mechanisms developed in 2001 in the act of *Mediació familiar de Catalunya* influenced the increase in separation agreements. Following the recent amendments (Act 8/1993 and Act 9/1998 of the Codi de Familia, *cfr.* Lamarca *et al.* 2003), the new marital contracts are strongly related to marriage crises, and as far as non-financial matters are concerned, they might relate to issues concerning children custody and education. According to Lamarca *et al.* (2003) other crucial factors explaining the substantial growth of marital contracts in Spain are: a) the increasing amount of divorces in the last few years and consequent remarriages; b) migration processes with resulting mixed-marriages even between Spanish people coming from different regions, and which lead to inter-regional conflicts of legislation; and c) no less importantly, changes in the system of the management and the inter-generational transmission of rural property which have been replaced by the middle-class system of purchase of real estate properties and investments of family savings in the capital market.

We argue here that, along with the causes indicated by Lamarca *et al.* (2003), recent changes in Spanish politics and society which have transformed a traditionally strong Catholic-rooted culture into an increasingly lay one have certainly contributed to the growing number of separations and divorces and to the consequent spread of marital contract stipulations. Spain has been by far the country with the greatest increase in the number of divorces over the years 1996-2006, almost tripling (290%) in number, rising from 32,571 divorces in 1996 to 126,952 in 2006 as indicated in the 2008 Report on the Evolution of the Family in Europe, an account presented annually in the European Parliament by the Institute for Family Policies.

4. The data

The gathering of official documents has not been easy or straightforward, due to the fact that despite the diffusion of many websites, forums and blogs on prenuptial agreements equipped with downloadable forms or online templates, these are almost always only obtainable at a cost, further underscoring the closure of the legal profession with the aim of maintaining its own prestige, privileges and control. Various types of samples with different names were found on the Web: premarital agreements, antenuptial agreements, prenuptial agreements or simply prenups in English, and *capitulaciones matrimoniales*, *capitulos matrimoniales*, *acuerdos prematrimoniales, convenio regulador pre-matrimonial* in Spanish. The majority of them follow the rules for the drafting of legal contracts, "based on preprinted forms with spaces for the parties' names and special clauses to meet individual requirements" displaying "a standard pattern, with certain sections arranged in a set sequence" (Gotti 2005: 116). The corpus in the present study includes and compares:

- a premarital agreement from the State of Illinois, an equitable distribution state (henceforth PREN1);
- a prenuptial agreement employed by the law firm Granstaff, Gaedke and Edgmon, P.C, San Antonio, Texas, a community property state (henceforth PREN2);
- a *modelo de Acuerdo Prematrimonial*, which can also be used as *postnupcial,* offered by a Spanish law firm specialized in divorces and separations on its Internet website (henceforth CAP1);
- a *modelo de capitulaciones matrimoniales* (henceforth CAP2).

The choice of the two American samples was influenced by the aim of comparing a document used in a community property state with one used in an equitable distribution state. The application of the UPAA in a way or another would have likely shown some differences as well, but this would have led us too far away from our main aim. In fact, notwithstanding the regime applied, and the choice by the parties to keep property separate, the core structure of these legal papers holds by and large. Another reason for our choice is the presence or absence of a notary. In PREN1, the only actors are the spouses negotiating the agreement on their financial assets, while in PREN2, in addition to the contracting parties, legal counsels, a notary (having the role of mediator) and witnesses are named and take action.

As for the Spanish documents, they are both employed in two law firms in Madrid, an area in Spain where *the derecho común* is applied and which were drafted according to the legislation in the *Código Civil.* We have not considered *las capitulaciones* from the Autonomous Communities of Catalonia, the Balearic Islands, Aragon, Pais Vasco and Navarra, because of the differences in the legislation mentioned above, and because of the language used, which, in the particular case of Catalonia, would be Catalan and not standard Castilian Spanish. The choice of the two Spanish *capitulaciones* has been more content-driven: CAP2 deals only with financial matters, following both the American model and the Spanish legislation which allows the parties to choose the economic matrimonial regime. CAP1 is a perfect example of *acuerdo prematrimonial* anticipating the consequences of separation and divorce (similarly to American prenups) and especially those regarding children's interests, custody and support (García Rubio 2008) which instead cannot be contemplated in American prenups.

5. Prenuptial agreements as contracts

Premarital agreements display many of the main features identified in contracts in that they are written texts with extremely formal traits, highly codified, characterised by standardised and easily predictable sentences and formulaic expressions (Gotti 2005: 20-21). Within the Spanish legislation, the articles of marriage "*son contratos y como tales quedan sometidos a las reglas generales de los contratos*" [are contracts and as such they have to comply with the general rules of contracts] (García Rubio 2004). Starting from the assumption that "as a legally enforceable contract, a prenuptial agreement can be as detailed and lengthy as necessary, and can cover as many specifics as the parties desire" (Greenstein 1992), the aim of this study is to analyse the prenups in the corpus in the framework of contracts considering as paramount the conditions set which make the agreement valid and enforceable.

"According to both common law and civil law practice, a contract is an agreement between two or more parties which is legally valid and enforceable when executed under specific terms and requirements agreed by the parties themselves" (Di Renzo Villata 2007: 136). Normally, a great deal of attention is dedicated to conditions (clauses) which should always be included in any agreement – such as parties' names and details, definitions and interpretation of conditions repeatedly used throughout the contract, duration of the contract, dispute resolution procedure to be followed if needed, i.e. arbitration or mediation – and which can serve as a background against which the description of the prenups textual organization can be carried out.

6. The textual organization

A first rough comparative analysis of the four documents has emphasized that their overall structure complies with the main formal elements of contracts but displays several variations, despite having in common some 'macro-structural' aspects corresponding to "instantiations of the same type of legal discourse and belonging to the same, well-defined text-genre" (Garzone 2003: 186-187). The data (computed using Wordsmith Tools 3.00) show some differences from a quantitative point of view (cf. Table 1). The American texts are longer, with a higher number of sentences, and a lower type/token ratio. This means a lower variance of the lexis. Moreover, while PREN1 and PREN2 have an average sentence length of around 23.5 words, the range for the Spanish *capitulaciones* is definitely broader, indicating widely different patterns. These inequalities may originate from the different "drafting experiences and conventions characterizing the diverse legal cultures" (Garzone 2003: 186). Besides being the longest text, PREN2 is also much more detailed and structured. One reason could be its source: it is the only document collected from a law firm and is not an online template.

	PREN1	PREN2	CAP1	CAP2
Tokens	2,695	6,130	1,474	606
Types	647	908	488	282
Type/Token Ratio	33.40	29.36	34.40	46.53
Number of sentences	68	220	21	11
Words per sentence	27.24	23.16	51.83	24.04
Average word length	4.95	4.83	5.01	5.01

Table 1. Quantitative data.

As regards the linguistic content, the presence or absence of certain articles, conditions or clauses can provide an account of its linguistic pattern and of its textual organization. Table 2 shows the main sequential semantic-pragmatic structures (Gotti 2005: 124), conceptual units (Garzone 2003: 188), topics which help the reader obtain a general overview of the texts but also identify the several parts or sections.

Textual organization and semantic units				
Semantic-pragmatic units	PREN 1	PREN 2	CAP 1	CAP 2
Definitions and interpretation of conditions repeatedly used throughout the contract	X			
Definition of terms applicable to this agreement	X			
Date and place of agreement	X	X	X	X
Introduction: party names and personal details	X	X	X	X
Reference to party age	X		X	X
Notary introduction of the parties				X
Object of agreement: intention to get married and to stipulate a premarital contract	X	X	X	X
Purpose: intent to define property rights or to choose the economic marital regime	X	X	X	X
Introduction of legal counsels for the agreement drafting		X		
Term of agreement		X		
Modification	X	X	X	
Ratification		X	X	X
Clauses or Clausulas - Agreement conditions				
Separate property to remain separate property (income included)	X	X		X
Separate liabilities to remain separate	X	X	X	X
Financial responsibilities during the marriage	X		X	X
Place of residence during marriage		X		
Place of residence in case of divorce			X	
Reference to alimony in case of divorce	X	X	X	
Reference to minor/children financial support	X		X	
Reference to minor children custody			X	
Visitation to the children			X	
Summary of the parties' financial statements	X	X		
Financial disclosure	X	X		
Reference to State law	X	X		
Resolution of dispute through mediation or arbitration		X		
Reciprocal acknowledgements by the parties	X		X	
Acknowledgements by notary	X	X		X
Presence of witnesses		X		

Table 2. Semantic-pragmatic units in premarital contracts.

Contracts, like all legal texts in general, are not compact texts: generally they are sub-divided and organized into chapters, or articles, sections, subsections, often signalled by numbers, letters, or introduced by titles or subtitles (Engberg/Rasmussen 2003: 126). As Table 2 shows, the structure of the four prenups follows different patterns. The semantic-pragmatic units identified do not always appear in the same order in the texts, being sometimes positioned in different clauses under different headings.

6.1. Semantic-pragmatic units in prenups

After the title 'Prenuptial agreement' and the introduction of the parties, in PREN1 the archaic verb form WITNESSETH introduces five premises, each one starting with the adverbial WHEREAS which normally "clusters at the beginning of the sentence" (Crystal/Davy 1969: 204). 'Whereas clauses' (or *consideranda*) are introductory statements meaning 'considering that', justifying the subsequent provisions and explaining and codifying the reasons for the execution of the contract (Jottini 2002: 256). The use of capitalized words has the main function of emphasizing the structure of the agreement. "The premises being considered" (PREN1), twelve clauses or articles of agreement are listed following Roman numbers, some of them divided into sections (1-5 maximum) and subsections. Clauses are always introduced by a title while sections are either introduced by Arabic numbers or sub-titles, and subsections are organized into alphabetical ordered lists (a, b, c…).

Article I underlines that the agreement will take effect only "upon the lawful solemnization of the marriage"; article II is devoted to the separation of property; articles III and IV deal with the waiving of certain rights and claims, distinguishing between the case of separation or divorce from that of death; articles V and VI are dedicated to debts and financial disclosure, while VI-X deal with the agreement validity and modifications. Differently from the Spanish *acuerdo* CAP1, 'Acknowledgments', stating the parties' understanding of the clauses and free will to sign, are located in Article XI at the end of the document, and XII makes reference to State Law.

A relevant pragmatic function within this genre (Gotti 2005: 127) is fulfilled by the section 'Definition of Terms Applicable to this Agreement' which specifies the meaning of some terms used throughout the agreement. The same pragmatic defining function is performed through the introduction of an alternative term to the conventional one such as in "The agreement is also known as a 'premarital agreement'" (PREN1). At times, an appropriate 'nomenclatory procedure' (Gotti 2005: 127) is used, for instance to define the actors in the agreement, such as in "[...] who shall be collectively known herein as 'the parties'" (PREN1).

After the 'Summary Financial Statements of the Parties', as an example of the semantic unit 'Financial Disclosure' (Table 2), the conclusive section states:

(1) IN WITNESS WHEREOF, we each sign the foregoing Prenuptial Agreement (also known as a Premarital Agreement), do it willingly and as our free and voluntary act for the purposes herein expressed, and further state that we are each eighteen years of age or older, of sound mind, and under no constraint or undue influence.

This statement ends the prenup, where emphasis is again put on the contracting parties' legal capacity and willingness to sign the covenant ('Reciprocal acknowledgements by the parties', Table 2). After the parties' signatures and dates, the last formality is the notary's declaration as public authority:

(2) IN WITNESS WHEREOF, I have hereunto subscribed my name and affixed my official seal this day of October, 2004.

This sentence is followed by his/her signature (corresponding to the semantic unit 'Acknowledgements by notary', Table 2).

In PREN2 the structure is somewhat more articulated and detailed. After the parties and their intention to get married are introduced, three broad articles are listed with Roman numbers and introduced by headings: PURPOSE (I), RECITALS (II), dealing with children from previous marriages, disclosure and marriage as a condition for the validity of the document, and AGREEMENTS (III), addressing separate property, credits and liabilities, the waiving of community property, joint accounts, release of marital rights, invalid provisions, term of the agreement, income taxes, modifications and miscellaneous. Provisions about tort, waiver, place of residence, confidentiality, ratification and mediation/arbitration conclude ARTICLE III. As in PREN1, each article is further divided into sections identified by Arabic numbers, and subsections listed by lower case letters.

The sentence in quotation (3) indicates the official status of the premarital agreement, and is followed by witnesses' signatures, two per party ('Presence of witnesses', Table 2).

(3) THIS AGREEMENT IS EXECUTED in two (2) original counterparts by the Parties on this day of____, 20__, to be effective as of the date of the marriage.

Acknowledgements follow by the Notary Public in and for the State of Texas, and the attorney certification for their clients' willingness to sign and to comply with the covenant. Exhibit A and B, at the end of the agreement, show each party's financial assets, while Exhibit C, entitled 'RATIFICATION OF PRENUPTIAL AGREEMENT of JOHN DOE and JANE DOE' certifies the marriage and the execution of the prenup, again acknowledged by the Notary and certified by the attorneys.

6.2. Semantic-pragmatic units in capitulaciones

As regards the Spanish documents, in CAP1, after the place of agreement, the parties' names and details and their reciprocal acknowledgment of their legal capacity to enter into a contract (quotation 4), the two parties express their intention to get married and to sign *capitulaciones matrimoniales* in order to select their matrimonial regime:

(4) [...] reconociéndose reciprocamente capacidad para otorgar el presente documento [...]
[reciprocally acknowledging legal capacity to stipulate the present agreement]

Then, the two verbs *CONVIENEN Y PACTAN* in capital letters, meaning "(the parties) agree and stipulate", introduce the several premises numerically listed, *PRIMERO*, *SEGUNDO*, *TERCERO* and so on up to *SEXTO* before the final statement. The articles of marriage or

(5) condiciones por las que se habrán de regir ante una eventual separación legal o de hecho o divorcio
[conditions that will apply in a possible legal or *de facto* separation or divorce]

are further subdivided into alphabetically ordered sections, each of which is developed in one or more sentences. Some of the articles are introduced by a short heading or title. The first article deals with the place of residence, *el domicilio conyugal*, for the children and the parent who has their custody in case of divorce. The second article, introduced by the heading *En cuanto a los hijos del matrimonio* deals with the issues concerning the custody of minor children, and their *patria potestad* i.e. parental responsibility or custody (Table 2). This second article is organized in five subsections (from A to E). Subsection E, dealing with *Régimen de visitas y estancias* [Visitation Rights], is further subdivided into four parts addressing the several available possibilities regarding child custody during school holidays, weekends, and summer holidays. The third article, *Alimentos y cargas del matrimonio*, addresses the financial responsibilities in case of divorce and alimony. In the fourth article, *De la pensión compensatoria*, the two parties agree on waiving any agreement regarding retirement contributions. The fifth article waives any agreement on common properties since the chosen regime is the separation of property in which each party contributes to the joint financial responsibilities during marriage *proporcionalmente a sus ingresos*, proportionally to their own income. In the last article, the sixth, addressing the semantic unit of Modification (Table 2), the document is recognized by the parties as the *convenio regulador de su posible separación o divorcio* [agreement regulating their possible separation or divorce] which has an irrevocable character, unless a joint agreement sets up different conditions for a 'Modification'. In the final, or closing, statement, *los reuni-*

dos [the parties] undertake to sign the necessary public and private documents and to appear before a notary for its ratification:

(6) obligándose los reunidos a firmar cuantos documentos públicos o privados sean necesarios y en todo caso a comparecer en la presencia judicial para su ratificación.
[the parties agree to sign any necessary private or public documents and in any case to appear before a court for their ratification.]

The second example of *capitulaciones,* CAP2, is shorter and, more traditionally, deals exclusively with the parties' choice of the economic matrimonial regime, and considers neither the eventuality of any divorce nor the issues of child custody and support in case of separation. The two parties are introduced by the notary public, *Notario del Ilustre Colegio de Madrid,* who lists their personal details and acknowledges their legal capacity to stipulate the *capitulaciones*. After this introduction, the verb *EXPONEN*, in capital letters, expresses the two parties' intention to marry on a certain date and the intention of *los futuros esposos* [future spouses] to establish their economic matrimonial regime according to some clauses which follow. There are five *CLAUSULAS* in total, each one introduced by a heading. The *PRIMERA clausula* deals with the *REGIMEN* chosen by the parties, corresponding to the semantic unit 'Purpose: intent to define property rights or to choose the economic marital regime' (Table 2) which is that of *separación absoluta de bienes*. This clause is developed into five sentences, the fifth of which is the longest since it lists the several financial rights which each party can exert without the other's consent.

The second clause accounts for the *RECONOCIMIENTO DE BIENES PRIVATIVOS*, ('Separate property to remain separate property', Table 2), and the third clause copes with *PRUEBAS AND PRESUNCIONES*, considering the possibility for each party to certify and prove the property of their assets. In the fourth clause, *CONTRIBUCION A LAS CARGAS DEL MATRIMONIO*, the participation to charges and expenses during marriage is proportional to each party's income and assets. In the fifth clause the parties *[s]olicitan la inscripción en el Registro Civil correspondiente* [file the agreement with the Registry Office]. This Spanish agreement ends with the declaration by the Notary public who testifies to the parties' identities, their legal capacity and their free consent to the agreement.

7. Participants or human actors

7.1. Human actors in prenups

The second part of this linguistic analysis focuses on the lexical choices used to refer to participants or legal subjects or, in Salmi-Tolonen's words, "the human actors" (2003: 324). In the two American prenuptial agreements, the actors can be classified into three groups: the contracting parties, the official authorities, and third parties. The contracting parties are either called by name or 'the Parties', either in capital letter: "It is the desire of the Parties [...]" (PREN2), or in lower case: "whereas, the parties are presently unmarried and intend to [...]" (PREN1). As Gotti puts it, "some common terms are capitalised in legal texts to mark a special meaning, while in lower case they denote a general referent" (2005: 127). However, the use of *party/ parties* (PREN1) and of *Party/Parties* (PREN2) is consistent throughout the documents denoting a specific choice by the drafter. The only exception in PREN1 is the use of *Party A* in the section devoted to the 'Definition of Terms Applicable to this Agreement', to better differentiate the parties in the display of general rules. Moreover, while PREN1 clarifies that the people named "[...] shall be collectively known herein as 'the parties'", PREN2 does not specify.

In the introduction to PREN1 each party is identified as a *resident of* and is, therefore, both geographically and legally located. PREN2 prefers using the adjective *residing*. In the subsection 'Contributions and accumulations in retirement plans and accounts' the party is referred to as the *beneficiary* (PREN1/2) or a *trustee* (PREN2). Further on, under the section 'Waiver of Rights Upon Death' (PREN1) the expressions *surviving spouse* and *deceased spouse* are found several times in contrast. Moreover, *spouses* or *owner-spouse* is used when referring to the assets or liabilities of the parties considered as a married couple (PREN2). The expressions *owner* alone and *non-managing spouse* are employed when dealing with separate property management. Further on, in PREN1 we find sentence (7) where the surviving spouse is given certain duties under the conditions stated. In PREN2 the proper names of the parties recur more frequently while the word *person* is employed with a general meaning:

(7) the right to act as executor or personal administrator of the deceased spouse's estate unless the deceased spouse's Last Will specifically names the other spouse as executor or personal administrator.

The second group of human actors includes the *attorney* or the *independent legal counsel*, named with reference to the possibility of consulting an expert, which gives the parties the opportunity to understand the agreement content and comply with the formalities which make it valid and enforceable. In PREN2 counsels' proper names appear. The *notary* (PREN1/2) and *witnesses* (PREN2) also hold an official role within the documents.

The third group of participants is that of a third party in general. Reference is made to *children* support but very concisely and simply states that "Nothing in this agreement shall be construed as relieving either party of an obligation to support their *minor children*" in PREN1, while in PREN2 *children from other marriages* are mentioned. In addition, provisions are written in case a *third party* "may donate gifts or inheritances to one of the parties" (PREN1).

In both documents a further actor is represented by *successors*:

(8) Each and every provision hereof shall inure to the benefit of and shall be binding upon the heirs, assigns, personal representatives, and all successors in the interest of the parties. (PREN1).

PREN2 also mentions *creditors* when dealing with joint debts and the *court*, a *mediator* and an *arbitrator* when coping with the resolution of a possible dispute or controversy through mediation or arbitration.

PREN1 ends with the declaration by the Notary Public where the first person singular pronoun is employed thus giving authority and validity to the whole document:

(9) I, the undersigned, a Notary Public authorized [...]. IN WITNESS WHEREOF, I have hereunto subscribed my name [...].

The closing formulas of PREN2 are introduced by "BEFORE ME, the Notary [...]" which achieves the same purpose in a less straightforward and involving way.

7.2. Human actors in capitulaciones

The human actors in *las capitulaciones* are the contracting parties and their future children, along with the Notary Public. As already indicated in the case of the American prenups, reference to them is made through the use of different lexical items according to their function in the text, implying those different actions they are supposed or required to perform in the context of the agreement they are signing. In the opening of CAP1 the parties are defined as *los reunidos* and they are introduced with proper names and personal details. The second person plural verbs *EXPONEN* and *CONVIENEN Y PACTAN* underline the joint action of meeting to reach an agreement and to make decisions which will govern their relationship in case of separation or divorce.

Starting from the first article in the agreement, in which *la separación* is contemplated, the parties are considered individually as in *el cónyuge que tenga la custodia* [the spouse who will obtain child custody], or *el cónyuge titular del domicilio conyugal* [the spouse who owns the matrimonial residence]. Having introduced *los hijos del matrimonio* in Section A of the first article, Art. 2 explicitly deals with the issues related to child custody; therefore the parties perform a different function: taken individually *la madre* will be responsible for child custody if she decides to reside in the same town where the matrimonial residence is situated, and if *el padre* decides to have his residence outside the town or even outside Spain.

In Art. 2, Section B, *los hijos mayores de 12 años* [children older than 12] will be able to choose the parent they prefer for their custody: here, each parent is expressed by means of the general term *progenitor*, both masculine and feminine singular. Joint custody, instead, *será compartida por ambos cónyuges,* meaning by this that some functions will be performed *de común acuerdo entre ambos esposos* [jointly by both spouses] in collaboration or cooperation. In Art. 2, Section D, each parent having child custody is required to perform some duties which affect the relationship between divorced parents and minor children, who are referred to as *los menores* from this point on.

When the parties are fulfilling their legal functions of meeting, discussing and agreeing on some potential future conditions in case of divorce, they are always referred to as *los reunidos*. The terms *los cónyuges, los esposos,* and *los consortes* are instead used to refer to the parties as a couple, either married or already divorced. In the role of parents who are supposed to agree on issues regarding their children, they are referred to as *los padres, los progenitores*, if taken collectively, and *el padre*, *la madre*, *el progenitor*, *el cónyuge no custodio* and *el progenitor no custodio,* when taken individually in the performing of their legal obligations.

The reference system to human actors in CAP2 seems to be simpler and more straightforward. The parties are always referred to as *los futuros esposos*, when taken collectively as a married couple who performs some joint actions, such as the contribution to *las cargas del matrimonio* [the burdens of marriage] in the fourth clause, and *cada uno de los futuros esposos* [each one of the future spouses] when their individual duties and legal obligations are listed in the agreement. The parties are referred to as *los comparecientes*, meaning the people appearing before the notary. In the closing statement, 'Acknowledgements by the notary public', the parties are referred to as *los otorgantes*, the parties that sign and execute a public instrument, or *los intervinientes*, a synonym of *los comparecientes.*

The Notary public in these *capitulaciones matrimoniales* becomes an active actor who introduces the parties, mediates and seals the agreements with the closing formula. CAP2 ends with the use of the first person singular pronoun *yo* at the end of the statement in which the notary public attests the parties' identities, their legal capacity and their free consent to the agreement:

(10) De la identidad de los otorgantes, de la capacidad y legitimación que, a mi juicio tienen, de que el consentimiento por parte de estos ha sido libremente prestado, así como que este otorgamiento se adecua a la legalidad y a la voluntad debidamente informada de los otorgantes y/o intervinientes, y del contenido de este instrumento público [...], yo, el Notario, DOY FE.
[I, the undersigned Notary Public, certify the parties' identity and their legal capacity. I certify that they have executed such instrument within their free and legal rights, that this agreement complies with the legally and duly informed will of the parties and that the agreement content is legal].

8. Conclusions

Due to the small quantity of data included in the analysis, it would be too ambitious to offer generalizations at this stage. What this small study does is to offer some insights into those linguistic features present in these types of contracts deemed to be the most significant. From an intercultural perspective, CAP1 in particular represents something of an innovation since it includes the issue of child custody, a matter which cannot be addressed in American prenups or even in traditional Spanish *capitulaciones matrimoniales*. These latter, up to some years ago, could not even include provisions agreeing upon any potential crisis in marriage. Agreements in the American sense of the word, namely those contemplating divorce, are gradually being introduced in the Spanish family law, so this may be a precursor of some important cultural change.

These texts, however much they are drafted for the layperson, remain difficult to understand, unclear and likely to be beyond the comprehension of the average layperson, requiring the presence of a legal counsel. The layperson does not have sufficient knowledge to understand the legal meaning of the words used, as compared with their lay values. At times the expressions may be unclear or unintelligible, at times misleading. The textual organization with headings and numbering and the reference system to the participants function as *textual-mapping devices* (Bhatia 1993: 141-142) which simplify the texts in both cultures and languages, reducing the information load. They help laymen to read and understand the text guiding them through it. Other examples of such devices are: "under the law" (PREN1), "by operation of Texas law" (PREN2), "by law" (PREN1), "*previstos por la Ley*" (CAP2), items referring to the legislation to be taken into account without being redundantly detailed.

However, in order to make these documents plainer and more accessible in their meaning, more *easification* (Bhatia 1993: 209) devices should be used especially from a lexical point of view. This does not mean that the document form and content should become simpler "sacrificing its originality, authenticity or generic integrity" (Bhatia 1993: 209). The main purpose remains that of balancing the need for simplicity and clarity on the one hand, with certainty on the other (Bhatia 1993: 210), especially in countries such as the USA where all-inclusiveness is required in contracts in order for the provisions to be valid and enforceable. This often results in a text overloaded with information, and therefore difficult to follow, and at the same time vague, making it hard to interpret.

References

Al Mureden, Enrico 2005. *I prenuptial agreements negli Stati Uniti e nella prospettiva del diritto italiano.* [Prenuptial agreements in the USA and in the framework of Italian law]. University of Bologna, Faculty of Law. <http://www.corsodirittofamiglia.it/allegati/contr_almureden.pdf>.

Bhatia, Vijay K. 1993. *Analyzing Genre: Language Use in Professional Settings*. London: Longman.

Bhatia, Vijay K. / Candlin, Christopher N. / Gotti, Maurizio (eds) 2003. *Legal Discourse in Multilingual and Multicultural Contexts. Arbitration Texts in Europe.* Bern: Peter Lang.

Bix, Brian H. 2001. Premarital Agreements in the ALI Principles of Family Dissolution. *Duke Journal of Gender Law and Policy* 8, 231-244.

Crystal, David / Davy, Derek 1969. *Investigating English Style.* London: Longman.

Di Renzo Villata, Maria Gigliola 2007. *Legal English.* Padova: Cedam.

Engberg, Jan / Rasmussen, Kirsten W. 2003. Danish Legal Language in International Commercial Arbitration. In Bhatia/Candlin/Gotti, 111-154.

García Rubio, María Paz 2004. Acuerdos prematrimoniales. De nuevo la libertad y sus límites en el derecho de familia. [Premarital agreements. Once again, freedom and its limitations in Family Law]. *XV Jornades de Dret català a Tossa, El nou dret successori del Codi Civil de Catalunya*, Tossa de Mar, 23 i 24 de setembre de 2004. <http://civil.udg.edu/tossa/2004/textos/pon/2/mpgr.htm#_ftn1>.

Garzone, Giuliana 2003. Arbitration Rules across Legal Cultures. In Bhatia/Candlin/Gotti, 177-220.

Gotti, Maurizio 2005. *Investigating Specialized Discourse.* Bern: Peter Lang.

Greenstein, Brian R. 1992. Prenuptial Agreements: What they can and cannot Accomplish. *The CPA Journal Online*, Sept. 1992, <http://www.nysscpa.org/cpajournal/old/13606725.htm>.

Jottini, Laura. 2002. L'Inglese Giuridico delle Comunità Europee: Aspetti testuali, lessicali e sintattici. [Legal English in the European Communities. Textual, lexical and syntactic aspects]. In *Due Codici a confronto: per un'analisi contrastiva dei sistemi linguistici inglese e italiano.* [A comparison of two codes: a contrastive analysis of the English and Italian linguistic systems]. Brescia: La Scuola, 247-298.

Lamarca I Marquès, Albert / Farnós Amorós, Esther / Azagra Malo, Albert / Artigot i Golobardes, Mireira 2003. Separate Property and Family Self-Determination in Catatonia: A Peaceful Model Under a Change? *Working Paper of Catalan Law* 164, Barcelona. <www.indret.com>.

Salmi-Tolonen, Tarja. 2003. Arbitration Law as Action: An Analysis of the Finnish Arbitration Act. In Bhatia/Candlin/Gotti, 313-336.

Stewart, William J. 2007. *Collins Dictionary of Law*. London: Collins.

The American Law Institute. 2002. *Principles of the Law of Family Dissolution: Analysis and Recommendations*.

Tiersma, Peter M. 1999. *Legal Language*. Chicago: University of Chicago Press.

Williams, Christopher 2005. Legal English and Plain Language: an Introduction. *ESP Across Cultures* 1, 111-124.

Primary sources

Sample of Premarital agreement from the State of Illinois, <http://www.docstoc.com/docs/2318082/Free-Prenuptial-Agreements>.

Prenuptial agreement, Law Firm Granstaff, Gaedke and Edgmon, P.C, 5535 Fredericksburg Rd # 110, San Antonio, TX 78229-3553.

Modelo de Acuerdo Prematrimonial <http://www.nuevodivorcio.com/acuerdos prematrimoniales. pdf>.

Modelo de capitulaciones matrimoniales. <http://tusasuntoslegales.blogspot.com/2009/05/casarse-con-separacion-de-bienes-con.html>.

LARISSA D'ANGELO*

Online Dispute Resolution in Italy: State of the Art and Future Perspectives

1. Introduction

In the present-day globalisation of trade and commerce, Alternative Dispute Resolution (ADR) has been increasingly seen as an efficient, economical and effective alternative to litigation for settling commercial and other disputes (Davis 2006). Within the ADR panorama, Online Dispute Resolutions (ODR) has become a new and recent way of dealing with disputes, which is slowly appearing on the Italian commercial scene. In the last few years this phenomenon has become more and more popular. In particular, in the years 2000-2003 there was a rapid growth of online sites set up for promoting the resolution of disputes online through the ODR system. When it appeared, some people considered ODR to be too innovative, destined to disappear in a short time; instead others believed it was suitable only for certain instances (Sali 2003). However, despite this criticism, ODR has developed constantly, gaining more and more attention from users. Nonetheless, although it is considered a faster and cheaper tool able to overcome geographical barriers, Italian consumers still seem to prefer the traditional mediation and arbitration practice (Katsh/Leah 2006). The experts think this is mainly due to cultural reasons and to the fact

* The research on which this chapter is based is part of an international research project entitled *International Commercial Arbitration Practices: A Discourse Analytical Study* (http://www.english.cityu.edu.hk/arbitration/), headed by prof. Vijay Bhatia of the City University of Hong Kong. It also contributes to the National Research Programme *Tension and Change in Domain-specific Genres* directed by prof. Maurizio Gotti of the University of Bergamo, funded by the Italian Ministry of University (COFIN Grant No. 2007JCY9Y9).

that, because ODR only uses written language, authority is more difficult to be established (Conley/Raines 2006; Hattotuwa 2006). Moreover, ODR requires a certain familiarity with long-distance communication instruments.

In the context of this situation the present chapter analyzes the evolution of ODR from ADR and focuses on ODR practice in Italy, comparing it with traditional forms of arbitration, litigation and mediation. While focusing on critical moments in the ODR process, particular attention is devoted to relevant cultural as well as linguistic characteristics of this phenomenon.

2. From ADR to ODR

In the last few decades in Europe, as well as in most civil law countries, there has been a strong and widespread increase in the use of ADR. This mainly includes the following methods: arbitration, mediation and conciliation. In Italy, mediation and arbitration are the most widely used ADR instruments, which are becoming increasingly popular among users as they have proved to meet different functional needs. Arbitration, the classic dispute resolution system for companies, represents a strong alternative to ordinary court cases. This procedure results in an arbitration award, which is as binding as the decision of a judge of a court of first instance. The dispute resolution system has been particularly appreciated by Small or Medium Enterprises (Sali 2003). Yet, as formal arbitration is getting increasingly similar to litigation in both time and expense, commercial mediation, which instead implies a negotiated agreement between the parties, is becoming the most attractive ADR option. In this procedure, agreement is reached by the parties through the work of a neutral party, the mediator, who helps them analyze the true interests involved in the dispute. He also identifies the differences implied in the parties' respective positions, leading them towards a resolution of the dispute, without imposing any decision.

The terms 'mediation' and 'conciliation' are often used as synonyms of the same concept, that is, an informal cooperation towards the solution of a controversy due to the neutral participation of a third and neutral participant. In reality, mediation and conciliation have their own specific fields of application deriving from the professional characteristics of these two instruments, the techniques and the tactics they employ and from the theoretical developments of the experts working in each field. The term 'conciliation' is generally used for civil, commercial and employment matters, whereas the term 'mediation' is often used for procedures involving family disputes as well as social matters (Uzqueda/Frediani 2002).

As mentioned above, one of the reasons for the relatively recent development and spread of ADR systems in Italy is that they are able to free courts from the burden of small cases that inevitably slow down the judicial process. The access to a traditional judicial process is also discouraged by the quantity, the complexity and the technical nature of legislative texts. In particular, as regards the Italian context, this pathological situation is the consequence of a number of correlated factors, such as the enormous amount of material that each process accumulates; the insufficient structures available and the limited familiarity with a computerized management of disputes; in consequence, the great amount of judicial work still to be processed inevitably hampers the Italian judicial system.

The complexity of the judicial system is particularly problematic in small-medium patrimonial controversies, where single consumers are involved; the average time needed to carry out a civil process and the costs of a lawyer often are not compensated by the benefits deriving from a favorable verdict. The consumer therefore often prefers renouncing his or her own rights. Negative consequences also derive from litigation between parties belonging to the same partnership or involved in a positive economic relationship; recourse to a judge might lead to a breakdown in the economic relationship, something that is less likely to happen in an extrajudicial resolution of the controversy.

Within this problematic context, ADR instruments have been shown to play an important complementary role as they are not simply an alternative to litigation, but they are often more suitable for commercial and civil controversies. Moreover, in ADR, parties can choose the method of resolution, playing a more active role in the procedure. This consensual approach augments the parties' possibility to maintain a commercial relationship once the issue has been settled.

In particular, ADR instruments have proved to be able to respond positively to the needs of medium-small disputes, such as those in B2B (business to business) and B2C (business to consumer) transactions over the Internet. E-commerce transactions are spreading quickly, with each of them potentially triggering a dispute (Hart 1999). Therefore, the growth of e-commerce greatly depends on the possibility of providing consumers with easy access to justice, also taking advantage of the opportunities provided by the online environment.

It is the aim of this chapter to provide an investigation of the most interesting innovations and experiences concerning ODR. In particular, the analysis will illustrate and evaluate the new procedure available to Italian consumers and businesses.

3. ODR in Italy

Before analyzing the main ODR services and experiences, it is worthwhile analyzing how such procedures work. Besides being the easiest and most innovative way of resolving problems deriving from transactions generated on the World Wide Web, ODR is also becoming popular in resolving off-line disputes. The reason for this popularity is that the online dispute resolution service is simple and easy to carry out as it allows users to overcome time and space barriers, offering them the possibility to communicate easily. In its brief history, the Italian ODR system has already been applied not only to the B2B and B2C market, but also to the C2C (consumer to consumer) transactions (Del Ninno 2008). All these are environments where both consumers and businesses need faster and more reliable instruments to solve disputes. The main functions performed by ODR are the following:

a. Assisted negotiation: Two parties exchange monetary offers, following an automatic system offered by a provider of ODR services. In this case no neutral party, meant to help the participants solve the controversy, is present.
b. Online conciliation or mediation: The participants communicate by e-mail or on a chat line, with the presence of a third party, the mediator, who helps them reach an agreement. This model is the one which most faithfully resembles the traditional process of face-to-face mediation.
c. Online arbitration: The participants rely on the decisions of an arbitrator, who not only helps them reach an agreement, but who also produces an award. This procedure is carried out exchanging all the relative documents by Internet. In essence, if online mediation is based on the dialogue between the participants, in online arbitration the parties mainly exchange documents online.

In Italy, ODR has been developed by the Milan Arbitration Chamber (cf. website at <www.risolvionline.it>). This procedure has been defined as an 'open model' (Sali 2003: 3) because it aims to favor a direct exchange of communication between participants; it is the mediator's duty to help parties discuss openly and find – through dialogue – a satisfactory solution to their dispute.

In the traditional model of nonvirtual mediation, to overcome the mistrust and the disagreements of the parties, the mediator applies several psychological techniques that allow him to interpret the nonverbal language of the participants as well as their attitudes, their emotions and their immediate reactions. Obviously, the reproduction of this model online is meeting some difficulties, at least at the present state of computer techniques. Indeed, the online mediation systems inspired by this open model are strongly limited by the scarce 'communicativeness' of the software now available. E-mail communication or chat-room conferences are the only devices which can be used to recreate, as far as possible, the typical situation of a hearing of conciliation in a virtual environment. As a real arbitration institution would do, the supplier of the mediation service makes available to the parties a virtual meeting place (resolution room) as well as an experienced and qualified mediator.

To begin the procedure, the provider presents a form on the webpage to be completed by the participants (cf. Figure 1). This form can also be submitted by the lawyer representing a consumer or an enterprise.

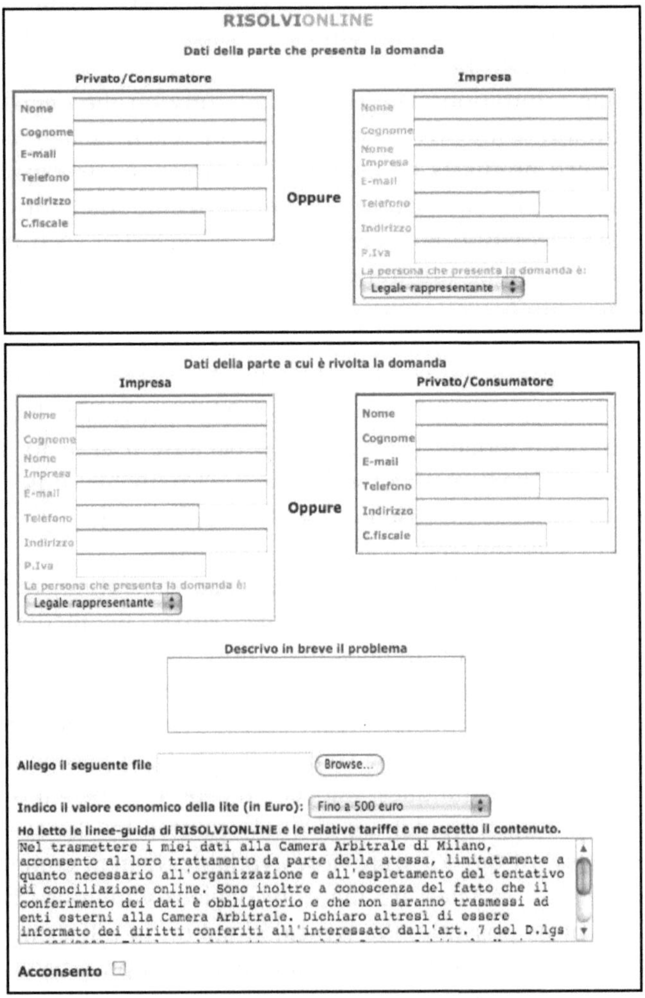
RISOLVIONLINE

Dati della parte che presenta la domanda

Privato/Consumatore: Nome, Cognome, E-mail, Telefono, Indirizzo, C.fiscale

Oppure

Impresa: Nome, Cognome, Nome Impresa, E-mail, Telefono, Indirizzo, P.Iva, La persona che presenta la domanda è: Legale rappresentante

Dati della parte a cui è rivolta la domanda

Impresa: Nome, Cognome, Nome Impresa, E-mail, Telefono, Indirizzo, P.Iva, La persona che presenta la domanda è: Legale rappresentante

Oppure

Privato/Consumatore: Nome, Cognome, E-mail, Telefono, Indirizzo, C.fiscale

Descrivo in breve il problema

Allego il seguente file Browse...

Indico il valore economico della lite (in Euro): Fino a 500 euro

Ho letto le linee-guida di RISOLVIONLINE e le relative tariffe e ne accetto il contenuto.

Nel trasmettere i miei dati alla Camera Arbitrale di Milano, acconsento al loro trattamento da parte della stessa, limitatamente a quanto necessario all'organizzazione e all'espletamento del tentativo di conciliazione online. Sono inoltre a conoscenza del fatto che il conferimento dei dati è obbligatorio e che non saranno trasmessi ad enti esterni alla Camera Arbitrale. Dichiaro altresì di essere informato dei diritti conferiti all'interessato dall'art. 7 del D.lgs

Acconsento

Figure 1. RisolviOnline Mediation Form.

There are no limits as to value: all the controversies can be submitted to the service, whatever their economic value may be. The party that intends promoting an attempt at conciliation completes and sends the submission form online. Besides indicating personal data, the claimant must also briefly describe the controversial matter from his or her point of view, adding any necessary attachments, and describing the nature and the value of the controversy. At the beginning of the mediation process, the claimant must also indicate his or her credit card number, because the procedure fee must be paid in advance.

After having received the completed form by e-mail, the supplier contacts the counterpart and sends him or her another form (Figure 2).

ADESIONE AL TENTATIVO DI CONCILIAZIONE ONLINE

FAC-SIMILE

ATTENZIONE : il modulo di adesione viene inviato via e-mail di volta in volta a cura della segreteria. Il presente fac-simile ha scopo puramente informativo.

Nome

Cognome

Nome Impresa

E-mail

Telefono

Indirizzo

P.Iva/Cod.Fiscale

(Se impresa) la persona che presenta la domanda è:

Legale rappresentante

Descrivo in breve il problema

Allego i seguenti file Sfoglia...

Ho letto le linee-guida di RISOLVIONLINE e le relative tariffe e ne accetto il contenuto.

Nel trasmettere i miei dati alla Camera Arbitrale di Milano, acconsento al loro trattamento da parte della stessa, limitatamente a quanto necessario all'organizzazione e all'espletamento del tentativo di conciliazione online. Sono inoltre a conoscenza del fatto che il conferimento dei dati è obbligatorio e che non saranno trasmessi ad enti esterni alla Camera Arbitrale. Dichiaro altresì di essere

Prosegui

Per eventuali informazioni sulla compilazione del modulo contattare Roberta Regazzoni allo 02-8515.4522

Figure 2. Facsimile of the submission form to be completed by the counterpart.

Online mediation is voluntary in nature; in the case that the counterpart contacted by the manager of the service does not accept participation, the mediation attempt will not take place. If he or she instead does accept, a mediator is named, a time and date for a meeting is set, and a reserved communication line is created (that only the parties and the mediator can access using personal passwords), on which the whole procedure will develop.

At the date and time arranged beforehand, the participants and the mediator link themselves to <http://www.camera-arbitrale.com/conciliazione/> and insert the code of the mediation case, the passwords and the usernames assigned by *RisolviOnline*. Once the virtual contact between the parties and the mediator is established, the procedure reproduces the traditional scheme of nonvirtual conciliation. The mediator introduces himself or herself and asks the parties to do the same; afterwards, each party will be asked to give his or her own version of the facts. The mediator may then ask for further explanations and subsequently will identify the controversial matters, and draft a resolution proposal. The system is pre-organised in such a way as to allow the parties to choose the type of negotiation that they prefer: an exclusive conversation with the mediator (using the available 'reply' command) or all the participants (using the command 'reply to all') (Figure 3).

As happens in traditional mediation, this system also allows the mediator to interact separately with each party to discuss in private the most delicate and confidential aspects of the controversy. As in traditional mediation, the virtual system must be able to guarantee confidentiality in the procedure, assuring privacy in the negotiation, and guaranteeing inaccessibility of all communications by third parties.

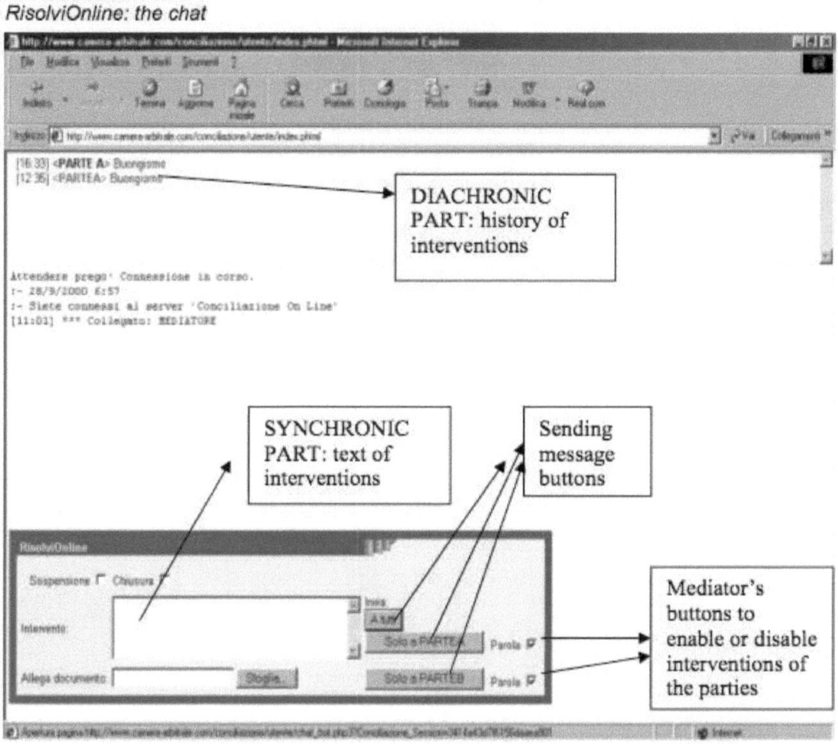

Figure 3. The chat-room made available by *RisolviOnline* (Sali 2003: 6).

At the end of the meeting, if the result is positive, the mediator sends the participants the Online Mediation Agreement (Figure 4) by mail. Two copies of the Agreement must be printed, signed and sent to *RisolviOnline* by fax. The service keeps a copy of the document and makes sure that each participant receives a copy signed by the other party. This last operation is necessary to make the online agreement binding, thus conferring on it the nature of a real contract enforceable by law.

Conciliazione online

Camera Arbitrale
Nazionale e Internazionale
di Milano

N. CONCILIAZIONE 123456

Controversia tra:

Sig. XY residente in...
e
Sig. KX residente in...

Sono intervenuti:
Sig. XY

Sig. KX
Conciliatore Bianchi

Oggetto della controversia:

Verbale:

Dopo ampia e approfondita discussione, le parti hanno deciso di conciliare la loro controversia alle seguenti condizioni ...

Le parti dichiarano di nulla avere più a pretendere l'una dall'altra in relazione all'oggetto della controversia in oggetto.

Redatto in (data)

Firma delle parti:

Firma del conciliatore:

Figure 4. Online Mediation Agreement.

4. The future of ODR in Italy

The service provided by the Arbitration Chamber of Milan offers several advantages: the use of e-mail and fax allows participants who are not able to, or do not want to meet in person the chance to communicate rapidly without incurring excessive costs. The system also allows the supplier of the service to name experienced and prepared mediators without worrying about travel distances and expenses, as well as renting a facility to conduct the mediation (Bordone 1998). Consequently, an important aspect of ODR is that international commercial relations are favored, because the solution of a controversy between international parties is not slowed down or impeded by long distances. As far as *RisolviOnline* is concerned, 45% of mediation requests have been initiated by foreign parties, demonstrating the international scope of the ODR instrument. As attorney's fees are perhaps the greatest expense in traditional litigation, and even sometimes in traditional mediation, in cyber-mediation parties are instead able to save a large amount of money, as hiring an attorney is often unnecessary (Lan 2001).

There are also several benefits that stem from the asynchronous nature of e-mail communication. Messages are not transmitted live, but can be written and sent later. Since e-mail and web posting can be written, posted and responded to at any time, taking part in cyber-mediation is very convenient. The scheduling difficulties that can arise in traditional mediation do not appear in ODR; parties are able to engage in the negotiation when they are ready and at convenient times. The mediator can contact either or both of the parties privately, without affecting the flow of the mediation. The idle downtime that disputants experience is similarly reduced because, in contrast to traditional mediation, the mediator can devote time to one party without wasting the time of the other party. As Melamed (2002) explains:

> Experienced mediators are well aware of the benefits of asynchrony. This is a big part of the reason that many mediators 'caucus' (meet separately) with participants. Mediators want to slow the process down and assist participants to craft more capable contributions. This concept of slowing the process down

> and allowing participants to safely craft their contributions is at the heart of caucusing. Surely, the Internet works capably as an extension of individual party caucus and is remarkably convenient and affordable. Internet communications take less time to read and clients do not hear a professional fee meter clicking. When the Internet is utilized for caucus, the 'non-caucusing participant' does not need to sit in the waiting room or library reading *Time* magazine or growing resentful at being ignored.

It may also be argued that more thoughtful, well-crafted contributions result from the ability of the parties to edit messages before sending them: "Asynchronous Internet communications have the advantage of being edited 'best' communications sometimes in contrast to 'first' (often impulsive) responses that can take place in real time face-to-face mediation discussions" (Melamed 2002). In addition, many of the cyber-mediation mechanisms, such as the fully automated cyber-mediation websites discussed above, are available all-day long, every day of the year. Disputants can therefore proceed with negotiating the settlement of disputes immediately, rather than waiting lengthy periods to go to trial. The cost of the service is also proportional to the value of the controversy. Although a payment is necessary to start the mediating process, in the case that the counterpart refuses to participate, the sum will be entirely refunded.

The system nevertheless has some drawbacks when compared with traditional mediation. As Eisen (1998: 1310) observes, the practice of mediation cannot easily be reproduced in the online environment because "cyberspace is not a 'mirror image' of the physical world." Virtual communication – at least as it is now – is not very 'communicative' from an emotional and nonverbal point of view. Negotiations are certainly more effective when parties are able to communicate freely facing one another. For example, helping parties to listen and understand concerns, empathize with each other, vent feelings and confront emotions is considered an important art in mediation:

> For many participants, mediation is about the 'venting' of feelings and emotions that they would be unable to express in a more formal setting such as a courtroom. The opportunity to tell one's version of the case directly to the opposing party and to express accompanying emotions can be cathartic for mediation participants. (D'Zurilla 1997: 1323)

Substituting e-mail for dialogue, for example, makes it difficult to give any weight to emotion in mediation. Additionally, communication online does not express the variable tone, pitch and volume of the participants and cannot convey personality traits or physical cues. It is therefore more difficult to evaluate the flexibility of a particular party, or the strength of a party's feelings or confidence on a particular issue. Consequently, some authors (Katsh *et al.* 2000) have argued that the lack of personal presence in cyber-mediation can make it more difficult for the mediator to maintain effective control over the negotiating parties:

> The online medium, at least the e-mail environment, makes it difficult for the mediator to manage or temper the tone of the interactions without sounding controlling and judgmental. The mediator, at least in the beginning, is a disembodied voice and cannot use her own physical 'personhood' to set the parties at ease and create an environment for sustained problem-solving. Similarly, absent the physical presence of the disputants, the mediator has difficulty using the intuitive cues of body language, facial expression, and verbal tonality that are part of face-to-face mediation processes. (Katsh *et al.* 2000: 714)

Experts in this sector agree in considering this model inadequate and believe that new efforts to improve the level of virtual communication are necessary. Some improvement can certainly derive from a greater diffusion of video and audio communication systems (web cams) that make long-distance visual communication possible between the participants and the mediator. Another important issue discussed by Katsch (1996: 971) is the concern over the protection of confidential material in ODR. While traditional mediation does not necessarily create a physical record, online mediation creates an electronic record. This could potentially enable a party to easily print out and distribute e-mail communications without the knowledge of the other party. This may hinder the development of open and honest exchanges in cyber-mediation. Finally, the familiarity of users with IT technologies becomes fundamental when Internet becomes the main vehicle through which mediation takes place. To take advantage of ODR, a user must be able to manage the software and hardware necessary to chat online, send emails and faxes, and at times, even to use a web cam.

Because of all these reasons, the *RisolviOnline* service provided by the Arbitration Chamber of Milan has had a difficult start and is only now beginning to receive a positive feedback from consumers and firms. In the first few years, many requests for online mediation that were submitted to *RisolviOnline* were not all related to its mission and focus. This was probably due to the fact that this innovative service was not defined clearly enough, and Italian web surfers were not familiar with its scopes, nature and modalities. As Figure 5 shows, 117 new requests for on-line mediation services were filed in 2007. This is an impressive result when compared to the 16 requests filed in 2003. On the other hand, if we consider the latest statistics available from the Arbitration Chamber of Milan, we notice that of the 117 requests filed in 2007, only eight parties have agreed to participate in an ODR, while 31 have decided to explore an agreement outside this procedure. Although the overall number of requests is constantly rising and ODR is becoming more and more known to the public, one cannot help noting that the service is still in its early phase, even if *RisolviOnline* has been active since 2002.

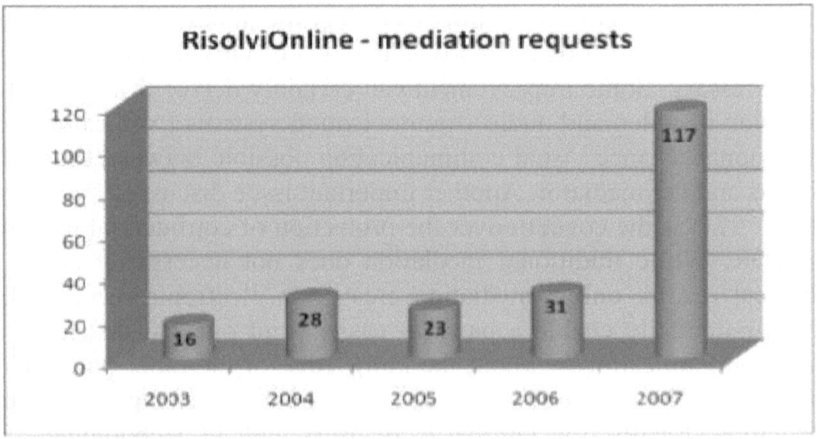

Figure 5. RisolviOnline mediation requests (2003-2007).

5. Conclusions

The reason that has impelled national and international legislators to foresee a way to solve controversies online is connected to the need to favour the development of a market on the web. The advantages of this instrument are clear both for relationships between firms, as well as for those between consumers and businesses. ODR does not merely translate traditional ADR instruments to be used on the web; rather, if ADR responds to the need to facilitate access to the instruments of justice, especially from an economic point of view, ODR responds to the ever-increasing need of businesses and consumers to solve economic disputes taking advantage of the rapidity and convenience of the online instrument.

Although cyber-mediation has been criticized because of its impersonal nature, it is likely to become more popular and better suited to resolving disputes as technology advances. Online mediation will probably not be fully developed until videoconferencing becomes commonplace, video cameras and microphones are built into every computer, videoconferencing software is easily accessible and modems are fast enough to allow videoconferencing. When this becomes a common reality, ODR will reach consumers on a wider scale, and users will familiarize themselves more with the many advantages offered by this virtual procedure.

References

Arbitration Chamber of Milan. *RisolviOnline Statistics 2002-2007.* <http://www.camera-arbitrale.com/consulta.php?sez_id=4&lng_id=7>.

Bordone, Robert C. 1998. Electronic Online Dispute Resolution: A Systems Approach – Potential Problems and a Proposal. *Harvard Negotiation Law Review* 175/3, 190-191.

Conley Tyler Melissa / Raines, S 2006. The Human Face of Online Dispute Resolution (Introduction to Special Issue). *Conflict Resolution Quarterly* 23/3, 333-342.

D'Zurilla, William 1997. *Alternative Dispute Resolution* 45 LA. B.J. 352.

Davis, Benjamin G. (ed.) 2006. Symposium on Enhancing Worldwide Understanding through Online Dispute Resolution, *The University Of Toledo Law Review* 38/1, 1-10.

Del Ninno, Alessandro 2008. Alternative Dispute Resolution Procedures: Online Mediation and Arbitration. <http://www.leggiweb.it/articoli/A5061696/Conciliazioneedarbitratoonline.html>.

Eisen, Joel 1998. Are we Ready for Mediation in Cyberspace?. *Bringham Young University Law Review* 4, 1305-1360.

Hart, Christine 1999. Online Dispute Resolution and Avoidance In Electronic Commerce. Draft Report. <http://www.law.ualberta.ca/alri/ulc/current/hart.htm>.

Hattotuwa, Sanjana 2006. Transforming Landscapes: Forging New ODR Systems with a Human Face. *Conflict Resolution Quarterly* 23/3, 371-382.

Katsh, Ethan 1996. Dispute Resolution in Cyberspace, *Connecticut Law Review* 28, 953-971.

Katsh, Ethan / Leah, Wing 2006. Ten Years of Online Dispute Resolution (ODR): Looking at the Past and Constructing the Future. In Davis (ed.), 19-46.

Katsh Ethan / Rifkin, Janet / Gaitenby, Alan 2000. E-Commerce, E-Disputes, and E-Dispute Resolution: In the Shadow of 'eBay Law'. *Ohio State Journal on Dispute Resolution* 15, 705-714.

Lan, Hang 2001. Online Dispute Resolution Systems: The Future of Cyberspace Law. *Santa Clara Law Review* 41, 837-855.

Melamed, Jim 2002. The Internet and Divorce Mediation. <http://www.mediate.com/articles/melamed9.cfm>.

Sali, Rinaldo 2003. Risolvionline Experience: A New ODR Approach For Consumers And Companies. *Proceedings of the UNECE Forum on ODR 2003.*

Uzqueda A. / Frediani P 2002. *Mediation: A Conflict Resolution Guide*. Milano: Giuffrè.

Linguistic and discoursal features of dispute resolution

CELINA FRADE

Linguistic Pathologies in Arbitration Clauses

Unclear writing is one of the oldest causes of litigation (Mellinkoff 1982: 61)

1. Introduction

International arbitration, as an alternative form of dispute resolution, is now firmly established worldwide involving multilegal and multilingual parties. Different from litigation, the parties expressly agree to settle any controversy arisen out of contracts out of court and invest arbitrators with the power to decide upon it. Among the numerous reasons to arbitrate rather than litigate, Woodbridge and Mason (1999: 260-1) point out privacy, finality, a superior quality tribunal, decreased costs and party participation in shaping procedures.

Arbitration agreements are composed of a series of interrelated genres which interact with each other resulting in what Bazerman (1994) calls a 'system of genres', ranging from the drafting of a valid and enforceable arbitration clause to the final award issued by the arbitral tribunal. The pressure for harmonization in international arbitration procedures has resulted in an attempt to standardize the discourse of arbitration by means of a large variety and number of multilingual ready-made model types of arbitration contracts and clauses designed to be used by the parties as a frame of reference. These model forms, mostly available in websites of well-established institutions and organizations, are usually simple, concise and all-inclusive and not concerned with specific characteristics and difficulties of each arbitration.

As the basis of arbitration, the arbitration clause requires more consideration and attention on the part of drafters and translators. Arbitration clauses are not as simple as they used to be a few years ago; they are becoming increasingly complex and multi-tiered due to the detailed specification of a series of interrelated steps the parties need to go through before finally indicating a choice for arbitration. As pointed out by Mellinkoff (1982: 101), the 'form disease' has the effect of overwhelming drafters with forms of everything and, though these may not always be entirely appropriate in every case, they are nonetheless invested with 'the sham authority' of the printed form 'discouraging detailed examination' by the users.

On the legal level, drafters should utilise their best efforts and skills to avoid ill-suited, equivocal or unhappily drafted clauses – also called 'pathological clauses' – which may result in another dispute and/or litigation between the parties (and even invalidity of the arbitration agreement by the arbitral tribunal) arising out of poor drafting. Furthermore, linguistic pathologies and inadequate and/or inaccurate translation from multilingual versions to English versions may increase the cost and duration of arbitration due to misunderstandings, errors and ambiguities.

This chapter provides an analysis of the identification of some linguistic pathologies in standard model clauses produced by international arbitral institutions. The investigation is part of an ongoing international and multidisciplinary project conducted by a group of linguists and legal practitioners who investigate the legal, linguistic and discoursal properties of the interrelated genres in international commercial arbitration contexts.[1] The claim is that not only pathologic clauses on the legal level, if not rendered invalid, but also linguistically defective clauses may jeopardize some advantages of arbitration and should therefore be avoided by drafters and translators. As there is no such *perfect* clause, we also have in mind to attempt to raise legal drafters/translators' awareness of such pathologies, particularly where drafters and translators are from civil law and non-English

1 RGC (HKSAR) Cerg Project (No. CityU1051/06H) on 'International Arbitration Practice: A Discourse Analytical Study'. (See the website: <http://www.english.cityu.edu.hk/arbitration/>.

speaking countries such as Brazil, so as to provide some guidelines in the decision-making process of drafting a clear and proper arbitration clause.

2. Arbitration agreements

Arbitration agreements can generally be regarded as normal contracts which contain an arbitration clause which provides that, if a dispute should arise, it will be resolved by arbitration. In the case where the agreement is signed after a dispute has arisen, and with the parties' agreeing that the dispute should be resolved by arbitration, it is sometimes called a 'submission agreement'.

Parties who decide to settle any dispute by arbitration in international contexts can make a choice between *ad hoc* and institutional arbitration. *Ad hoc* arbitration is administered by the arbitrators themselves who have the burden of scheduling all the events and providing for much of the necessary administration of the process, including the drafting of the arbitration clause. On the other hand, institutional arbitration is administered by a functioning arbitral institution or association covering all legal and procedural aspects of arbitration, including multilingual versions of standard model clauses, and the scrutiny of arbitration awards.

Multiple and varied types of rules, procedures and/or processes of administering arbitration are available in a number of treaties, conventions, supranational model laws (United Nations Commission on International Trade Law-UNCITRAL Model Law on International Commercial Arbitration),[2] national statutes (Arbitration Act 1996, the Brazilian Arbitration Law 9.307/1996)[3] and reputed arbitration asso-

---

2 The original version of the Model Law dates 1985, with amendments adopted in 2006 with Explanatory Notes at <http://www.uncitral.org/uncitral/en/uncitral_texts/arbitration/1985Model_arbitration.html>.

3 Homepages: <http://www.opsi.gov.uk/Acts/acts1996/ukpga_19960023_en_1> and <http://www.planalto.gov.br/ccivil_03/leis/l9307.htm> (in Portuguese).

ciations and organizations (such as American Arbitration Association-AAA, International Chamber of Commerce-ICC, Brazil-Canada Chamber of Commerce-CCBC).[4] The general aim is to provide for the uniformity of arbitral procedures and "the desired harmonization and improvement of national laws" (UNCITRAL).

The 2006 amended version of the UNCITRAL Model Law[5] adopts two options which "reflect two different approaches on the question of definition and form of the arbitration agreement":

Option I *Article 7. Definition and form of arbitration agreement*

> (1) 'Arbitration agreement' is an agreement by the parties to submit to arbitration all or certain disputes which have arisen or which may arise between them in respect of a defined legal relationship, whether contractual or not. An arbitration agreement may be in the form of an arbitration clause in a contract or in the form of a separate agreement.
> (2) The arbitration agreement shall be in writing.
> (3) An arbitration agreement is in writing if its content is recorded in any form, whether or not the arbitration agreement or contract has been concluded orally, by conduct, or by other means.
> (4) The requirement that an arbitration agreement be in writing is met by an electronic communication if the information contained therein is accessible so as to be useable for subsequent reference; 'electronic communication' means any communication that the parties make by means of data messages; 'data message' means information generated, sent, received or stored by electronic, magnetic, optical or similar means, including, but not limited to, electronic data interchange (EDI), electronic mail, telegram, telex or telecopy.
> (5) Furthermore, an arbitration agreement is in writing if it is contained in an exchange of statements of claim and defence in which the existence of an agreement is alleged by one party and not denied by the other.
> (6) The reference in a contract to any document containing an arbitration clause constitutes an arbitration agreement in writing, provided that the reference is such as to make that clause part of the contract.

4 Homepages: <http://www.adr.org/> and <http://www.iccwbo.org/> and <http://www.ccbc.org.br/ingles/default.asp>.

5 <http://www.uncitral.org/pdf/english/texts/arbitration/ml-arb/07-86998_E-book.pdf>.

Option II *Article 7. Definition of arbitration agreement*

> 'Arbitration agreement' is an agreement by the parties to submit to arbitration all or certain disputes which have arisen or which may arise between them in respect of a defined legal relationship, whether contractual or not.

Option I follows the original 1985 text (article 7), closely followed by the New York Convention (article II (2)[6]), which confirms "the validity and effect of commitment by the parties to submit to arbitration an existing dispute (*compromise*) or a future dispute (*clause compromissoire*), according to Explanatory Note 19. It states that the arbitration agreement is in written form though also allowing the court to recognize the agreement in "any form", including orally, as long as the content of the agreement is recorded. This new approach "modernizes the language", according to the Note, in the era of electronic communication in international contracts. In item (6), it states the binding effect of the arbitration agreement allegedly made "by reference" in a contract. More flexibly, Option II "defines the arbitration agreement in a manner that omits any form requirement" (Explanatory Note 19).

The reason for such amendments is to "better conform to international contract practices" since, as pointed out by some practitioners, the drafting of a written document is "impossible or impractical" in various situations (Explanatory Note 19). Moreover, as the willingness of the parties to arbitrate is not in question, the validity and enforceability of the arbitration agreement are preserved in both options.

Nevertheless, it seems that the basis of the arbitration agreement still lies in the written arbitration (or arbitral) clause included in a contract or an arbitration agreement, signed by the parties under the New York Convention. As there is no such *perfect* arbitration clause, the drafting of a complete and valid clause is the "primary pre-condition and safeguard for parties" to settle disputes among them "smoothly and timely" in the course of arbitral procedure afterwards (Liu 2006: 33-37). On the other hand, an arbitration clause which is poorly-drafted and/or does not comply in such a way that, if not rendered

---

6 <http://www.uncitral.org.pdf/english/texts/arbitration/NY-conv/XXII_1_e. pdf>.

invalid, may threaten the main tenets of arbitration, is considered an imperfect or a pathological clause.

3. Arbitration clauses

Appropriately called *midnight-clauses* or *airport-express-bus clauses*, arbitration clauses are often the last ones to be inserted in the contract, "at around 2:00 a.m. on the morning of the day of the closing" and so drafters do not pay sufficient attention to the circumstance which it relates to and "paste[d] in a copy of the nearest clause available" (Townsend 2003: 1). According to Debattista (2005: 233), arbitration clauses are not as simple as they used to be and are becoming increasingly multi-tiered and

> may spell out in detail a litany of steps which the parties need to go through, for example seeking amicable settlement, then formal mediation through specified institution; and only then arbitration.

A very large number of well-known institutions have prepared multilingual standard model clauses (usually available online) "as a safeguard against defective arbitral clauses" (Šarčević 2008: 293). These model clauses are short and simple and embody all "requisite elements" (Liu 2006: 35) and wording required for an arbitration clause to be valid, such as *all disputes*, *resulting from* and *definitely*. Also, they often provide for the "recommended elements" (Liu 2006: 35) that may or may not be included into them by the parties, such as the place of arbitration, substantive law etc. Although rarely operating with any models at all, Child (1992: 295) claims that standard model clauses may foster the drafter's "temptation to accept something that looks all right under cursory inspection".

In *ad hoc* arbitrations, the parties have substantial but not unlimited freedom to design the structure of their arbitration, and they should be encouraged to turn to experts to draft their arbitration clauses who will produce a clause "which will create as few difficulties as possible for the arbitrators and consequently be valid and effective" (Liu 2006: 35).

International commercial practice shows that a valid and enforceable arbitration clause should contain at least some of the following substantial elements: the intention of arbitration clearly expressed in the clause, matters which may be arbitrable, the arbitration institution or rules for *ad hoc* arbitration, the place of arbitration, arbitral rules and effects of the arbitral award. On the whole, standard and all-purpose arbitration clauses, whether detailed or otherwise, are often unhappily drafted and may result in another unwanted dispute and/or litigation. An arbitration clause which fails to satisfy the substantial elements before mentioned is called a pathological clause.[7] As defined by Bishop (undated: 18):

> Pathological arbitration clauses might be defined as those drafted in such a way that they may lead to disputes over the interpretation of the arbitration agreement, may result in the failure of the arbitral clause or may result in the unenforceability of an award.

In terms of legal criteria, there are many features that make for pathological arbitration clauses, but inattention and anxiety to close the deal seem to be the main reasons why the parties disregard the importance of drafting a clear and proper arbitration clause (see Towsend 2003, Liu 2006, Šarčević 2008). For Lemes (2003), pathological clauses may result in a type of 'parasite litigation' in order to elucidate the parties' real intention to settle their disputes by arbitration.

In terms of linguistic criteria, pathological clauses are poorly-drafted in such a way that, if not rendered invalid, they do not meet the requirements of syntactic consistency, conventionalized terminology, for example, an adequate and/or accurate English translation into/from various languages. Within the current multilingual and multi-legal context of international arbitration, not only drafters but also legal translators play a key contribution in "the globalization of arbitration by removing linguistic and cultural barriers" (Šarčević 2008:

7 The term 'pathological clause' is said to have been coined by former Secretary General of the ICC International Court of Arbitration Frédéric Eisemann.

292). As English has become the *lingua franca* of international arbitration, for non-English speaking drafters/translators, such as Brazilians, the challenge is to be able to recognize "whether a provision is mandatory or discretionary in the source text and possess the know-how to formulate the provision as such in the target language" (Šarčević 2008: 301) to avoid linguistic pathologies al all costs.

4. Method and material

Founded in 1973, the Brazil-Canada Chamber of Commerce (in Portuguese, Câmara de Comércio Brasil-Canadá, hereafter 'CCBC')[8] is a bi-national organization which represents Brazilian and Canadian companies operating in all major economic sectors, both in Brazil and Canada. Concerning its arbitration and mediation center,

> The Brazil-Canada Chamber of Commerce was a pioneer in Brazil in terms of arbitration. As early as July 26, 1979 it had already created its Arbitration Committee with the purpose of providing comprehensible and expeditious means to settle litigation, whether between individuals or, more importantly, between corporate persons in matters related to contracts.

The CCBC displays a four-language (Portuguese, English, French and Spanish) version of regulations for mediation and arbitration and suggested model clauses in its website. The analysis was conducted to identify linguistic pathologies (and provide remedies) in a) the standard clause in both Portuguese and English versions and b) three examples of suggested model clauses in English version. The justification for the choice of the data is the fact that, in accordance with Giannoni's (2005:443) viewpoint, "albeit limited in number, the clauses are representative of thousands of international [and domestic] commercial contracts drafted every year with their inclusion". In particular, for Brazilian drafters and/or translators, the analysis aims at

8 Official website in English <http://www.ccbc.org.br/ingles/quemsomos.asp>.

drawing their attentions to such pathologies and suggests alternatives by means of which to draft a relatively perfect and valid arbitration clause.

5. Linguistic pathologies in arbitration clauses

In order to achieve harmonization and standardization, international arbitration practice has conventionalized some of its norms, routines and features so that it becomes possible to group them all under the general term of 'arbitration clause', which can be viewed as a genre. However, as there is no uniform wording, we find acceptable generic variations which cannot be adequately made use of keeping in mind the contractual context in which they will be likely to operate (see Frade 2004).

In particular, arbitration clauses may invariably lead to misunderstandings, errors or ambiguities if the drafter/translator is careless and not aware of potential linguistic pathologies embodied in standard model clauses. Next, we will identify some linguistic pathologies embodied in both the Portuguese and English model clauses and then will focus on the suggested model clauses.[9]

5.1. The Portuguese/English versions of the CCBC model clause

5.1.1. Wording

The wording of the English version of the CCBC model clause (App. 1 §1) seems to follow the standard model clauses provided by arbitration institutions worldwide: short, simple and concise as it is "designed for use by parties as a frame of reference [to promote] their capability to settle disputes among them by arbitration" (Liu 2006: 34-35). The short sentence length, as explained by Gotti (2008: 246), "en-

9 The integral versions of the clauses are in Appendix 1 and Appendix 2.

hances [its] level of readability and makes [it] easier to process and more user-friendly" particularly for the non-native English speaking user. Nevertheless, clause (1) displays unnecessary legal English jargon (*hereunder*, *pursuant to*) and the characteristic lack of adequate punctuation which may result in unnecessary delay and reading effort.

(1) Any litigation resulting from the contract hereunder, including its interpretation or execution, shall be definitely settled by arbitration, in accordance with the Guidelines of the Arbitration Center of the Brazil-Canada Chamber of Commerce by three (03) arbitrators appointed pursuant to said Guidelines.

5.1.2. Translation

The English translation was made word-for-word (see App. 1) without apparently resulting in any error or ambiguity as the Portuguese version contains "no system-bound terms that would limit aspects of its application to a particular legal system or systems" (Šarčević 2008: 303). However, the clause lacks consistency in reference as there are no such *Guidelines* available on the CCBC website, but rather *Regulation of the Arbitration Center of the Brazil-Canada Chamber of Commerce*. Interestingly, the version in Portuguese (App. 1 §2) displays the term *Regulamento*. Although both terms may be considered synonyms or near synonyms in general language, this stylistic choice should be avoided in legal drafting as it may be misleading. It is highly recommended that the bilingual drafter strives to be "consistent and precise in using only one term for each concept" (Chroma 2008: 321).

5.1.3. Terminology

The choice of terminology involves the identification of its legal origin and convention of use to see if they can be adequately borrowed and employed in the context of arbitration. This is not the case of the term *litígio* which, in legal Portuguese, acts as a superordinate term to include lawsuits and also other types of dispute resolution, whereas in common law use *litigation* is related to lawsuits and not to alternative dispute resolutions such as arbitration. On the pragmatic level, the convention of avoiding terms denoting 'stronger' conflicts, such as *litigation* and *conflict*, for the sake of politeness, is not followed. As

Frade indicates (2002: 17), such strong terms are conventionally replaced by *softer* terms like *dispute*, *claim*, *dissatisfaction*, *discrepancy*, *contradiction*, *difference* and *disagreement*, as in clause (2):

(2) 3.4 - Any issue, controversy, doubt or pendency shall be settled by arbitration in the event success shall not be attained by an extrajudicial settlement, as referred to in the preceding clauses.

In other words, the convention is to integrate two or more terms within the idea unit of *litigation* to neutralize any potentially offensive act without using the term *litigation* itself.

Particular consideration should be given to the choice of prepositions either in isolation or in multinomials. In clause (1) the expression *resulting from* is restrictive in nature (only disputes relating to the contract itself) and may either lead to its invalidation or conflict with Brazil's arbitration law 9.3097, which reads in Chapter I. - General Provisions Article 1: "Any person capable of contracting may settle any dispute by arbitration related to patrimonial rights over which they may dispose". If a controversy not related to patrimonial rights *results from* the contract, arbitration cannot be even considered. It is advisable in such a case to broaden the scope of the clause with the inclusion of the prepositional phrase *in relation to*, for example. Brazilian drafters must be very careful not to provide exact (or unsatisfactory) translation of all Portuguese legal terms into English without considering their semantic, legal and cultural values between legal systems.

5.2. The CCBC 3-models of arbitration clauses

5.2.1. Consistency

Consistency is regarded as one of the most highly valued principles in drafting legal documents, including arbitration agreements and clauses. A well drafted document is the one that "the drafter always says the same thing the same way and different things differently" (Child 1992: 376). In our data, syntactic inconsistencies are displayed in all examples of model clauses. The first clauses, for instance, all start each with different syntactic structures and different 'agents' of *shall*: " Any discrepancies resulting from this contract shall be settled by arbitration" (App. 2 1), "should there be significant discrepancies [...], they shall be settled by resorting to..."(App. 2.1) and "the parties shall make their best efforts to extrajudicially settle [...]" (App. 3.1) which may result in the reader's understanding that the clauses are dealing with different subject matter. The clauses also display two categories of agents of *shall*: passive sentences with non-human 'agents' in subject position and 'suppressed' human agent (Trosborg 2008:209), as in "settlement shall be reached by arbitration" (App. 2.2) and "Any controversy, discrepancy or claim shall be settled pursuant to the legislation of" (App. 2.6); and active sentences with human and non-human 'agents' as subject, as in "The arbitration venue shall be" (App.2.4) and "The parties shall each appoint an arbitrator" (App. 2 §1).

5.2.2. Terminology

Inconsistent terminology is further displayed in all clauses (as well). Terms such *contract*, *instrument* and *agreement*; *solve* and *settle*, *attained* and *reached*; *provisions* and *norms*; *according to* and *pursuant to* are used interchangeably as synonyms or near synonyms:

(3) 3.6 - Arbitration shall be supervised by the Arbitration and Mediation Center of the Brazil-Canada Chamber of Commerce by enforcing the corresponding Guidelines and the provisions of this instrument, i.e., the terms herein set forth shall prevail. The Guideline shall be an integral part of this contract, whereas the version in force on the date of the request to initiate arbitration proceedings shall apply.

Some of these terms are also used inconsistently either alone or as part of a list – multinomials – in the examples below, respectively: *discrepancies* (App. 2 §1); *litigation, controversy, disagreement or claim* (App. 2.2) and *issue, controversy, doubt or pendency* (App. 3.4).

(4) 1 – Any discrepancies resulting from this contract shall be settled by arbitration, whereas the arbitration court shall comprise three (03) arbitrators.

(5) 2.2 – In the event of unsolvable discrepancies, in addition to any non-settlement of litigation, controversy, disagreement or claim resulting from, or related to, this contract […].

(6) 3.4 – Any issue, controversy, doubt or pendency shall be settled by arbitration […].

(7) 2.6 – Any controversy, discrepancy or claim shall be settled pursuant to the legislation of … (country, in the case of an international or national contract, according to Article 2 of the Arbitration Law).

Although there seems to be no problem in using nouns or noun phrases alone, "legal writing is full of synonyms and near synonyms, some distinctly legal, some not" (Mellinkoff 1982: 22). The conventional practice is either to repeat them or to place them sequentially in the same multinomial throughout the clause for the sake of precision, accuracy and explicitness so as to avoid ambiguity. Therefore, the remedy to avoid ambiguity is to choose one word to express the same meaning, and not switch to a synonym or near synonym.

Using a term in singular and plural interchangeably is apparently unproblematic as this "is a matter of language and will not affect the results" (Šarčević 2008: 297). Our data display various examples of terms used both in singular and plural as in *proceeding* (App. 3.7) and *proceedings* (App. 1.3, 2.5, 2.7, 3.3, 3.6, 3.7); *Guideline* (App. 3.6) and *Guidelines* (App. 1.1, 2.2, 3.6); *controversy* (App. 2.2, 2.6, 3.4, 3.7) and *controversies* (App. 3.1, 3.2, 3.3). However, unless the drafter/translator is aware that this 'mistake' will not affect interpretation of the clause and "arbitrators familiar with the legislative intent" (Šarčević 2008: 297), it should be avoided.

A particular case of terminology misuse, or rather non-use, is *whereas* and *while* as in App. (3.2) and (3.5), respectively.

(8) 3.2 – In the event of controversies, any of the parties shall forthwith request a meeting with the other party to discuss the issue in question in up to twenty-four (24) hours, whereas they shall have the right to appoint a mediator to assist them in such meeting

(9) 3.5 – The Arbitration Board shall be comprised of three (03) arbitrators and within a five (5) day period, each party shall be obliged to appoint one (01)

arbitrator, while the third arbitrator shall jointly be appointed by the two (02) arbitrators previously appointed..

In the legal tradition, *whereas* is conventionally placed at the beginning of contracts – recitals – where it takes on a particular value and has the immediate purpose "to serve as preamble to establish the conditions of the commitment between the parties" (Frade 2002: 14).

5.2.3. The use of shall

The restricted use of the "legal or quasi-legal" *shall* (Quirk *et al* 1985: 230) is invariably redundant and excessive and misused in the following clauses:

(10) 1 – Any discrepancies resulting from this contract shall be settled by arbitration, whereas the arbitration court shall comprise three (03) arbitrators. The parties shall each appoint an arbitrator of their trust who shall, in turn, appoint the third arbitrator.

(11) 1.2 – The party that shall resort to arbitration shall be required to notify the other party of its intent and shall inform the name of its arbitrator, whereas the other party shall have fifteen (15) days to appoint its own arbitrator.

What drafters/translators must be aware of is that, in addition to stipulating regulations or legal requirements, *shall* has nothing to do with precision and is only an old formalism restricted to legal contexts. The question here is the drafter/translator's decision "whether the presence of *shall* genuinely create[s] serious problems of misinterpretation" (Williams 2008: 211) or its absence reduces the degree of ambiguity in the clause. In the latter case, *shall* can very often be appropriately replaced by either the present indicative or the semi-modal *be to* without reducing the effectiveness of the clause itself.

5.2.4. Linguistic packaging

As pointed out by Chafe (1976: 21), linguistic or information packaging has less to do with the content than "with the way that content is wrapped up and presented to the [reader]". The contents of arbitration clauses can be designed in one single clause or in various clauses following the interrelated sequence of events making up a system of genres. From the organizational viewpoint, the information packaging of an arbitration clause is "the process of gathering all the promises and policies into groupings that will serve as sections" (Child 1992: 131). The division of three CCBC possible arbitration clauses does not seem technically sound. In (App. 2 §1), for example, information about the appointment of arbitrators is spread over practically each clause. In App. (2), there is reference to both arbitral and court jurisdiction in section (2.2): "[...] settlement shall be reached by arbitration pursuant to the Arbitration Guidelines [...]" while section (2.6) reads that "[...] claim shall be settled pursuant to the legislation of [...]". In (App. 2 §3), before even establishing who will administer arbitration (section 3.6), the appointment of the arbitrators is provided (section 3.5).

The way information is packaged in the clauses is confusing and sometimes redundant with the result of "information-overlap and a lack of logical sequence" (Frade 2004: 53) likely to mislead the reader. It seems that the drafter started writing provisions without considering organization at all and that these are typical examples of *midnight clauses*. Child (1992: 131) provides some organizational remedies for such types of clauses claiming that "the sections should be mutually exclusive" and the drafter should apply one consistent principle to govern the division of information throughout the clause.

6. Final remarks

As international arbitration is becoming increasingly popular and its use consolidated in various branches of law other than international commerce, some of its advantages are put at risk as a consequence of extensive production of ready-made multilingual model forms which are meant to provide safeguards for parties to begin effective arbitration proceedings.

In particular, model arbitration clauses prepared by arbitration institutions are drafted for use by the parties as a frame of reference, are usually translated into various languages, and available on their websites. One of the many challenges drafters face is how to draft valid and enforceable arbitration clauses so as not to result in another dispute and/or litigation arisen out of poor drafting – a pathological clause. Also, translating these model forms to/from English, the *lingua franca* of international arbitration, raises the issue of how to deal with foreign concepts and conventionalized terminology in the original text.

This chapter has discussed some linguistic pathologies in model arbitration clauses produced by an international arbitral institution. When compared with the concept of pathological clauses found in the legal literature, such ill-suited and equivocating linguistically clauses may result in misunderstandings, delays and even occasion a further dispute between the parties arisen out of poor drafting. The findings evidence the relevance, as pointed out by Bhatia (2008: vii), of a "multidisciplinary understanding of the use of language in international arbitration" in an attempt to provide all actors involved with decision making and problem solving strategies on both linguistic and legal levels in order to strengthen arbitration itself.

References

Bazerman, Charles 1994. Systems of Genres and the Enactment of Social Intentions. In Freedman, Aviva / Meadway, Peter (eds) *Genre and the New Rhetoric*. UK: Taylor & Francis, 79-104.

Bhatia, Vijay J. / Candlin, Christopher, N. / Engberg, Jan 2008. *Legal Discourse across Cultures and Systems*. Hong Kong: Hong Kong University Press.

Bishop, R. Doak undated. *A Practical Guide for Drafting Arbitration Clauses. King & Spalding*. Houston, Texas. <www.kslaw.com/library/pdf/bishop5.pdf>.

Chafe, William 1976. Giveness, Contractiveness, Definiteness, Subjects, Topics, and Point of View. In Li, Charles, N. (ed) *Subject and Topic*. New York: Academy Press, 27-55.

Child, Barbara 1992. *Drafting Legal Documents: Principles and Practices*. St. aul, Minn.: West Publishing Co.

Chroma, Marta 2008). Translating Terminology in Arbitration Discourse. In Bhatia/Candlin/Engberg (eds), 309-327.

Debattista, Charles 2005. Drafting Enforceable Arbitration Clauses. *Arbitration International*, 21/2, 233-204.

Frade, Celina 2002. Mitigating Conflict in Arbitration Clauses through Language. *LSP & Professional Communication*, 2/1, 8-25.

Frade, Celina 2004. Generic Variation across Legislative Writing: a Contrastive Analysis of the UNCITRAL Model Law and Brazil's Arbitration Law. *Hermes, Journal of Linguistics* 32: 45-75.

Giannoni, Davide Simone 2005. 'Any dispute shall be settled by arbitration': A Study of Vagueness in International Model Arbitration Clauses. In Bhatia, Vijay K. / Engberg Jan / Gotti, Maurizio / Heller Dorothee (eds) *Vagueness in Normative Texts*. Bern: Peter Lang, 437-468.

Gotti, Maurizio 2008. Cultural Constraints on Arbitration Discourse. In Bhatia/Candlin/Engberg (eds), 221-252.

Lemes, Selma Ferreira 2003. As Cláusulas Arbitrais Omissas e Defeituosas. *Jornal Valor Econômico*, 22.08.03, Caderno Legislação & Tributos, São Paulo, E-2. <http://www.mundojuridico.adv.br/cgi-bin/upload/texto713.pdf>.

Liu, Xiaohong 2006. Achieving Effectiveness of Arbitration Clauses-A Practical Survey from a Chinese Legal Perspective. *US-China Law Review* 3/6 (Serial Number 19), 33-41.

Quirk, Randolph / Greenbaum, Sidney / Leech, Geoffrey / Svartvik Jan 1985. *A Comprehensive Grammar of the English Language*. London: Longman.

Mellinkoff, David 1982. *Legal Writing: Sense & Nonsense*. St. Paul, Minn.: West Publishing Co.

Šarčević, Susan 2008. Translation in International Arbitration. In Bhatia/Candlin/Engberg (eds), 291-307.

Townsend, John M. 2003. Drafting Arbitration Clauses: Avoiding the 7 Deadly Sins. *Dispute Arbitration Journal* 58/1, 1-8.

Trosborg, Anna 2008. Rhetorical Strategies in Arbitration Law. In Bhatia/Candlin/Engberg (eds), 201-220.

Williams, Christopher 2005. Vagueness in Legal Texts; Is There a Future for *Shall*? In Bhatia, Vijay K. / Engberg Jan / Gotti, Maurizio / Heller Dorothee (eds) *Vagueness in Normative Texts*. Bern: Peter Lang, 202-224.

Woodbridge, Frederick Jr. / Mason, Paul E. 1999. Arbitration in the United States: Background, the American Arbitration Association, and a Comparison of AAA and Other International Rules. In Garcez, José Maria R.(ed) *A Arbitragem na Era da Globalização*. Rio de Janeiro: Forense: 255-299.

Appendix 1

CCBC- ARBITRATION CONVENTION
Typical Arbitration Clause

1- English version

Any litigation resulting from the contract hereunder, including its interpretation or execution, shall be definitely settled by arbitration, in accordance with the Guidelines of the Arbitration Center of the Brazil-Canada Chamber of Commerce by three (03) arbitrators appointed pursuant to said Guidelines.

2- Portuguese version

Qualquer litígio originário do presente contrato, inclusive quanto à sua interpretação ou execução, será definitivamente resolvido por arbitragem, de acordo com o Regulamento do Centro de Arbitragem da Câmara de Comércio Brasil-Canadá por três árbitros, indicados de acordo com citado Regulamento.

Appendix 2

CCBC- Possible arbitration clauses

1 - Any discrepancies resulting from this contract shall be settled by arbitration, whereas the arbitration court shall comprise three (03) arbitrators. The parties shall each appoint an arbitrator of their trust who shall, in turn, appoint the third arbitrator.
1.1 - Arbitration shall take place in the Capital City of São Paulo and shall follow the norms set forth in the Arbitration Guidelines of the Arbitration and Mediation Center of the Brazil-Canada Chamber of Commerce, whose provisions shall be an integral part of the contract hereunder.
1.2 - The party that shall resort to arbitration shall be required to notify the other party of its intent and shall inform the name of its arbitrator, whereas the other party shall have fifteen (15) days to appoint its own arbitrator.
1.3 - Following the appointment of the arbitrators, the parties shall initiate arbitration proceedings before the Arbitration and Mediation Center of the Brazil-Canada Chamber of Commerce. The proceeding chosen shall be Arbitration.

2. CLAUSE ... – ARBITRATION
2.1 - Should there be significant discrepancies in the interpretation and enforceability of this contract, they shall be settled by resorting to advisory services of the highest level in order to find an acceptable solution for the parties.
2.2 - In the event of unsolvable discrepancies, in addition to any non-settlement of litigation, controversy, disagreement or claim resulting from, or related to, this contract and, furthermore, if there shall be any event of default, rescission or annulment of the contract hereunder, settlement shall be reached by arbitration pursuant to the Arbitration Guidelines of the Arbitration and Mediation Center of the Brazil-Canada Chamber of Commerce.
2.3 - The number of arbitrators shall be .... (one sole arbitrator or three arbitrators);
2.4 - The arbitration venue shall be … (city and country in the case of an international contract);
2.5 - The official language(s) to be used during the arbitration proceedings shall be … (in the event of an international contract);
2.6 - Any controversy, discrepancy or claim shall be settled pursuant to the legislation of … (country, in the case of an international or national contract, according to Article 2 of the Arbitration Law);
2.7 - The arbitral award shall be proffered within a period of … counted from the initiation of arbitration proceedings.
2.8 - The parties shall immediately comply with the arbitral award.

3. Arbitration

3.1 - The parties shall make their best efforts to extrajudicially settle controversies resulting from this agreement;

3.2 - In the event of controversies, any of the parties shall forthwith request a meeting with the other party to discuss the issue in question in up to twenty-four (24) hours, whereas they shall have the right to appoint a mediator to assist them in such meeting;

3.3 - Unless otherwise set forth in specific mediation proceedings, the parties shall have ten (10) days subsequent to the first meeting to extrajudicially solve the controversies referred to in Clause 1.2 above.

3.4 - Any issue, controversy, doubt or pendency shall be settled by arbitration in the event success shall not be attained by an extrajudicial settlement, as referred to in the preceding clauses.

3.5 - The Arbitration Board shall be comprised of three (03) arbitrators and within a five (5) day period, each party shall be obliged to appoint one (01) arbitrator, while the third arbitrator shall jointly be appointed by the two (02) arbitrators previously appointed. The alternate arbitrators shall be appointed by the Chairman of the Arbitration and Mediation Center of the Brazil-Canada Chamber of Commerce. The venue of the Arbitration shall be in São Paulo.

3.6 - Arbitration shall be supervised by the Arbitration and Mediation Center of the Brazil-Canada Chamber of Commerce by enforcing the corresponding Guidelines and the provisions of this instrument, i.e., the terms herein set forth shall prevail. The Guideline shall be an integral part of this contract, whereas the version in force on the date of the request to initiate arbitration proceedings shall apply.

3.7 - Upon the appointment of the arbitrators, the parties shall initiate the proceedings before the Arbitration and Mediation Center of the Brazil-Canada Chamber of Commerce. In view of the complexity of the controversy, the parties may choose either normal or expeditious arbitration proceedings. However, in the event of a controversy during the execution phase of a case, expeditious arbitration shall, at all times, be the chosen proceeding.

3.8 - The parties shall immediately comply with all the terms of the arbitral award.

MICHELE SALA*

Arguing the Case: Discoursal Aspects of Italian Commercial Arbitration

1. Introduction

The arbitral procedure is a dispute resolution method aimed at the drafting of an award which is intended as a definitive measure for the settling of disputes. Based on the free will of the conflicting parties to agree and settle their disputes without resorting to legal action, arbitration is meant as a time-saving and economical alternative to ordinary jurisdiction (Nariman 2000, Marriott 2004, Bocchini 2006). While quite frequently used in international contexts (Bhatia *et al.* 2003), in Italy, up to 1994, the arbitral practice was almost non-existent (cf. Maci forth.), also due to the fact that, before that date, arbitration laws lacked specific provisions to make awards unchallengeable, therefore entailing the possibility of various forms of appellate review (Ceccon 2000, Belotti 2003). The reform of the Italian Code of Civil Procedure in 1994 and new laws enacted in recent years (Legislative Decree 5/2003, Legislative Decree 40/2006, Legislative Decree 113/2008) have served the purpose of promoting arbitration in civil and commercial matters, and reinforcing the definitiveness of the arbitral decision by circumscribing the possibilities of challenge (Gotti/Anesa forth., Maci forth.). Nonetheless, arbitration proceedings can still be appe-

* The research on which this chapter is based is part of an international research project entitled *International Commercial Arbitration Practices: A Discourse Analytical Study* (http://www.english.cityu.edu.hk/arbitration/), headed by prof. Vijay Bhatia of the City University of Hong Kong. It also contributes to the National Research Programme *Tension and Change in Domain-specific Genres* directed by prof. Maurizio Gotti of the University of Bergamo, funded by the Italian Ministry of University (COFIN Grant No. 2007JCY9Y9).

aled for nullity, revocation or third party opposition (Consolo 2006, Lino 2006, Cutolo/Esposito 2007). This makes the validity of the procedure problematic, especially when the award is perceived as being non-coherent or lacking authoritativeness. On this basis, the main purpose of this chapter is to analyse the methods arbitrators use to reinforce the validity of awards as judicial acts. More specifically, the main focus is on the argumentative and interdiscursive strategies used by the drafters to express epistemic and interactive meanings in order to confer efficacy and definitiveness to their pronouncements, and deontic value to the whole text.

2. Material and methodology

The analysis is based on a corpus of 20 commercial arbitration awards written in Italian between 2000 and 2006, and available in the archives of the Chambers of Arbitration of Bergamo, Milan and Reggio Emilia (totalling over 900,000 words). Wordsmith Tool 4.0 (Scott 2004) and Portable Document Format (PdF program) search options were used for word counts and the results were subsequently filtered through manual correction to rule out non-relevant occurrences.

For an in-depth investigation of the discourse strategies of arbitration it is necessary to point out that the Code of Civil Procedure (*Codice di Procedura Civile in materia di processo di Cassazione e di Arbitrato*) accounts for the possibility of appeals and challenges (Cutolo/Esposito 2007, Gotti/Anesa forth.). For instance, awards can be appealed as null for either purely formal or procedural factors (i.e. the arbitrators were not appointed in the form and manner laid down by law; the award failed to meet mandatory formal requirements or was delivered outside the prescribed time limit), or else for reasons closely pertaining to the matter of the dispute (i.e. the award exceeds the scope of the arbitration agreement, it contains contradictory provisions, or there is justifiable doubt as to the arbitrators' impartiality). As a consequence, although arbitration is meant as a definitive resolution, its outcome does not have (or is not perceived as having) the same juridical weight as a court sentence. This has a considerable impact on the definitiveness of this procedure and bears a significant influence on its discourse. As a matter of fact, to overcome the obstacle represented by the possibility of challenge, the award needs to be presented and perceived as a coherent and convincing whole, more specifically, it has to be:

- persuasive as to the meaning: the argumentation of the motivations leading to the final decision should be (or sound) compelling and, as a consequence, the award pronouncement should be perceived as necessary, expected and unquestionable;
- authoritative as to its textualization: the presentation of the meaning should be worded in a way that is appropriate to the context, showing the drafter's competence both in the field of the dispute and as a legal expert (Gotti/Anesa forth.), thus conferring on the text the impact and deontic force of a normative act.

The text of arbitration awards is usually modelled according to three macro-moves which are also found in the court judgement template (Bhatia 1993, Santulli 2006, Maci forth.):

1. The *Fatto* [Facts] move, with the function of identifying and establishing the facts of the case: this is the most typically narrative part of the award, representing the various stages of the arbitral procedures and the syntheses of the *Memorie* [Memorial or Memories] presented to the Board by the parties;
2. The *Motivazioni* [Motivations] move, aimed to present the arguments and derive the *ratio decidendi* (i.e. reasons for award pronouncement) this is the argumentative part of the award, devoted to the examination of the dispute and the illustration of the reasons leading to the final decision;
3. The *Decisione* [Final decision] move, pronouncing the judgement: usually introduced by the formula *PQM* (acronym of *Per Questi Motivi* [For these reasons]), this is the core part of the award with a distinctive performative character.

Given its argumentative nature and its function as a preparatory step for the award pronouncement, the focus of this investigation is on the *Motivazioni* move. This chapter analyses epistemic (cf. § 3.1) and interactive aspects (cf. § 3.2) of arbitration discourse to see how drafters present interpretations and evidence, account for the parties' expectations, and exploit different and recognizable voices in arguing their claims and articulating their meanings.

3. Results

3.1. Markers of argumentation

In the *Motivazioni* move arbitrators discuss the *ratio decidendi* of the case, resorting to rhetorical strategies aimed at making the final decision clear, coherent, convincing, and accepted as binding for the resolution of the dispute at issue, and the whole award certain and unchallengeable. This section investigates the use of markers of textual and semantic coherence which are used to express arguments in an effective way.

3.1.1. Evidentiality and epistemic markers

The presentation of informative material in the *Motivazioni* section is fundamental. The operation of selection and distribution of information plays a significant role in supporting given views and influencing interpretation. This subsection examines the way evidence is introduced and organized in order to construct meanings. Evidentiality is a phenomenon widely studied in linguistics (Givón 1982, Chafe/Nichols 1986, Wierzbicka 1994, Nuyts 2000) and refers to any linguistic expression of attitude towards the truth of a state of affairs indicating either the nature of evidence or the source of knowledge. For the purpose of this chapter, formulations used by the arbitrators to represent knowledge claims and interpretations have been divided into two main categories:

- Mediated resources: when the evaluating agent *Collegio* or *Arbitro* [Board or Arbitrator] – either with the grammatical function of subject or (direct and indirect) object – is lexicalized and claims are explicitly framed within a subjective perspective through formulations such as *il Collegio ritiene, viente ritenuto da questo Collegio, a parere del Collegio, X ha portato il Collegio a...,* etc. [The Board thinks, it is thought by the Board, according to the Board, X has led the Board to, etc], as in (1) and (2) below;
- Non-mediated resources: when meanings are represented and the parties' views are accepted or rejected without any reference to the semantic agent, through formulations like *è chiaro, è possible, sembra, si presume, si può ritenere,* etc. [it is clear, it is possible, it seems, it is believed, it can be observed, etc.], as in (3) and (4) below.

Both resources are fairly common in the *Motivazioni*, as can be seen in the following extracts:

(1) *Non ritiene l'arbitro unico* meritevole di accoglimento [...] la richiesta di condanna.
[The Arbitrator feels that the request for conviction should not be granted.]

(2) Anche tale eccezione [...] è, *a giudizio del Collegio*, affatto priva di pregio.
[Also such an exception, in the opinion of the Board, is devoid of any worth.]

(3) *È pacifico* [...] che nella fattispecie in esame lo sconto fiscale ottenuto non ammonta a € X.
[It is certain that in the case in point the tax reduction does not correspond to € X.]

(4) Tale richiesta *appare dunque fondata.*
[The request appears well-founded.]

The table accommodates the frequencies of such expressions both in absolute and normalized figures (per 10,000 words).

	Absolute figures	Normalized figures
Mediated resources	99	21.7
Non-mediated resources	235	51.7

Table 1. Frequency of mediated and non-mediated resources in the *Motivazioni* section.

The data in the table show the high frequency of non-mediated evidentiality markers, irrespectively of their pragmatic function as boosters (i.e. *è chiaro, è ovvio,* etc.) or hedges (i.e. *sembra, è possibile,* etc.). This seems to be indicative of the tendency to present evidence in a detached way, from an external perspective rather than as the arbitrator's view.

3.1.2. Markers of causality

The way causality is represented for deriving the *ratio decidendi* is crucial for the articulation of meaning. This subsection investigates the discursive interactive dimension (Thompson 2001, Hyland 2005) found in the *Motivazioni* move, examining the ways arbitrators account for the parties' knowledge, expectations and processing abilities to guide their interpretation. The focus is on conjunctions, adverbs and adverbial structures used to express textual and semantic coherence and introduce cognitive relationships between meanings. Such strategies are distinguished into consecutive and contrastive logical markers, signalling respectively causality and contrast or concession.

3.1.2.1. Consecutive logical markers

According to studies of Italian legal language (Ferrari 1999, Mortara Garavelli 2001) the expression of causality can differ according to two modes of linking cause and effects, namely:

- a *regressive mode*, pointing to the cause starting from the results, thus making explicit the link between a final state and its original condition through expressions such as *perché, poiché, giacché, siccome, dal momento che,* etc. [because, since, given that, etc.], as in (5) and (6) below;
- a *progressive mode*, pointing to the consequence starting from its original condition through formulations like *perciò, quindi, dunque, di conseguenza, conseguentemente,* etc. [so, thus,

therefore, as a consequence, consequently, etc.], as in (7) and (8) below.

(5) X è d'altra parte escludibile, *poiché* il rilascio dei titoli costituiva obbligazione prevista nell'ambito del contratto.
[X is, however, to be excluded, since the issue of the securities was foreseen as part of the contract.]

(6) Contrariamente a quanto da X si sostiene, il Collegio ha ampio potere: giacché materia di interpretazione ed applicazione di legge.
[Contrary to what is claimed by X, the Board has full authority since it is a matter of interpretation and application of the law.]

(7) [Il debito] superava l'importo che la banca doveva garantire. Appare *dunque* fondata la richiesta [...] riguardante l'accertamento.
[The debt was higher than the sum the bank was to grant. Therefore the request made by [x] as to verification seems well-founded]

(8) Quanto alle domande [...] per danni da eventi atmosferici o da terzi, il C.T.D. ne ha escluso l'esistenza e *quindi* nulla compete a X.
[As to the request for damages due to weather conditions or a third party, the C.T.D. excluded such a possibility, thus nothing is due to X.]

3.1.2.2. Contrastive markers

These are formulations representing opposition or concession between different meanings and are expressed by connectors such as *ma, sebbene, per quanto, nonostante,* etc. [but, although, even though, nonetheless, etc.]. More specifically, by voicing alternative views about a state of affairs, on the one hand, these markers are meant to infer a sense of impartiality and semantic exhaustiveness in relation to a given idea and, on the other hand, they rhetorically mark the preferred meaning, thus biasing interpretation (see (9) and (10)).

(9) Assenza di colpa, intesa come ineluttabilità dell'evento impediente *nonostante* l'adoperarsi diligente dello stesso X.
[Absence of responsibility, intended as unavoidability of the impediment *despite* the diligent effort of X.]

(10) *Pur non potendo escludersi* in linea puramente teorica [questo], non va dimenticato che [...].

> [Although from a purely theoretical viewpoint this cannot be excluded, it must be remembered that […].]

The different logical connectors are quite frequent in our corpus. The table below lists the frequencies of the various types of logical markers found in the *Motivazioni* move of our corpus.

	Absolute figures	Normalized figures
Consecutive markers: *regressive mode*	88	19.36
Consecutive markers: *progressive mode*	189	41.58
Contrast markers	91	20

Table 2. Frequency of logical markers in the *Motivazioni* move.

A significant piece of evidence emerging from Table 2 is the high number of consecutive markers (19.36 + 41.58). Also worth noting is the fact that progressive markers are used twice as much as either regressive or contrastive markers (respectively 41.58 vs. 19.36 and vs. 20), signalling the preference for an orderly and consequential sequencing of the informative material in the *Motivazioni* move.

3.2. Interdiscursive features

The textualization of the arbitral procedure in general, and especially the organization of the *Motivazioni* move, has a markedly interdiscursive character (Giner 2009, Maci forth.). Interdiscursivity (Bhatia 2007, 2008) has a two-fold function: on the one hand, it creates intertextual relationships between the views expressed by the parties (in the *Memorie*) and the norms established by the legislator through an elaborate scaffolding of references and quotations (cf. §3.2.1); on the other, it emphasizes the dialogistic positioning (Martin/Rose 2003, Martin/White 2005) of the award within the domain of legal communication by resorting to specialized wording and exploiting recognizable rhetorical standards which are distinctive of traditional legal discourse (Mellinkoff 1963, Tiersma 1999, Williams 2005) (cf.

§3.2.2). The present section focuses respectively on the intertextual and dialogistic dimension of arbitration discourse.

3.2.1. Intertextual references

As already remarked, in the *Motivazioni* move arbitrators present their interpretation of the *Fatto* leading to the final pronouncement. Since interpretation is to some extent a subjective activity, often based on objective evidence in order to mark their distance and impartiality, very often drafters choose to represent claims through the original words used respectively by the parties in the *Memorie* and by the legislator in the codification of the norm. On several occasions, rather than synthesizing or paraphrasing meanings – which is in itself a hermeneutic activity – arbitrators create a sort of virtual dialogue between the voice of the parties and the voice of the law, ultimately presenting their interpretation as implicitly resulting from this interaction. Especially when confronted with problematic and controversial meanings, drafters seem prone to present the parties' claims through quotations of whole sentences, expressions or single terms when they are semantically crucial, as in the following examples:

(11) Si accennava a '*prezzi pattuiti in difformità dei simulati contratti*'.
[A mention was made of 'prices fixed not in accordance with the simulated contracts'.]

(12) Il Collegio non riteneva di poter esaminare la questione della asserita '*simulazione*'.
[The Board considered it impossible to examine the question of the alleged 'simulation'.]

13) A proposito dell'asserito *'errore'* [...].
[As to the alleged 'error' (...).]

The parties' voice is often introduced to provide an informative basis for a counterclaim or a comment based on the law. Articles of the Civil Code or court sentences are sometimes used to respond to the claimants, as is clear in the following extract:

(14) In senso contrario la difesa [...] ha espresso l'opinione che si dovrebbe *"trovare un criterio alternativo a quello contrattuale"* [...] Ma un tale concorso pare da escludere dovendosi interpretare l'*art. 73 del contratto* come esaustivo della disciplina del recesso.
[The defense stressed the necessity of "finding an alternative criterion to the one fixed by the contract". But such a measure does not seem to apply since article 73 of the contract is to be taken as exhaustive as to the withdrawal regulation.]

The search for intertextual indicators has been based on quotation marks (inverted commas), on the occurrence of terms such as *Memorie* [Memorial], *il/la* + name of either party, *articolo, legge, sentenza del Tribunale* [article, law, court sentence, etc.] used to report respectively the words of the parties and the norm. Table 3 reports the results found in our corpus and compares the occurrences in the *Motivazioni* move with those in the *Fatto* and *Decisione* moves so as to build up evidence to highlight the typically intertextual character of the *Motivazioni* move.

	FATTO		MOTIVAZIONI		DECISIONE	
	Absolute figures	Norm. figures	Absolute figures	Norm. figures	Absolute figures	Norm. figures
Mention of the parties	399	103.7	227	60.1	–	–
Mention of the law	95	24.7	250	55.0	11	15.4

Table 3. Frequency and distribution of intertextual references in the corpus.

As can be seen, the total references in the *Fatto* and in the *Motivazioni* moves do not differ much in purely quantitative terms. Those in the *Fatto* move depend primarily on the specific function of the section, which is intended to represent the content of the *Memorie*. For this reason, the majority of mentions in this move (399 vs. 95) mainly reproduce the claimants' view through their own words. The situation is different in the *Motivazioni* move, where the voice of the parties is less frequent and quantitatively balanced by a similar number of mentions reporting the content of the law. In this respect this move reproduces a sort of virtual dialogue between the litigants and the legislator rhetorically orchestrated by the drafters.

3.2.2. Dialogue with the tradition

The analysis of the linguistic features indicating the dialogistic positioning of arbitration discourse within the continuum represented by traditional legal language investigates both the use of Latinisms and of marked constructions. These features, which are distinctive of legal rhetoric in general (Tiersma 1999, Gotti 2003, Williams 2005), are also commonly found in arbitral discourse, in fact: "In writing awards, arbitrators seem to display a certain level of awareness of the importance of their linguistic choices. […] It is not possible to explore new writing styles; it is important to write within a certain traditional and accredited style." (Gotti/Anesa forth.)

3.2.2.1. Latinisms

Latin terms and expressions are widely used in the legal domain, both in the international context (Mellinkoff 1963, Williams 2005) and Italian jurisdiction (Fiorelli 1998, Mortara Garavelli 2001). They are frequently exploited not only to represent specific juridical concepts, but also to confer a "sense of formality and traditionalism" (Gotti/ Anesa forth.) on the texts. Latinisms may have either a domain-specific or generic value, respectively when they are meant to stress the legal specificity and significance of a given meaning – as in formulations like *artifex additus artifici, perpetuatio jurisditionis, causa petendi,* etc. – as opposed to more general meanings as in expressions such as *de quo, de qua, ex novo, in primis*, etc. Very often both usages are found within the same section of text, as exemplified in the following extracts:

(15) A prescindere dal *nomen juris* utilizzato dalle parti (permuta) l'*in idem placitum consensus de quo* si appalesa più propriamente quale espressione di un mutamento dell'oggetto dell'originario contratto di compravendita del natante. [Aside from the juridical denomination used by the parties (barter) the agreement on the point at issue manifests itself more properly as the expression of a change of the object in the original purchase contract.]

(16) Ai fini della pertinente applicabilità della disposizione *de qua* alla presente fattispecie, […] la regola della *perpetuatio iurisdictionis* di cui all'art.5 c.p.c. va intesa nel senso che il processo deve continuare davanti al giudice.
[As to the applicability of the provision at issue, the rule of *perpetuatio iurisdictionis* in Art. 5 in the Code of Civil procedure is to be taken to mean that the trial should continue before the judge.]

Table 4 lists the occurrences of Latin expressions in the three macro-moves of the awards.

	FATTO		MOTIVAZIONI		DECISIONE	
	Absolute figures	Norm. figures	Absolute figures	Norm. figures	Absolute figures	Norm. figures
Latinisms	54	14.04	84	18.48	5	7

Table 4. Frequency and distribution of Latinisms in the corpus.

Irrespectively of their domain-specific or general use, it is remarkable to note that the *Motivazioni* move features the highest number of such expressions. This tendency becomes meaningful if interpreted in relation to the specific preparatory function of this move towards the final decision. In fact, by using Latinisms, arbitrators ensure their familiarity not only with specific procedures and practices, but also with the appropriate language through which such activities are carried out. This confers greater authority on them, and legal validity on their texts.

3.2.2.2. Markedness

As to the use of marked or non-standard forms used to elicit a sense of formality, authoritativeness and a specific legal (or 'legalistic') connotation to arbitral awards, this section focusses, first, on argumentative connectors pointing to cause-effect and addition discourse relations and, secondly, on subject-verb ordering in formulations having the terms *Collegio* and *Arbitro* as grammatical subject.

3.2.2.2.1. Argumentative markers

To distinguish between the standard and the marked use of consecutive (i.e. *perché, poiché, dunque*, etc. [because, since, so, etc].), contrastive (i.e. *benché, sebbene,* etc. [although, even though, etc.]) and additive connectors (i.e. *invero, altresì, inoltre*, etc. [indeed, also, moreover, etc.]), the level of their markedness has been established after a search through a reference corpus of Italian written language (CoLFIS, Corpus of written Italian, cf. Laudanna *et al.* 1995). Connectors with a frequency rate below 0.1 per 10,000 words in CoLFIS have been selected as markedly infrequent in written Italian and their occurrence has been compared to the one resulting from word counts in our corpus (Table 5). Also markers whose frequency ratio is higher than 1 occurrence per 10,000 words in CoLFIS have been considered and accommodated in a separate table (Table 6) to provide a sample of standard argumentative expressions in written Italian and compare them with their use in arbitral awards. The tables below list the frequency of, respectively, the markedly infrequent (below 0.1) and most common connectors (above 1) in standard Italian, and their distribution across the award moves.

	CoLFIS		FATTO		*MOTIVAZIONE*		DECISIONE	
	Abs. fig.	***Norm. fig.***	Abs. fig.	Norm. fig.	*Abs. fig.*	*Norm. fig.*	Abs. fig.	Norm. fig.
Purtuttavia	***1***	***0***	1	0.3	*2*	*0.4*	0	0
Quantunque	***2***	***0***	0	0	*1*	*0.2*	0	0
Altresì	***6***	***0***	32	8.3	*48*	*10.5*	9	9.8
Orbene	***6***	***0***	0	0	*8*	*1.8*	0	0
Invero	***8***	***0.01***	1	0.3	*21*	*4.6*	0	0
Ancorché	***11***	***0.02***	2	0.5	*3*	*0.7*	0	0
Seppur	***19***	***0.03***	1	0.3	*2*	*0.44*	0	0
Senonché	***41***	***0.08***	3	0.8	*5*	*1.1*	0	0
TOTAL	***104***	***0.2***	*40*	*10.4*	*90*	*19.8*	*9*	*9.8*

Table 5. Frequency and distribution of marked argumentative connectors.

	CoLFIS		FATTO		*MOTIVAZIONE*		DECISIONE	
	Abs. fig.	***Norm fig.***	Abs fig.	Norm . fig.	*Abs. fig.*	*Norm. fig.*	Abs .fig.	Norm . fig.
Così	***4512***	***9.0***	30	7.8	*43*	*9.5*	28	39.2
Infatti	***1621***	***3.2***	8	2	*44*	*9.7*	2	2.8
Comunque	***1278***	***2.6***	27	7	*30*	*6.6*	2	2.8
Anche se	***1183***	***2.4***	0	0	*6*	*1.3*	0	0
Dunque	***947***	***1.9***	12	3.1	*40*	*8.8*	2	2.8
Pure	***561***	***1.1***	2	0.5	*9*	*1.9*	0	0
Tuttavia	***525***	***1.1***	4	1	*7*	*1.6*	4	5.6
Nonostante	***466***	***1***	2	0.5	*12*	*2.6*	0	0
TOTAL	***11,093***	***22.2***	*85*	*22.1*	***191***	***42***	*38*	*53.2*

Table 6. Frequency and distribution of unmarked argumentative connectors.

A quick glance at the results shows that the least common connectors in written Italian (Table 5) are used twenty times more frequently in the *Motivazioni* move of awards (0.2 vs. 19.8), whereas the difference in the use of more standard formulations (Table 6), if conspicuous – given the argumentative character of the *Motivazioni* – is less significant (22.2 vs. 42.02) and corresponds to the one noted between the use of such markers in the *Fatto* (where they are in line with standard written Italian) and the *Motivazioni* move (22.1 vs. 42.02).

3.2.2.2.2. Subject-verb inversion

The markedness of verb (henceforth V) and subject (henceforth S) constructions in Italian legal discourse has often been noticed (Rovere 2000, Mortara Garavelli 2001, Garzone/Santulli 2008) and these collocations are found also in our corpus. Given the major role of arbitrators as arguers in the *Motivazioni* move, this section investigates those expressions where drafters chose to textually represent their *persona* in structures where the verb is associated with the grammatical subject *Collegio* or *Arbitro*, as in the following examples:

(17) *Può* [...] *il Collegio*, al contempo rigettando ogni contraria eccezione, definitivamente statuire in punto di validità della clausola compromissoria e di sussistenza della propria giurisdizione.
[The Board, rejecting at the same time any exception to the contrary, can declare the validity of the arbitral provision and of its own jurisdiction.]

(18) *Ritiene in proposito il Collegio* di non potere condividere [questo] criterio.
[As to this matter, the Board thinks it impossible to share this criterion.]

(19) *Accerti il Collegio Arbitrale* [...] i seguenti crediti.
[The Board should ensure the following credits.]

The occurrence of sentences depending on the subject *Collegio* and *Arbitro* is shown in Table 7. To provide a basis for comparison and discussion, instances of both the standard S+V construction and of the marked V+S formulations are considered.

	FATTO		MOTIVAZIONI		DECISIONE	
	Abs. fig.	Norm. fig.	Abs. fig.	Norm. fig.	Abs. fig.	Norm. fig.
S+V forms	59	15.3	20	4.4	19	26.6
V+S forms	9	2.3	25	5.5	–	–

Table 7. Frequency and distribution of *Collegio/Arbitro* + verb constructions.

As can be seen, V+S constructions are remarkably more frequent in the *Motivazioni* move than in the other moves (5.5 vs respectively 2.3 and 0) and, quite significantly, these marked formulations are more numerous than the unmarked ones within the text of the *Motivazioni* section itself (5.5 vs. 4.4). The use of inversion in this move can serve the purpose of conferring legal formality and tone on the reasoning leading to the final pronouncement. What may appear peculiar is the lack of such structures in the *Decisione* move, despite its normative character. This may depend on the fact that its deontic and statutory function is normally expressed in an explicit way, as in this section arbitrators do not feel they have to prove their juridical competence by using a language which is typical of the legal domain. On the contrary, in order to be effective, they try to encode meaning in a clear way, accessible also to the layman.

4. Discussion and conclusion

In the light of the results presented above it is possible to discuss such findings especially in consideration of the particular nature of arbitration. In fact, as noted by Maci (forth.), "the arbitral tribunal is not the court: there is neither a judge nor a jury, nevertheless decisions with verdict-like efficacy are pronounced". As has already been said, the validity of the *Decisione* section which closes the arbitral proceedings depends to a great extent on the way such a judgement is prepared and presented, in other words, on how arguments are discussed both in cognitive and rhetorical terms. For an award to be convincing and certain there seem to be specific requirements to be respected, namely the need of impartiality, semantic coherence, and conformity to a recognizable accredited style: the former as a guarantee of a judgement which is fair; the latter to strengthen the legal and binding quality of the text itself.

According to the evidence examined here, the sense of impartiality seems to be elicited both through the handling of markers of evidentiality and the use of intertextual resources. As to evidentiality, the findings in Section 3.1.1 reveal the quite marked predominance of non-mediated forms for the presentation of claims. Arbitrators tend to construct meanings in a depersonalized, distanced, almost axiomatic way – through formulations like *sembra, appare, è chiaro*, etc. [it seems, is appears, it is clear, etc.] rather than *il Collegio/L'Arbitro ritiene che* [the Board/Arbitrator believes that, etc.] – as if the truth of the content were self-evident and necessarily resulting from observation, shared knowledge, or common sense. Moreover, the discrepancy between mediated and non-mediated resources (21.7 vs. 51.7) also seems to suggest that arbitrators are prone to offer their own interpretations (through verbs of opinion such as *ritenere, osservare, stimare*, etc. [believe, observe, deem, etc.]) only once the truth of a state of affairs has been established through non-mediated strategies, as is clear in the following extracts:

(20) *Questa [...] deve considerarsi* la vera materia del contendere. [...] *Il Collegio non condivide, pertanto, l'interpretazion*e offerta sul punto da parte convenuta.

[This is to be considered as the true matter of the dispute. As a consequence, the Board does not share the interpretation on the point at issue provided by the claimant.]

(21) *Noto è*, peraltro, che i suddescritti principi hanno riguardato le concessioni X; *è parimenti noto* [che] la regola della *perpetuatio iurisdictionis* [...] va intesa nel senso che il processo deve continuare davanti al giudice inizialmente adito. [...] *Il Collegio pertanto* [...] *può concludentemente ritenere* sussistente la propria giurisdizione.
[It is also known that the above defined principles have concerned grants X; it is equally known that the *perpetuatio iurisdictionis* is to be taken to mean that the process must continue before the judge originally appointed. Thus the Board can ultimately consider its jurisdiction valid.]

In both cases drafters textually manifest themselves and their views (*Il Collegio non condivide, il Collegio può ritenere* [the Board does not share, the Board can consider]) as arguing on the basis of evidence presented as empirical (i.e. *questa deve considerarsi, noto è che* [i.e. this is to be considered, it is known that]). In other words, to avoid the risk of ideological bias, arbitrators represent their *persona* not as (subjectively) evaluating a state of affairs, but as commenting and discussing objective and observable truths.

Another step towards impartiality is represented by the tendency found in the *Motivazioni* section to express different, even conflicting views in articulating the reasons leading to the final decision (party vs. party, party vs. law, party vs. arbitrator). These are rhetorically introduced by connectors of contrast and markers of intertextuality (see respectively Sections 3.1.2 and 3.2.1). Both strategies are meant to confer a sense of completeness and objectivity on the argumentation. In the specific case of contrastive markers the purpose is to include in the discussion of the case any relevant view that the parties may have, also those which appear to be detrimental to the establishing of the arbitrator's point of view. This removes any suspicion of a subjective and possibly biased principle of selection of the content to be examined, which is likely to undermine the perception of impartiality. The pragmatic function of such connectors is then to infer a semantic hierarchy between meanings, thus favouring preferred interpretations, as can be seen in this short example:

(22) *Pur* non potendo escludere *X* non va dimenticato Y.
[Although X cannot be excluded, Y must be taken into consideration.]

The contrastive marker *pur* [although] is used to concede the possibility of X, and at the same time it modifies its meaning by connoting it as weaker in relation to Y. In this way the arbitrator manages to lexicalize both concepts rather than omitting one, but assigning them different semantic values.

A similar function is performed by intertextuality, through which not only different meanings but references to different voices and texts are used as argumentative devices to construct claim-counterclaim sequences, where the claimants' view is subsequently neutralized or framed within the boundaries established by the law. As already observed in § 3.2.1, by using the parties' and the legislator's very own words, the drafters signal their distance and present meanings from an external perspective rather than through paraphrases which could to some extent reveal their attitude or bias. Also, by creating this interplay, arbitrators rhetorically represent themselves as being responsible for emphasizing dichotomies between the parties' expectations and the requirement of the law, thus opting for the role of arguers rather than evaluators, which is ultimately the role taken in the *Decisione* move.

For the coherent argumentation of the *Motivazioni* section, logical markers – both consecutive and contrastive – are crucial (see §3.1.2). They are meant to simplify decodification by stressing the links between meanings, thus making the text (relatively) reader-friendly. In fact "a lower number of logical markers in a text entails a greater decoding effort on the part of the readers as they need to work out the semantic relationship between different parts of the discourse" (Mur Dueñas 2007: 50). Such strategies are distinctive of a rationalistic thought style (as opposed to empiricist, scholastic, etc., cf. Chafe/Nichols 1986, Taavitsainen 2001) and of an argumentative attitude towards the creation of meaning which also accounts for the possibility of rhetorically negotiating it with the recipient, in consideration of his/her needs and expectations. The relatively high frequency of these devices (see Table 2) in a performative text can also be interpreted in terms of politeness (Goffman 1967, Brown/Levinson 1987): in fact, they mitigate the threat which is implicit in a legally binding text such as the award. As a matter of fact, since the *Motivazioni* section serves the purpose of preparing and justifying the final pronouncement delivered in the *Decisione* move, through these mechanisms the drafters manage to discuss ideas, combine conflicting claims (those of either party vs. the provisions of the legislators) and expound controversial meanings (expressing disagreement with one of the parties or rejection of their requests) without sounding overimposing, too assertive or arrogant. As a matter of fact, in the *Motivazioni* move rarely is the arbitrator's view or the law itself asserted as an absolute truth (as in the *Decisioni* section), but it is usually rhetorically shaped within the text.

Since the interplay between meanings and their sequential ordering is so important, the predominance of progressive over regressive markers (respectively 41.58 vs. 19.36) is also significant for the purpose of coherence. In fact, the organization of the informative material in cause-effect or condition-consequence sequences, on the one hand, reflects a reader-friendly textualization and reduces the decoding effort and, on the other, it minimizes considerably the possibility of semantic ambiguities and contradictions, thus making the text understandable and eventually more easily accepted as binding.

At odds with this trend towards 'reader-friendliness' is the necessity for arbitrators to conform to an accredited formal style. As has already been mentioned, arbitration is a practice external to traditional tribunals. Although it is meant to settle disputes between potential litigants without recourse to the litigative procedure of a court, in Italy this procedure is grounded in litigation or, at least, highly influenced by its practices, especially in terms of discourse. Elements which are characteristic of traditional jurisdiction – which eminently avoids the use of non-standard language – are often imported into the arbitral procedure so as to enhance the validity and effectiveness of the proceedings (Gotti/Anesa forth., Maci forth.).

The respect of conventional lexical and morpho-syntactic standards to codify legal meanings, especially when very specific or complex, is a general feature of legal discourse at large. In the case of awards, the use of archaisms, Latinisms, formulaic or marked expressions seems to be primarily aimed at connoting the text, and simply confers on the arbitral pronouncement the same stylistic formality and impact of court sentences, rather than denote juridical concepts (Maci forth., Sala forth.). This becomes clear if we consider the use of SV inversion and of archaic markers of argumentation (§3.2.2.2).

Table 7, for instance, shows the predominance of the marked V+S collocations over the unmarked S+V in the *Motivazioni* move. However, in semantic terms there is no significant difference between the two structures if not in terms of connotation or illocutionary force (Searle 1969): they are easily associated with the style and register used in formal legal contexts, and for this reason they are exploited to signal and highlight the authority of the drafter and enhance the legal value of his/her claim (Mortara Garavelli 2001). A similar function is performed by the archaic or non-standard markers of argumentation listed in Table 5, each of which could easily be substituted by a more conventional one (i.e. *purtuttavia* with *tuttavia*, *seppur* with *anche se, quantunque* with *nonostante*, *ovvero* with *cioè* etc.). Unmarked forms would indeed introduce the same syntactic relationships, but would also dissipate the aura of legal formality from which the award and its perceived value benefit considerably.

Finally, the case of Latinisms is symptomatic in this respect. In fact, apart from the use of Latin wording to refer to particular legal concepts whose complexity is transparent and concisely elicited by crystallized expressions (i.e., *perpetuatio iurisdictionis*, *artifex additus artifici,* etc.), searches through our corpus revealed the use of Latinisms with no juridical specificity, some of which are also found in standard Italian (i.e. *in primis* [firstly], *una tantum* [one-off], *pro capite* [per person]) and many others could be replaced by standard expressions without losing much of their efficacy (i.e. *lapsus calami* [typographical error], *pro die* [per day], *tempus* [time or time span]).

Sentences combining all of these legally connoted or connotative resources are quite frequent in the *Motivazioni* move, as exemplified by the following extracts:

(23) *Stima il Collegio* che, ad un siffatto procedere, si opponga il fatto che non rientra nei poteri del giudice né dell' arbitro […] operare non come interprete ma come *artifex additus artifici*, sostituendo così scelte proprie a quelle riservate alle parti.

[The Board believes that, against this way of proceeding, is the fact that it is the faculty neither of the judge nor of the arbitrator to operate as *artifex additus artifici* rather than interpreter, thus substituting its own decisions to those pertaining to the parties.]

(24) *Orbene*, alla stregua degli svolgimenti e delle statuizioni che precedono, e in conformità peraltro delle modalità di calcolo [...], *ritiene il Collegio* di potere affermare che a quegli spetti la invocata 'maggiorazione'. Considerato, infatti, che la maggiorazione *de qua* è dovuta "per ogni anno intero previsto per l'ultimazione dei lavori" (così l'art. 33 [...]), deve per l'appunto conseguirsi che il *dies a quo* vada fissato al 07.02.92.
[Thus, in relation to the preceding processes and situations, and also in conformity with the modality of computation [...] the Board thinks it is possible to claim that to those is due the requested 'increase'. Considering the fact that the increase at issue is due "for each full year foreseen for the completion of the work" (according to Art. 33), it follows that the day at issue should be 07.02.09.]

As can be seen, both examples feature cases of V-S inversion (*stima il collegio, ritiene il Collegio*), of Latinisms (*artifex additus artific*, *de qua, dies a quo*) and archaic connectors (*orbene*). With the exception of the expression *artifex additus artific*, none of the others has a juridically specific meaning. Although devoid of any distinct semantic purpose, such strategies have a foregrounded perlocutionary function of emphasizing the impact of the award by making it sound like a court judgement and marking it as a fully-fledged legal text.

References

Belotti, Ulisse 2003. Generic Integrity in Italian Arbitration Rules. In Bhatia/Candlin/Gotti (eds), 19-40.

Bhatia, Vijay 1993. *Analyzing Genre: Language Use in Professional Settings*. London: Longman.

Bathia, Vijay 2007. *Interdiscursivity in Critical Genre Analysis,* Paper given at the 4th International Symposium on Genre Studies, Unisul,

Brazil, <http://www3.unisul.br/paginas/ensino/pos/linguagem/cd/English/36i.pdf>.

Bhatia, Vijay 2008. Genre Analysis, ESP and Professional Practice. *English for Specific Purposes* 27, 161-174.

Bhatia, Vijay / Candlin, Christopher / Gotti, Maurizio (eds) 2003. *Legal Discourse In Multilingual and Multicultural Contexts: Arbitration Texts in Europe*. Bern: Peter Lang.

Bocchini, Ermanno (ed.) 2006. *L'Arbitrato*. Padova: CEDAM.

Brown, Penelope / Levinson, Stephen 1987. *Politeness: Some Universals in Language Usage*. Cambridge: Cambridge University Press.

Ceccon, Roberto 2000. La Corte Arbitrale di Venezia, una nuova istituzione per attrarre l'arbitrato internazionale in Italia. *Le prospettive dell'arbitrato interno ed internazionale: il Regolamento della Corte Arbitrale di Venezia*. Torino: Giappichelli, 7-12.

Chafe, Wallace / Nichols, Johanna (eds) (1986). *Evidentiality: The Linguistic Encoding of Epistemology*. Norwood, NJ: Ablex.

Consolo, Claudio 2006. *Le impugnazioni delle sentenze e dei lodi.* Padova: CEDAM.

Cutolo, Daniele / Esposito, Antonio 2007. The Reform of the Italian Arbitration Law. The Challenging of Arbitrators and the Setting of Time Limits. *Journal of International Arbitration* 24/1, 49-62.

Ferrari, Angela 1999. Tra rappresentazione ed esecuzione: indicare la 'causalità testuale' con i nomi e con i verbi. *Studi di Grammatica Italiana* 18, 113-144.

Fiorelli, Piero 1998. L'italiano giuridico dal latinismo al tecnicismo. In Domenighetti, Ilario (ed.) *Con felice esattezza. Economia e diritto fra lingua e letteratura.* Bellinzona: Casagrande,139-183.

Garzone, Giuliana / Santulli, Francesca (eds) 2008. *Il linguaggio giuridico. Prospettive interdisciplinari. Milano:* Giuffrè.

Giner Diana 2009. The Presence of Persuasive Interactional Elements in the Construction of Argumentation in Investment Arbitral Awards. Paper presented at the Conference. *Researching Language and the Law.* Bergamo (Italy), 18-20 June 2009.

Givón, Talmy 1982. Evidentiality and Epistemic Space. *Studies in Language* 6, 23-49.

Goffman, Erving 1967. *Interaction Ritual: Essays on Face-to-Face Behavior*. New York: Anchor Books.

Gotti, Maurizio 2003. *Specialized Discourse. Linguistic Features and Changing Conventions*. Bern: Peter Lang.

Gotti, Maurizio / Anesa, Patrizia forthcoming. Professional Identities in Italian Arbitral Awards: The Spread of the Lawyers' Language. *Proceedings of the Conference 'Issues of Identity in and Across Cultures and Professional Worlds'*, Rome (Italy), 25-27 October 2007.

Hyland, Ken 2005. *Metadiscourse*. London: Continuum.

Lino, Vincenzo 2006. *Cassazione e Arbitrato*. Cercola: Edizioni Giuridiche Simone.

Laudanna, Alessandro / Thornton, Anna Maria / Brown, Giorgina. / Burani, Cristina / Marconi, Lucia 1995. Un corpus dell'italiano scritto contemporaneo dalla parte del ricevente. In Bolasco, Sergio / Lebart, Ludovic / Salem, André (eds), *III Giornate internazionali di Analisi Statistica dei Dati Testuali*. Volume I. Roma: Cisu, 103-109.

Maci, Stefania M. forthcoming. Arbitration in Italy. Litigation Procedures in Arbitral Practice. *Proceedings of the Conference 'Issues of Identity in and Across Cultures and Professional Worlds'*, Rome (Italy), 25-27 October 2007.

Marriott, Arthur 2004. Less is More: Directing Arbitration Procedures. *Arbitration International* 16/3, 261-278.

Martin, James / Rose, David 2004. *Working with Discourse: Meaning Beyond the Clause*. London: Continuum.

Martin, James / White, Peter 2005. *The Language of Evaluation: Appraisal in English*. New York: Palgrave Macmillan.

Mellinkoff, David 1963. *The Language of the Law*. Boston: Brown & Co.

Mortara Garavelli, Bice 2001. *Le parole e la giustizia*. Torino: Einaudi.

Mur Dueñas, Pilar 2007. Same Game, Same Discipline; However, There Are Differences: A Cross-Cultural Analysis of Logical Markers in Academic Writing. *ESP Across Cultures* 4, 37-53.

Nariman, Fali S. 2000. The Spirit of Arbitration: The Tenth Annual Goff Lecture. *Arbitration International* 16/3, 261-278.

Nuyts, Jan 2000. *Epistemic Modality, Language, and Conceptualization*. Amsterdam: John Benjamins.

Rovere, Giovanni 2000. L'avverbiale strumentale nel linguaggio giuridico. In Schena, Leandro / Snel Trampus, Rita (eds) *Traduttori e giuristi a confronto. Interpretazione traducente e comparazione del discorso giuridico*. Bologna: Clueb, 25-35.

Sala, Michele forthcoming. Linguistic and Textual Features of Italian Commercial Arbitration Awards. *Proceeding of the International Workshop 'Linguistic and Discursive Aspects of International Arbitration'*. University of Milan (Italy) 22-23 September 2008.

Santulli, Francesca 2006. Strutture argomentative e scelte lessicali nel linguaggio della giurisprudenza. In Cresti, Emanuela (ed.) *Prospettive nello studio del lessico italiano, Atti SILFI 2006*. Firenze: FUP, 461-469.

Scott, Mike 2004. *WordSmith Tools – Version 4*. Oxford: Oxford University Press.

Searle, John 1969 *Speech Acts: An Essay in the Philosophy of Language*. Cambridge: Cambridge University Press.

Taavitsainen, Irma 2001. Evidentiality and Scientific Thought-Styles: English Medical Writing in Late Middle English and Early Modern English. In Gotti, Maurizio / Dossena, Marina (eds) *Modality in Specialized Texts*. Bern: Peter Lang, 21-51.

Thompson, Geoff 2001. Interaction in Academic Writing: Learning to Argue with the Reader. *Applied Linguistics* 22/1, 58-78.

Tiersma, Peter M. 1999. *Legal Language*. Chicago: University of Chicago Press.

Wierzbicka, Anna. 1994. Semantics and Epistemology: The Meaning of 'Evidentials' in a Cross-Linguistic Perspective. *Language Sciences* 16, 81-137.

Williams, Christopher 2005. *Tradition and Change in Legal English*. Bern: Peter Lang.

CHIARA DEGANO

Indicators of Argumentation in Arbitration Awards: A Diachronic Perspective

1. Introduction

International commercial arbitration is being increasingly criticized for losing its distinctive character, while resembling litigation more and more closely (Mustill 1997; Nariman 2000; Browner 2007). In particular, what is regretted is the loss of its original drive towards a swift and satisfactory solution for the parties, in line with the needs of the commercial community, in favour of a more legalistic approach. This in turn has been laid at the door of lawyers, who have, it is felt, appropriated the practice of arbitration, transferring their litigative skills and strategies from national courtrooms to the resolution of disputes in arbitral tribunals.

From a linguistic point of view, this state of 'instability' in the practice of arbitration offers an opportunity to investigate genre variation, on the assumption that changes at the level of practice are likely to produce changes in discourse. Assuming that arbitration and litigation are characterized by different discursive features as a consequence of their different macro-functions, this chapter aims to provide some evidence as to whether arbitration awards present elements of hybridization as an effect of the influence of litigation. The scope of this study is restricted to argumentation, a discursive practice central to litigation, by virtue of the need to justify courts' decisions in relation to existing laws. In order to discover whether such elements of hybridization, can be traced in the text, the chapter analyses an electronic corpus of awards spanning over 20 years diachronically with the theme of questioning whether it reveals any intensification in the use of indicators of argumentation over time.

2. Background

Rivkin (2008: 375) summarizes the goals of international commercial arbitration as

> i) a fair and neutral process, (ii) conducted by intelligent and experienced arbitrators, (iii) resulting in a timely and well-reasoned decision, and (iv) benefiting from an effective enforcement mechanism.

According to some critical voices, the mission of the arbitration institution as expressed by these goals is being betrayed in more than one respect due to the legalistic turn taken by ICA. On the one hand, Rivkin expresses concern especially with regard to timeliness, arguing that the huge increase in recourse to ICA, resulting in arbitrators being too busy to schedule timely hearings, as well as the highly complex procedures involving "more extenuated proceedings, mountainous written submissions, longer hearings, document discovery" (2008: 377), are harming arbitration making it less efficient than it was supposed to be. On this ground, he argues for a return to what he calls the *town elder model*: "two business people taking their dispute to a wise business person in whom they both trusted [...] asking the arbitrator to provide them with the best solution to their dispute", thus making the case for a default simplified procedure as a starting point, to which additional procedures can be added if need be.

On the other hand Nariman draws attention to what he perceives as a betrayal of the original 'spirit of arbitration', defined – quoting Michel Gaudet – as follows:

> The dominant feature of arbitration is mutual understanding so as to be able to solve the conflict that has occurred. The aim of arbitration is not to draw from the applicable law a decision against the parties involved but to clarify, together with the parties, what should be done in a given situation to achieve justice with co-operation. (Nariman 2000: 261)

Co-operation, then seems to be a key word, as remarked on also by Bernardini (2004: 117), who recalls that arbitration should be animated by the will to find a solution to the problems through the interaction between the parties and the arbitrator, and not by a confrontational attitude. According to Nariman, however, modern ICA, far from embodying this spirit, is floundering under the burden of too much legal baggage, with the result of being 'almost indistinguishable from litigation'. In particular, the origins of this drift are to be found in the increasing publication of awards which came with the flourishing of literature on arbitration. Deprived of their original private nature, international arbitration awards tend to lose the original 'lightness of touch' and simplicity, which responded to the need of being understood by the parties for which they were exclusively intended. The original function of reaching a result which applies to a particular case is now associated with the intention of establishing a body of 'legal opinion' which can inspire future decisions of arbitral tribunals. Motivated or reasoned decisions tend to be longer and to contain much learned legal reasoning and reference to previous cases, thus turning awards into international jurisprudence.

The emphasis on co-operation, originally a defining aspect of arbitration, seems to be preserved in other Alternative Dispute Resolution techniques. Hunter (2000) points out that the outcome of arbitration is generally 'rights-based', as lawyers, trained for litigation, tend to focus on their clients' legal rights, while a focus on 'interest' might serve them better: while litigation aims at victory over 'enemies', clients might benefit more from continuing commercial relations, an outcome that, as things are, is more likely to be achieved through mediation than through litigation-influenced arbitration.

That argumentation and legal discourse are closely related is almost self-evident. Following the pragma-dialectic perspective, argumentation can be defined exactly as a process aimed to solve a 'difference of opinion' by justifying one standpoint (or refuting the other party's standpoint) through valid arguments. Van Eemeren *et al.* consider it as

> a verbal and social activity of reason aimed at increasing (or decreasing) the acceptability of a controversial standpoint for the listener or reader, by putting forward a constellation of propositions intended to justify (or refute) the standpoint before a rational judge. (van Eemeren *et al.* 1996: 5)

A key premise for such a process to take place is that behind each attempt at resolving a difference of opinion through argumentation there is an appeal to rationality, since the parties implicitly accept to rely on logical reasoning in order to find a solution to the dispute. In the legal context, in order not to sound arbitrary any judicial decision needs to be justified against the body of existing normative texts, be they statutory sources of law or previous decisions with the value of precedent. In common law legal systems, and with the court's attempt to present decisions as fair and consistent with the law, this confers on them an essentially argumentative nature.

Comparing the functions of litigation and arbitration respectively – judging a case against a set of rules vs. finding a solution through the co-operative interaction of the parties – it can be concluded that while in litigation discourse is primarily argumentative, in arbitration emphasis is expected to fall not so much, or not only, on rationality, but rather on cooperation and mutual understanding.

From a discursive point of view, such a difference of function is expected to determine different discursive strategies which influence the selection of textual structures both at the macro and the micro-linguistic level. Limiting the scope to legal English, a functional variety which has been thoroughly investigated (cf. among others Gibbons 1994; Garzone 2001, 2008, Gotti 2005: Bhatia *et al.* 2008,), an important feature of judicial discourse is the presence of what Stati (2002: 63) calls 'auxiliary argumentative lexis'[1], i.e. expressions which signal the argumentative function of propositions within the

1 Stati (2002) identifies five categories of auxiliary argumentative lexis: connectives, meta-argumentative expressions, modalizers, reference operators and, finally, para-argumentative expressions. Connectives are conjuncts, adverbs or phrases that link, argumentatively, two parts of a text. Meta-argumentative expressions are nouns or verbs which indicate the argumentative role of the part of text to which they are referred (e.g. *reason*, *objection*, *proof* or *refute*, *hypothesise* etc.). Modalizers encompass expressions which codify the author's stance towards the propositional content, in terms of epistemic modality (*must, may, likely*) or commitment (*definitely, tentatively* etc.). Reference operators attribute statements to others, and para-argumentative expressions present statements as true without supporting them through argument, either because they are considered self-evident or on the ground of the speaker's authority.

text, thus fulfilling the twofold purpose of enhancing its clarity while at the same time presenting the text as argumentatively sound, and therefore more persuasive.

In light of the above, a conspicuous presence of typical traits of argumentation in arbitration awards might be seen as a linguistic clue of its bending towards litigation. This chapter aims at verifying whether in a time span of about 20 years (1984-2003) indicators of argumentation have increased in arbitral awards, limiting attention to the category of connectives, as they can be more readily identified though automatic routine searches of electronic corpora.

3. Materials and method

The study is carried out on a selection of ICC awards included in the Kluwer Bank <http://www.kluwerarbitration.com>. An *ad hoc* corpus was created downloading all the ICC awards which reported the heading 'final award' (73 files), for a total amount of about 445,000 words, distributed across years as follows:

1984	1	1991	5	1998	2
1985	1	1992	8	1999	6
1986	–	1993	3	2000	2
1987	4	1994	7	2001	2
1988	3	1995	6	2002	1
1989	8	1996	4	2003	2
1990	7	1997	1		

Table 1. Corpus composition.

Using Wordsmith Tools 4 (Scott 2004), a general wordlist was extracted for the whole corpus, in order to identify the indicators of argumentation (van Eemeren/Houtlosser/Snoeck Henkemans 2007) which occur most frequently, limiting the scope – as already said – to connectors. As a second step, concordances were extracted for the most frequent connectors, focusing then on the respective dispersion plots, with the aim of visualizing trends of distribution (if any) for each indicator throughout the corpus. The visual impression thus obtained was then checked against numbers, by grouping the files in three periods of time: 1984-1990, 1991-1997 and 1998-2003. More specifically, starting from the dispersion plot data of each connector, the average p.1000 ratio was calculated for each period of time, and the average values for the three time spans were compared. The insights from quantitative analysis thus obtained were then integrated with qualitative analysis, with special regard to lexico-grammar and textual structure, relying also on notions of text grammar (Werlich 1983).

4. Results

The general wordlist presents *but*, *therefore*, *however*, *because* and *thus* as the most common connectors in the corpus, with the following ranking:

Word	%
But	0.16
Therefore	0.13
However	0.12
Because	0.08
Thus	0.07

Table 2. Connectors.

The extraction of the concordances for each of them allowed to calculate and visualize the dispersion plot, which shows "where mention is made most" of the search word in each file"(Wordsmith Tools Manual, Scott 2004). The dispersion plot referred to the word *but* is reported below for the purpose of exemplification:

N	File	Words	Hits	r 1,000	persion
1	2003_2.txt	8.430	17	2,02	0,724
2	2003_1.txt	184	1	5,43	-0,069
3	2002_1.txt	8.818	15	1,70	0,800
4	2001_3.txt	1.735	2	1,15	-0,069
5	2001_2.txt	8.660	16	1,85	0,774
6	2001_1.txt	8.480	9	1,06	0,622
7	2000_2.txt	10.702	19	1,78	0,746
8	2000_1.txt	5.059	11	2,17	0,642
9	1999_6.txt	4.529	4	0,88	0,300
10	1999_5.txt	10.425	14	1,34	0,776
11	1999_4.txt	4.243	9	2,12	0,785
12	1999_3.txt	8.261	6	0,73	0,478
13	1999_2.txt	9.443	15	1,59	0,871
14	1999_1.txt	10.170	48	4,72	0,784
15	1998_2.txt	5.630	10	1,78	0,687
16	1998_1.txt	7.046	4	0,57	0,429
17	1997_1.txt	5.438	1	0,18	-0,069
18	1996_4.txt	5.210	10	1,92	0,648
19	1996_3.txt	3.124	1	0,32	-0,069
20	1996_2.txt	4.844	2	0,41	-0,069
21	1996_1.txt	5.160	7	1,36	0,640
22	1995_6.txt	7.125	8	1,12	0,650
23	1995_5.txt	5.302	6	1,13	0,478
24	1995_4.txt	6.581	13	1,98	0,753
25	1995_3.txt	7.203	11	1,53	0,613
26	1995_2.txt	3.546	4	1,13	0,429
27	1995_1.txt	6.592	3	0,46	0,478
28	1994_7.txt	11.477	40	3,49	0,819
29	1994_6.txt	3.572	14	3,92	0,679
30	1994_5.txt	5.893	5	0,85	0,550
31	1994_4.txt	5.803	15	2,58	0,773
32	1994_3.txt	7.755	4	0,52	0,429
33	1994_2.txt	9.978	15	1,50	0,706
34	1994_1.txt	7.847	20	2,55	0,838
35	1993_3.txt	1.919	9	4,69	0,667
36	1993_2.txt	2.514	2	0,80	0,300
37	1993_1.txt	13.326	28	2,10	0,817
38	1992_8.txt	4.502	13	2,89	0,628
39	1992_7.txt	7.531	16	2,12	0,825
40	1992_6.txt	4.493	12	2,67	0,596
41	1992_5.txt	3.853	9	2,34	0,581
42	1992_3.txt	19.955	31	1,55	0,903
43	1992_1.txt	5.190	4	0,77	0,429
44	1991_5.txt	6.303	7	1,11	0,514
45	1991_3.txt	4.038	5	1,24	0,687
46	1991_2.txt	10.895	44	4,04	0,774
47	1991_1.txt	1.829	3	1,64	0,250
48	1990_7.txt	6.811	9	1,32	0,785
49	1990_6.txt	8.540	7	0,82	0,723
50	1990_5.txt	3.537	4	1,13	0,429
51	1990_4.txt	2.928	3	1,02	0,478
52	1990_3.txt	5.620	10	1,78	0,522
53	1990_1.txt	2.833	3	1,06	0,478
54	1989_8.txt	2.327	2	0,86	-0,069
55	1989_7.txt	2.320	3	1,29	0,250
56	1989_6.txt	4.124	5	1,21	0,446
57	1989_5.txt	9.314	7	0,75	0,514
58	1989_4.txt	5.214	4	0,77	0,300
59	1989_3.txt	3.833	4	1,04	0,429
60	1989_1.txt	2.409	5	2,08	0,550
61	1988_3.txt	7.890	11	1,39	0,795
62	1988_2.txt	6.605	16	2,42	0,733
63	1988_1.txt	4.317	7	1,62	0,514
64	1987_4.txt	2.261	4	1,77	0,429
65	1987_3.txt	4.717	3	0,64	0,478
66	1987_2.txt	2.064	1	0,48	-0,069
67	1987_1.txt	7.292	13	1,78	0,589
68	1985_1.txt	1.963	5	2,55	0,550
69	1984.txt	4.993	7	1,40	0,640

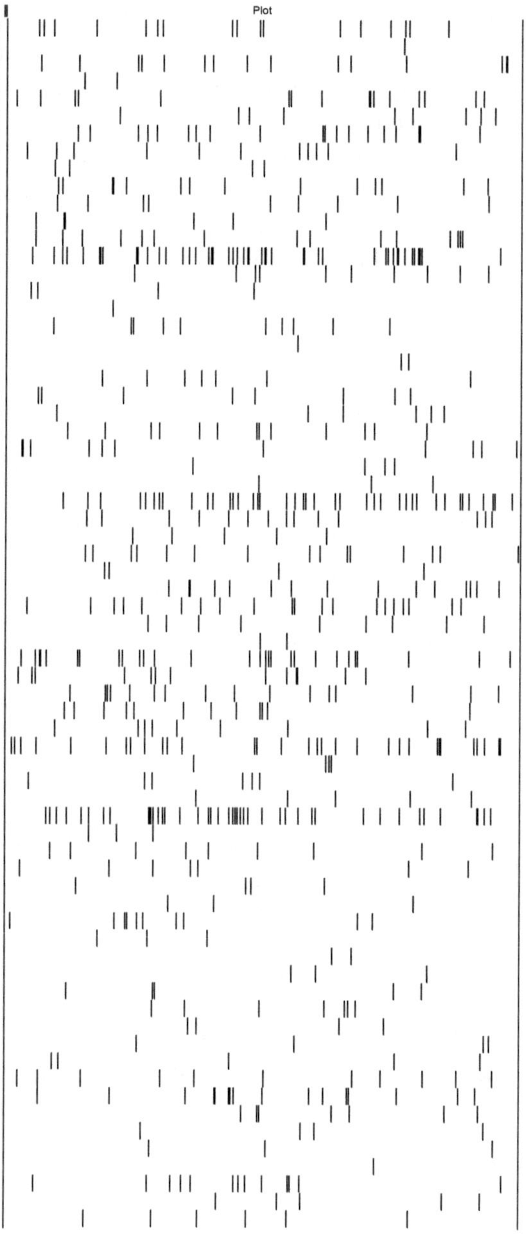

Figure 1. Dispersion plot.

The impression drawn from the plot representation is that a lower concentration of bars (each one representing an occurrence of the search word) roughly corresponds to the years 1984-1990. However, this intuition needs to be confirmed by the figures reported in the columns on the left of Figure 1, where each line represents a file. As all the files have different dimensions, they are only comparable by looking at the p.1000 word value. Grouping the files into three time-spans, the average of the p.1000 word value was calculated for each file group, with the following results:

	1984/90	1991/97	1998/03
but	1.33	1.77	1.93

Table 3. Breakdown of *but* frequency throughout the corpus.

As shown in the table, data confirm that *but* occurs more frequently in the most recent files. Following the same procedure as illustrated for the word *but*, the breakdown for each connector was calculated, giving the following output:

	1984/90	1991/97	1998/03
Therefore	1.29	1.24	*1.54*
However	1.19	*1.46*	1.16
Because	0.71	0.91	*1.13*
Thus	0.79	0.81	*0.93*
Although	0.38	*0.58*	0.48

Table 4. Breakdown of the frequency of other connectors.

As shown in Table 4, all the connectors present an increase in frequency during time, with respect to the earlier files, with a peak (in italics in the table) either in the second or in the third time span.

5. Qualitative analysis

The quantitative analysis presented so far has highlighted an increase in the frequency of contrastive and resultative connectors. In order to check these data against textual evidence, the first and the last awards in the corpus have been analysed in more detail, thus integrating a quantitative with a qualitative approach. In particular, attention has been devoted to the sections which summarise facts, looking for extended textual patterns which might classify them as more or less argumentative.

Resting on the categorization proposed by Werlich (1983), the function of argumentative texts is that of "proposing relations between concepts of phenomena, [...] in opposition to deviant or alternative propositions", such text type being connected to the cognitive process of "judging in answer to a problem" (Werlich 1983: 40.). The judgemental dimension thus involved in argumentation is reflected in a number of linguistic aspects, many of which can be subsumed under the broad notion of 'evaluation', which Hunston and Thompson (2001: 5) define as

> the broad cover term for the expression of the speaker's or writer's attitude or stance towards, viewpoint on, or feelings about the entities or propositions that he or she is talking about.

The expression of stance in a context of opposition – be it explicit or implicit – to deviant or alternative proposition gives rise to a situation of polyphony, drawing on a concept developed with reference to academic writing (cf. especially Breivega/Dahl/Fløttum 2002; Fløttum 2005; Fløttum/Kinn/Dahl 2006). Elements of evaluation, either mono or polyphonic, can be found at all levels of language description, the most obvious one being the lexical level.

Looking at the lexicon of both texts through the lens of wordlists, a first difference between them can be detected in respect of verbs: the 2003 award presents a significant recurrence of the modal *should* (0.51%) and of the verb *argued* (0.39%), *vis-à-vis* a lower frequency of *should* (0.36%) in the 1984 text and the absence of the verb *argue/argued*.[2] While the verb *argue* explicitly refers to an argumentative process, *should* points into the same direction, albeit more overtly, by virtue of its obligational nature, which reveals the stance of the locutor (most often the Arbitral Tribunal) as to what someone else (mostly claimant or defendant) should do. A similar point can be made for nouns, with the nominalised form *claims* ranking among the top lexical words in the 2003 wordlist (1.03%) as opposed to zero occurrence in the 1984 text.

Moving on to the lexico-grammatical level, attention was devoted to the semantic patterns associated with the main actors in both texts, i.e. claimant/defendant in the 1984 text and buyer/seller in the 2003 one. The respective concordance lines are reported below:

N	Concordance
1	payments. On 17 November, claimant gave notice terminating the
2	made by defendant to claimant. Claimant pledged to the issuing bank the
3	of Justice of Geneva. Furthermore, the claimant proved unable, as a practical
4	defendant gave claimant notice. Claimant thereupon initiated the
5	of performance under the contract. Claimant was unable to meet various

Concordance 1. 'Claimant' as subject (1984).

N	Concordance
1	Payment Guarantee. In consideration, defendant caused a "Risk Exposure
2	of significant procedural developments. Defendant entered bankruptcy, and its
3	the contract, and on 18 November defendant gave claimant notice. Claimant
4	by its trustees in bankruptcy. Defendant initiated criminal proceedings
5	to meet various milestones, and the defendant made deductions from the
6	of certain sums due under the contract. Defendant objected that the amount
7	was a member. In January 1977, the defendant subcontracted part of the
8	and a Belgian consortium of which the defendant was a member. In January

Concordance 2. 'Defendant' as subject (1984).

2 In the 1984 text, on the other hand, the verb *held* features with considerable frequency (0.53%) while occurring only once in the 2003 text.

What emerges from these concordance lines is a pattern of the kind *subject + verb of action*, with the exception of one metadiscursive verb signalling disagreement (i.e. "defendant objected"). Quite different is the case in the 2003 text, as shown by the concordance lines below:

N	Concordance
1	several counterclaims. Because the seller argued that most of the claims
2	of Licences specified in the MA. The seller argued that the Licences could not
3	compensation from the seller. The seller asserted several counterclaims.
4	not be able to be used by buyer. The seller had not provided such a list and
5	the SA, the buyer alleged that the seller had violated representations,
6	as part of the business. Moreover, the seller had not included them on the list
7	approach including follow-up problems. Seller sought to reduce the
8	appear to be intentional. However, the seller was aware of the problems

Concordance 3. 'Seller' as subject (2003).

N	Concordance
1	(SA). Notwithstanding the SA, the buyer alleged that the seller had violated
2	was to be reduced by one third. The buyer also claimed compensation for
3	to Sects. 7 and 8 of the MA. The buyer argued that it was entitled to
4	rejected the seller's argument that the buyer had not suffered any damage, but
5	be made using judicial discretion. The buyer had been under a duty to inform
6	any damage, but did find that the buyer had been negligent as it had been

Concordance 4. 'Buyer' as subject (2003).

Consistently with the function of the 'facts' section, also in this concordance lines we note a core set of action verbs (*seller* 'had not provided', 'had violated', 'had not included', 'sought to reduce'; *buyer* 'had not suffered', 'had been under a duty'). Alongside this core pattern, however, another one is well represented, featuring metadiscursive verbs with a clear argumentative connotation, such as 'argued' and 'asserted' referred to *seller* and 'alleged', 'claimed' and 'argued' to *buyer*.

Finally, with reference to the same section, the textual level was taken into account, still relying on Werlich's (1983) model of text grammar, with a view to add a qualitative perspective to what electronic tools highlighted as regards connectors. From the perspective of text grammar, connectors are part of what Werlich calls 'sequence forms', i.e. lexical or grammatical expressions signalling progression and coherence in the textual structure. Each text type is characterised by specific sequence forms 'selected' on the basis of the function of the text and of the cognitive process activated by the text type.

In the 1984 award, sequence forms suggest that textual progression is mainly chronological, quite in tune with the function of the section, i.e. to sum up previous facts which are relevant for the judgement rendered in the award itself. Relevant facts are mentioned in a chronological order, through temporal reference, in the form of precise dates. The occurrences of these sequence forms are highlighted in italics in the text extract below:

1984: narrative text type

(1) This arbitration was the subject of a partial award rendered *14 June 1979*, and reported in Yearbook, Vol. VII (1982), pp. 96-106. A related dispute between the claimant and the bank which issued a "risk exposure guarantee" in its favor was decided by an award made *23 October 1979*, Case No. 3316 (published in Yearbook, Vol. VII (1982) pp. 106-116).
The dispute related to a construction contract entered into *in June 1976* between a Saudi Arabian government entity and a Belgian consortium of which the defendant was a member. *In January 1977*, the defendant subcontracted part of the project to claimant.
[...]
Difficulties arose in the first few months of performance under the contract. Claimant was unable to meet various milestones, and the defendant made deductions from the sixth and seventh installment payments. *On 17 November*, claimant gave notice terminating the contract, and *on 18 November* defendant gave claimant notice.
Claimant *thereupon* initiated the arbitration. The partial award made 14 June 1979 found in favor of claimant on a certain number of points. [...]
Subsequent to this partial award, there were a number of significant procedural developments. Defendant entered bankruptcy, and its case was thereafter conducted by its trustees in bankruptcy. Defendant initiated criminal proceedings in Belgium against claimant, and sought a review of the partial award pursuant to Art. 41 of the Swiss Concordat. [...] *After extensive negotiations*, amounts due to claimant under the Risk Exposure Guarantee, and to defendant under the various performance guarantees, were deposited into va-

rious escrow accounts, and held subject to the final disposition of the case by the arbitral tribunal.

Not only does the occurrence of chronological sequence forms, but also the representation of events rendered by the groups of subjects and predicates (underlined in the text), allow us to classify these text units as examples of narration. As already remarked when discussing concordances, the majority of verbs in this extract belong to the category of actions, as for example *to decide* (a dispute), *to subcontract* (a project), *to meet* (milestones), *to make* (deductions), *to give* (notice), and so on, with few exceptions in the introductory paragraphs which are typical of the expository text type ('the arbitration *was* the subject' and 'the dispute *related to'*). Also the textual structure is typical of the narrative text type, as both sequence forms and predicates present actions in a relation of cause and effect (e.g. "On 17 November, claimant gave notice terminating the contract, and on 18 November defendant gave claimant notice"; "Subsequent to this partial award, there were a number of significant procedural developments"). All these elements taken together construct a texture which is essentially narrative.

In the 2003 text, on the other hand, chronological sequence forms account for a scant minority of the occurring sequence forms – essentially limited to the time reference in the first paragraph ("in 1998" and "in 1999") –, while for the most part they are contrastive or resultative, as is typical of the argumentative text type (Werlich 1983):

2003: argumentative text type

(2) In 1998, the parties entered into a Master Agreement (MA) by which the respondent sold its business to claimant. For the determination of the final purchase price the MA provided a purchase price adjustment mechanism based on a Consolidated Financial Statement (CFS). *Because of* discrepancies between the auditors' reports with regard to the CFS, <u>the parties entered into negotiations</u> which resulted in 1999 in a Settlement Agreement (SA).
Notwithstanding the SA, the buyer alleged that the seller had violated representations, warranties and other obligations arising out of the MA and initiated ICC arbitration, claiming compensation from the seller. The seller asserted several counterclaims.

(3) *Because* the seller argued that most of the claims were covered by the SA, the arbitral tribunal first established its scope, using a systematic approach to determine the intention of the parties. [...]
The arbitral tribunal noted that: "If experienced business people advised by high-profile lawyers conclude a Settlement Agreement that comprises a whole bundle of claims based on Representations and Warranties – the core element of the MA and any such transaction – *it is hardly conceivable* that this is not reflected in the text of the SA." *Hence*, the settlement clause of the SA comprised only claims within the framework of the price adjustment procedure and claimant was not precluded from founding its claims of breach of Representations and/or Warranties pursuant to Sects. 7 and 8 of the MA.
The buyer argued that it was entitled to compensation from the seller for the renewal of non-transferable software licences (the Licences). In the view of the buyer, the Licences were assets and should be transferred as part of the business. *Moreover*, the seller had not included them on the list of Licences specified in the MA. The seller argued that the Licences could not be qualified as assets and that it only was required by the MA to give the buyer "reasonable assistance" regarding the licences. [...]
The arbitral tribunal rejected the seller's argument that the buyer had not suffered any damage, *but* did find that the buyer had been negligent *as* it had been aware that there might be a problem. *Therefore*, the damage was to be reduced by one third.
The buyer also claimed compensation for expenses incurred as a result of computer problems related to the change from 1999 to 2000 (the Y2K-problem or -phenomenon). The arbitral tribunal held that also this claim did not fall under the SA, but was a claim for a breach of representations and warranties. [...] The arbitral tribunal found that the damages could be mitigated if the reduction did not constitute an unbearable burden for the buyer and that this determination should be made using judicial discretion. The buyer had been under a duty to inform the seller of facts which could be the basis for claims, *but* had not done so, *although* this did not appear to be intentional. *However*, the seller was aware of the problems '128' and the failure to notify was without financial consequences. Any added value had, *however*, been taken into account by the deduction of one third.

In this case, chronological sequence forms are concentrated in the very first part of the text, to locate the beginning of the dispute in time, while the development of the dispute itself is presented in a way which emphasises relations of causality by making them explicit through the use of resultative/causal sequence forms (*therefore, because, hence, as*). These add to the text a flavour of logical soundness which is generally typical of the argumentative text type, a connotation which is further reinforced by the use of contrastive sequence forms (*however, although, but*) which are genuinely argumentative.

To conclude, the comparison of the two 'facts' sections reveals that the first presents the textual features of narrative text types, while the latter presents the typical traits of the argumentative text type. Considering that the section under review has the same function in both texts, i.e. summing up the previous stages of a dispute, it is reasonable to expect that it bears some of the features of the narrative text type and some of the argumentative text type. However, in the 1984 award, the focus conveyed by text structuring is on narration, while the content still reports of a difference of opinion, whereas in the 2003 text the narration of facts is embedded in a structure that is predominantly argumentative.

6. Conclusion

Starting from the premise that an increase of argumentation indicators in international awards over time might be the reflection of an increased influence of litigation practices, this study has highlighted a trend in this direction. Both quantitative analysis conducted on the whole corpus and qualitative analysis carried out more deeply on the 'facts' sections of the texts at the two poles of the temporal span, have revealed a difference in the linguistic texture which characterises the 1984 extract as narrative, while the 2003 excerpt combines contents which remain necessarily narrative, summing up the main events in the dispute, with an argumentative form.

Tentative as they are, due to the limited nature of the sample on which the analysis was conducted, these results suggest an influence of litigation practices on arbitration at two levels. First, the argumentative focus in the 2003 text emphasises the adversarial positioning of the parties typical of court cases, whereas in the 'spirit of arbitration' there would be no point in such an action, since the aim should be the reaching of a solution which can be acceptable for both parties. On a second level, an increasingly argumentative effort on the part of the Arbitral Tribunal might suggest a desire to justify their decision as sound on the basis of existing legislation, which, as pointed out by Nariman (2000: 262), does not fall within the purview of arbitration, rather than as "just in the particular case".

References

Bernardini, Piero 2004. The Role of the International Arbitrator. *Arbitration International* 20/2, 113-122.

Bhatia, Vijay / Candlin, Christopher / Engberg, Jan (eds) 2008. *Legal Discourse Across Cultures and Systems*. Hong Kong: Hong Kong University Press.

Breivega, K. Robgen / Dahl, Trine / Fløttum, Kjersti 2002. Traces of Self and Others in Research Articles. A Comparative Pilot Study of English, French and Norwegian Research Articles in Medicine, Economics and Linguistics. *International Journal of Applied Linguistics* 12/2, 218-239.

Browner, Charles 2007. W(h)ither International Arbitration? *Arbitration International* 24/2, 181-198.

Fløttum, Kjersti 2005. The Self and the Others – Polyphonic Visibility in Research Articles. *International Journal of Applied Linguistics* 15/1, 29-44.

Fløttum, Kjersti / Kinn, Torodd / Dahl, Trine 2006. 'We now report on …' versus 'Let us now see how …' Author Roles and Interaction with Readers in Research Articles. In Hyland, Ken / Bondi, Marina (eds) *Academic Discourse Across Disciplines.* Bern: Peter Lang, 203-224.

Garzone, Giuliana 2001. Deontic Modality and Performativity in English Legal Texts. In Gotti, Maurizio / Dossena Marina (eds) *Modality in Specialized Texts*. Bern: Peter Lang, 153-174.

Garzone, Giuliana 2008. Gli enunciati performativi nel testo giuridico inglese: la prospettiva linguistica. In Garzone, Giuliana / Santulli, Francesca (eds) *Il linguaggio giuridico. Prospettive interdisciplinari.* Milano: Giuffré, 57-87.

Gibbons, John (ed.) 1994. *Language and the Law*. London: Longman.

Gotti, Maurizio 2005. *Investigating Specialized Discourse.* Bern: Peter Lang.

Hunston, Susan / Thompson, Geoff (eds) 2001. *Evaluation in Text.* Oxford: Oxford University Press.

Hunter, Martin 2000. International Commercial Dispute Resolution: the Challenge of the Twenty-first Century. *Arbitration International* 16/4, 379-391.

Mustill, Lord Michael 1997. Too Many Laws? *JCI Arb.* 63, 248.

Nariman, Fali S. 2000. The Spirit of Arbitration. *Arbitration International* 16/3, 261-278.

Rivkin, David W. 2008. Towards a New Paradigm in International Arbitration: the Town Elder Model Revisited. *Arbitration International* 24/3, 375-386.

Scott, Mike 2004. *Wordmith Tools*. Oxford University Press.

Stati, Sorin 2002. *Principi di analisi argomentativa.* Bologna: Pàtron.

van Eemeren, Frans H. / Grootendorst, Rob / Snoeck Henkemans, Francisca 1996. *Fundamentals of Argumentation Theory. A Handbook of Historical Backgrounds and Contemporary Developments.* Mahwah (NJ): Lawrence Erlbaum.

van Eemeren, Frans H. / Houtlosser, Peter / Snoeck Henkemans, Francisca 2007. *Argumentative Indicators in Discourse: A Pragma-dialectical Study.* Dordrecht: Springer.

Werlich, Egon 1983. *A Text Grammar of English.* Heidelberg: Quelle & Meyer.

Patrizia Anesa

Spoken Interaction in Arbitration: An Analysis of Italian Arbitration Proceedings

1. Introduction

Effective oral communication is an essential aspect of arbitration proceedings. This analysis focuses, therefore, on the role played by spoken interaction in the arbitration process with particular reference to the current Italian context. This form of dispute resolution is often considered a relative novelty, but its importance in Italy has increased significantly in the last few years. Drawing on unpublished authentic data recorded in professional settings, and not on simulation materials, the study describes the main communicative and linguistic features that come into play in a particular phase of the arbitration proceedings, which is represented by the informal party examination *(interrogatorio libero delle parti)* taking place within business-related disputes in Italy. Formal and informal interviews have also been carried out with professional arbitrators, their colleagues and collaborators, as well as other legal experts. This has been of fundamental importance in gaining a more accurate understanding of the nature, the structure and the aim of arbitration procedures, as well as the legal principles applied, and the strategic techniques used.

The first part of this chapter focuses on the nature of one specific area of legal language, i.e. arbitration, and it explores the possibility of applying certain concepts derived from the field of Conversation Analysis (CA) to the spoken interactional process taking place in arbitration proceedings. The second part of the study provides an analysis based on a small corpus of authentic party examinations, and describes their main linguistic and communicative features. The aim is to offer an attempt of a descriptive and explanatory account of the complex speech situations that take place in a specific phase of the arbitration procedure.

2. Arbitration discourse

2.1. Background

Within the field of legal language, the study of arbitration discourse has in recent years received a growing level of scholarly interest (Bhatia/Candlin/Gotti 2003, Bhatia/Candlin 2004). This can be seen as a consequence of the development of this type of alternative dispute resolution both at a national and at an international level. However, studies focusing on spoken arbitration language still represent only a minor percentage, in comparison with their written counterparts. One of the main reasons underlying this substantial gap is often related to difficulty of finding authentic material of this type.

In contrast, the analysis of spoken legal discourse in other contexts has been extensively studied (Atkinson/Drew 1979, Drew 1985, Atkinson 1992, Heffer 2005), focusing particularly on the features that characterise this type of conventionalised speech compared to more spontaneous conversation. Arbitration proceedings still represent a relatively new research area, even though the spread of their use has contributed to a significant increase in the attention devoted to this branch of legal language in the last few years.

2.2. Arbitration as 'institutional talk'

At its outset, conversation analysis focused on the analysis of naturally occurring spoken interaction (Sacks/Schegloff/Jefferson 1974) and, in particular, on what has been defined as 'ordinary conversation', which identifies some forms of spoken interaction which are not restricted to settings with a high level of specialisation or to specific tasks

(Heritage 1998). Since the late '70s some significant scholarly interest has also been devoted to the analysis of spoken interaction in domain-specific settings, for example as regards legal discourse (Atkinson/ Drew 1979). The relationship between CA and applied linguistics has recently become an important research area (Boden/Zimmerman 1991, Hutchby/Woofitt 1998, ten Have 1999, Richards/Seedhouse 2005, Schegloff 2007) and in recent years some research has specifically focused on the application of Conversation Analysis to more specialised contexts (Bowles/Seedhouse 2007). The application of CA to standardised and heavily pre-structured communicative situations, as opposed to purely spontaneous discussion remains a key distinction.

Spoken interaction in professional settings is characterised by specific features that need to be taken into consideration when CA is applied. Firstly, the participants have communicative purposes which are more specific and specialised than in ordinary conversation and, secondly, interactions are more strictly related to specific restrictions and constraints; therefore, this kind of discourse is included in a more standardised framework (Drew/Heritage 1992). As Heritage (1998: 4) suggests, "The relationship between 'ordinary conversation' and 'institutional talk' can be understood as that between a 'master institution' and its more restricted local variants". Indeed, 'ordinary conversation' displays a vast scope of practice and communicative purposes, whereas 'institutional interaction' is generally characterised by a more limited variation of the interactional practices that are used, and by significant contextual restrictions (Drew/Heritage 1992, Heritage 1998). Furthermore, in ordinary conversations the order in which parties speak, how long for, and the content of the talk all vary significantly according to the speech situations, the participants and several other factors, and these aspects are not specified in advance (Atkinson/Drew 1979: 37). In more specialised settings, certain constraints and restrictions are evidently present and the allocation of turns also seems to be less varying and respects some sort of standard features, as will be seen in Section 5.

3. Methodological issues

3.1. Sources of information

From a methodological perspective, some of the basic concepts derived from CA have been used here as a tool in order to explain a few of the interactional dynamics that characterise arbitration. The aim of the study is to offer new insights into arbitration language and procedures, by also using sources of information that are not always typical of CA. As the target audience of this contribution includes members of the linguistic community as well as of the legal community, the approach has been interdisciplinary and presents different perspectives. Indeed, this study takes into consideration different sources of information, such as formal and informal interviews with the participants as well as with other members of the legal community, or references to laws and procedures. This approach is not commonly adopted in studies specifically following the tenets of CA, because, as ten Have (1990: 11) explains:

> There is no way to know how an interpretation of an action by a participant, produced in a setting different from the original one, relates to the action so interpreted. […] It may be very hard, for the participants, to reconstitute after the fact the moment-by-moment interweaving of meanings in interaction. They may be prone to present rather partial accounts, putting their actions in a favorable light.

The reliability of interviews, their arbitrariness and subjectivity, clearly constitutes a crucial point, whose discussion is particularly complex. However, in this case interviews do constitute a precious tool to better understand some of the practices to be followed and the legal procedures to be applied. Members of the legal profession involved in the conversation showed a great ability to recall and explain the meaning and the purpose of different utterances within a certain context, and they were very helpful especially as regards the explanation of how the conversation developed in relation to the specific legal framework.

Ten Have (1990: 11) adds that "the attention of CA is not directed at uncovering hidden meaning, strategic projects, and the like, but in the meanings that actually and observably are produced in and through the interaction". The approach used in this analysis is obviously different, as the aim is also to understand some of the organisational strategies, the communicative purposes, the persuasion techniques that lie behind spoken interaction in arbitration. The interaction is therefore not analysed as if it had a life of its own, but starting from the assumption that "[f]ragments of discourse materials always are shaped and constrained by the larger organizational settings in which they emerge" (Cicourel 2007: 736), with the awareness that describing the ways a specific organizational context impinges on the participants is often a very difficult task (Cicourel 2003).

3.2. Data collection

As regards the writing of the minutes or the video/audio recording of an arbitral hearing, it is up to the arbitrator or the arbitral tribunal to decide if and how this should be carried out. However, the standard practice is to consult the parties first. Recording arbitration hearings is indeed a standard practice in arbitration procedures. Therefore, I did not carry out the recording personally but I used the official recordings. This procedure has the advantage of avoiding the 'observer's paradox' (Labov 1972: 209), according to which the observation of an event or experiment is inevitably influenced by the presence of the observer/investigator. The examples presented here have not been transcribed according to all the conventions generally used in the application of Conversation Analysis (Jefferson 1983, 2004). This choice does not aim by any means to minimize the importance of these conventions in the preparation of the material to be analysed. Simply, considering the inevitable trade-off between accuracy and readability, the latter has been prioritised, as this study is not aimed at analysing specific linguistic features such as phonetic or prosodic elements, but investigates the communicative events that take place in an Italian oral arbitration procedure from a more general perspective.

The use of transcriptions in the analysis of talk-in-interaction has been the object of significant research projects (e.g. Peräkylä 1997) and calls for a series of considerations. It is true that by not using symbols referring to intonation contours, for example, one is deliberately excluding these aspects from his/her analysis. Nevertheless, there are also some practical considerations to take into account. Transcript systems are inevitably based on "approximations based on the target language's alphabet" (Pallotti 2007: 41) as it is extremely difficult to describe phonetic features, especially without using the International Phonetic Alphabet. Moreover, it is important to highlight the fact that transcribed data are not authentic, natural data, but inevitably undergo a transposition (Pallotti 2007: 41-42).

As regards non-verbal features, the importance of taking these elements into account while analysing spoken speech is certainly undeniable (Heath/Hindmarsh 2002), but they do not represent the focus of this analysis. This decision derives in the first place from the choice to focus on verbal interactional strategies, and from the practical difficulty of obtaining video material.

4. Analysis

Before analysing the communicative exchange taking place in an informal party examination, it is important to describe some of the elements on which the process is based.

4.1. The data

The analysis is based on a small corpus composed of two hearings recorded in 2006 and 2007. This corpus does not aim to be comprehensive but is nonetheless of use in examining oral interaction in arbitration procedures. The problem of representativeness, related to "the extent to which a sample includes the full range of variability in a population" (Biber 1993: 243), is crucial in a corpus-based analysis. However, despite their limited representativeness the examples analysed in the study can be helpful to identify some of the several linguistic and communicative features that come into play in this communicative event.

4.2. The participants

In the first recording the speakers involved are the arbitrator, the claimant and his lawyer, and the respondent and his lawyer. A secretary is also present but he does not intervene in the conversation. As regards the second recording, the participants are the claimant and his lawyer, the respondent and his lawyer and the arbitration panel, which consists of the President and two arbitrators. The conversation is mainly guided by the President. Indeed, of the two arbitrators, one takes an active part in the conversation only once, whereas the other does not intervene verbally at all. Here too the secretary is present but does not take part in the conversation.

4.3. The setting

Both examinations take place in the arbitrator's office. The participants are sitting around an oval table, with some water and a few glasses on it. Other elements of informality are sometimes introduced, as will be shown in the following sections.

4.4. Official transcripts

As commonly occurs in arbitration, the official recordings of the hearing were transcribed by an external company specialised in data transcription. This affords the arbitrator easier accessibility to a written document. The relationship between the authentic spoken data and their official transcriptions is particularly interesting, as transcripts constitute important legal elements and therefore a precise and extremely accurate transcription is fundamental. However, a written transcription on its own is not a sufficient subject for linguistic analysis without audio-recordings. Firstly, oral and written data are clearly not easily comparable; secondly, a transcription is inevitably mediated by another agent, and thirdly the transcription is not meant for linguistic analysis but as an official document that is of legal importance in the development of the proceedings. Nonetheless, in official transcripts certain prosodic elements seem to be introduced, but they obviously do not generally follow CA transcription conventions. For examples, dots (…) are indiscriminately used to indicate a pause or hesitation.

As the transcription must correspond exactly to the words spoken, grammatical mistakes are maintained. They are not particularly evident in spoken speech, but are clearly noticeable in a written document, as they seem to break the linguistic conventions which characterise written language, especially the conventions that we would expect to be typical of legal documents.

The metalinguistic reference to the importance of the transcription is clearly stated at the beginning of the transcription itself:

(1) Si dà atto che l'arbitrato sarà registrato su supporto digitale mediante stenotipia a cura di società specializzata incaricata dalla Camera Arbitrale di (omissis); la predetta trascrizione costituirà parte integrante del verbale, così come i fogli contenenti le generalità dei testi dai medesimi compilati e sottoscritti.
[Please note that the arbitration will be recorded digitally and stenotyped by a specialized company appointed by the Arbitral Chamber of *;[1] the aforesaid transcription will constitute an integral part of the minutes, along with the documents including the personal particulars of the witnesses, compiled and undersigned by the witnesses themselves].

This introduction confirms the fundamental role these documents play within the proceedings, as they are not additional or optional documents but an integral part of the records on which the arbitrators will base their decisions. The linguistic formality and technicality of this passage echo the complexity that is typical of the language of litigation.

---

1 For privacy reasons, names and other sensitive data have been replaced with *.

4.5. "Please speak into the microphone": recording talk

The participants involved are clearly aware that they are being recorded, as this represents a standard procedure in arbitration. At the very beginning of the hearing the President reminds the parties that it is important to switch on their microphone and asks them to repeat their names before speaking.

(2) A[2]: allora io chiedo a ognuno di schiacciare il proprio microfono, dire il proprio nome e dopodiché di esporre
[A: well, I'd like to ask you all to switch on your microphone, say your name, and then speak]

This apparently obvious process is particularly important, because it facilitates the transcribing process and allows the transcriber to identify who says what. This procedure has important consequences for the decisional process, as arbitrators need to be sure that every word has been attributed to the right person. With this in mind, it is easy to understand the importance of the physical presence of the microphone, which confers the right to speak. Whatever is not said into the microphone will not be recorded, and therefore may not be transcribed, and thus not taken into consideration. As a consequence, the President constantly reminds the speakers to use the microphone:

(3) A: Parliamo pure nel microfono
[A: Please speak into the microphone]

---

2 In order to identify the speakers, the following codes have been assigned:
A: arbitrator (President of the panel)
C1: claimant (dispute 1)
CL1: claimant's lawyer (dispute 1)
R1: respondent (dispute 1)
RL1: respondent's lawyer (dispute 1)
C2: claimant (dispute 2)
CL2: claimant's lawyer (dispute 2)
R2: respondent (dispute 2)
RL2: respondent's lawyer (dispute 2)

Moreover, references to the recording process are quite common throughout the hearing:

(4) A: Allora io direi che possiamo chiudere la registrazione
[A: Well, I think we can stop the recording]

The awareness of the speakers that their words are being recorded may lead them to increase their level of formality, because they are aware that the legal validity of their words is crucial. This happens in particular with the parties involved, when they are not legal experts, whereas, according to the interviews carried out, legal experts are accustomed to this procedure and the formality of their speech does not seem to be influenced significantly by the recording process.

5. Talk-in-interaction in arbitration

This section analyses the sequential organisation of talk-in-interaction in arbitration hearings, with particular reference to the definition offered by Schegloff (2007: 2), for whom talk-in-interaction refers to "any kind of organisation which concerns the relative positioning of utterances or actions".

5.1. Turn taking

The turn-taking sequence in informal party examination in an Italian arbitration proceeding is, on the one hand, extremely standardised and even predictable, but, on the other hand, it can display substantial differences which may derive from several factors, such as the nature of the dispute, the participants involved, the development of the hearing, etc. The allocation of turns is often pre-established and the arbitrator plays a very important role in this context as (s)he assigns the speaking turn. Turn allocation has been extensively discussed (Sacks *et al* 1974, Lerner 2004, Schegloff 2007) especially as regards casual conversation, and it is interesting to observe how the allocation of turns works in a partially pre-organised type of talk, such as the informal party examination.

Being in a legal context in which the parties are asked questions may suggest a parallelism with the examination process carried out in courts. This type of speech event clearly differs from ordinary conversation because the turn order and the type of turn are fixed (Atkinson/ Drew 1979: 61). Namely, the types of turn should be either questions or answers. The turns are allocated by the examiner, who usually self-selects after the party's answer. This is further explained by Atkinson and Drew (1979: 62) who state:

> The turn-taking system for examination is therefore characterized by the *pre-allocation* of the types of turns, and the distribution of those types to the respective parties. Because the sole right to ask questions belongs to the examiner, the techniques for allocating next turns are restricted in examination: they are operated by one party only, who allocates next turns through the production of questions, and then self-selects following answers, until completion. To the extent that the order in which speakers' talk is fixed by virtue of the turn allocation restrictions, speaker selection is built into the system, and therefore is *not* locally managed. (Original emphasis)

The communicative situation in which the parties are interrogated by the arbitrator nevertheless shows some significant differences in comparison with a party examination taking place within a different legal context, such as that of litigation. First of all, in an examination turns tend to include only two speakers, the examiner and the examinee. The system based on a pre-allocation of turns "restricts the talk to those two parties, so that the number of participants does not vary as it may do in conversation" (Atkinson/Drew 1979: 62). However, in informal examinations in the context of arbitration different speakers may be included in a turn, for example when the arbitrator asks a question to all the participants or asks if anybody has anything to add. However, it is important to remember that the number of participants involved in a turn is generally more limited than in ordinary conversation.

5.2. Selecting the next speaker

Different criteria have been defined to describe the allocation of turns (Sacks *et al* 1974). In a simplified way, it is possible to identify some main patterns that underlie the allocation of turns (Atkinson/Drew 1979), although several variants can obviously be present. First of all, the current speaker can use some speaker allocation techniques to select the next speaker. The selection of speaker can of course be made through non-verbal elements, but this analysis will focus on the allocation of turns determined by verbal interactions. This derives, firstly, from the fact that the corpus is based on audio-recordings, and therefore the analysis of non-verbal selections could only be based on the researcher's observation and not on video-recorded data, and that is not the approach used in this study; secondly, non-verbal selection is not the standard procedure in this context. According to the interviews carried out, when non-verbal selection takes place, it is simply because the current speaker forgets the importance of selecting by name, especially considering that the conversation is being recorded and transcribed. Moreover, it is important to underline the fact that in the legal field words assume a level of importance that is often not comparable with other talk situations; therefore it is easy to understand why turns are clearly organised through an evident verbal allocation of turns and a clear selection of speaker. In most cases the arbitrator clearly selects the next speaker by calling him/her by name:

(5) A: *Chiedo ora al dott. R2* se ci vuole illustrare l'attività della società.
[A: *I'd like to ask Mr. R2* if he can describe the company business.]

(6) A: Seconda domanda a chiarimento, che *chiedo al sig. R2*: Quale attività svolge e svolgeva, per quanto a lui consta, la società *?
[A: Second clarifying question, that *I'd like to ask Mr. R2*: What is, and what used to be, as far as you know, *'s business?]

Example 6 also shows that the sequence of questions has been pre-established by the lawyer, who is following a specific order.By highlighting the order of the questions (remarking that this is the second question) he conveys a sense of accuracy, rationality and logical order.

Even when different questions are asked to the same person, his name is always repeated, in order to achieve clarity and precision:

(7) A: Per finire, *sempre al sig. R2*, chiederei di illustrare brevemente invece in che cosa consiste la sua attività lavorativa.
[A. To conclude, I'd like to ask *Mr. R2* to briefly describe what his job is.]

In certain cases the same question is asked to both parties, always identifying the order of response in a very clear way. This approach is taken in order to avoid overlapping answers and convey transparency. Turns are generally not assigned randomly in communication, and neither are in a legal context:

(8) A: Bene, io rivolgo anzitutto ad entrambe le parti, quindi *prima al signor C1* quale attore e *poi al signor R1*, la domanda relativa alla società *. Se poteva descrivere questa società.
[A: Well, I'd like to ask both parties, so *first Mr C1* as claimant *and then Mr. R1*, the question related to company *. Could you describe the company?]

In other cases in which the question is asked to both parties, the previous order is generally maintained:

(9) A: Poi suggerirei che poniamo la stessa domanda ad entrambe le parti, *seguendo questo ordine* che abbiamo seguito per queste domande.
[A: Then I would suggest asking the same question to both parties, *following the order* we have followed for these questions.]

Only when the arbitrator is addressing the last speaker is it sometimes unnecessary to repeat the name of the speaker selected:

(10) A: Ecco, riproponevo la stessa domanda: a suo avviso [...]?
[A: Well, I'd like to ask the same question again: in your opinion [...]]?

Whenever a question is asked to someone who was not the last speaker, his/her name is clearly stated:

(11) A: Bene, adesso chiedo innanzitutto al *signor C1* che attività svolge.
[A: Well, now first of all I'd like to ask *Mr C1* what his job is.]

(12) A: *Chiedo ora al dott. C2* se vuole precisare quando è giunto a conoscenza dell'attività che il sig. R2 svolgeva.
[A: Now *I'd like to ask Mr. C2* if he would like to specify when he learnt about Mr. R2's activity.]

Formal and informal interviews with practitioners have confirmed that the procedure of selecting the speaker by name is clearly part of a set of conventions which belong to the legal tradition. Moreover, as this type of examination is not carried out with one party at a time, but with all the parties sitting around the same table, stating the name allows the arbitrator to make sure that the question is clearly addressed to the right interlocutor. On a more practical note, this procedure also helps to facilitate an accurate transcription and avoid potential cases of ambiguity. In some cases the next speaker is not explicitly selected, but this possibility is mainly limited to some questions asked by the arbitrators to the other interactants, such as the following:

(13) A: Io su questo non avrei altre domande. Ci sono delle altre domande?
CL1: Non ho domande.
RL1: Nessuna domanda.
[A: I don't have any other questions about this point. Are there any further questions?
CL1: I don't have any questions.
RL1: No questions.]

Even though a question of this type is apparently asked to all the people who are present, it is clear that the privileged interlocutors are the lawyers involved. This aspect is made explicit in another example where the two lawyers are selected jointly:

(14) A: I Difensori hanno qualcosa da aggiungere su queste dichiarazioni […]?
[A: Do the lawyers have anything to add about these statements […]?]

As has been mentioned, non-verbal elements may also play an important role as regards the selection of speakers, but this process is not common in an institutionalized context such as arbitration. However, in some cases the parties show through non-verbal signals (especially by raising their hands and through eye contact) that they would like to intervene and the arbitrator acknowledges this desire and makes it verbally explicit:

(15) A: […] R1 mi fa cenno che vuole a sua volta rendere dei chiarimenti.
[A: […] R1 is signalling that he would like to provide some clarifications.]

(16) A: Vedo anche che R1 chiede la parola per delle precisazioni.
[A: I see that R1 would like to speak in order to provide some clarifications.]

(17) A: Vedo che anche C1 vuole aggiungere qualcosa.
[A: I see that C1 would like to add something too.]

In these cases the parties do not automatically self-select, but to some extent ask to be selected, as they ask (even if not verbally) for the right to speak, and intervene only when the arbitrator has explicitly assigned the turn to one of the parties. This kind of selection does not generally occur in the context of litigation, where turns are pre-established and the order of turns is clearly defined. Beyond procedural conventions, it is also plausible to affirm that the relatively intimate setting in which the arbitration takes place and the limited number of people involved make it possible for the arbitrator to interpret non-verbal signals quite easily. Such an approach would not be feasible in the context of a busy courtroom, not only from a conventional but also from a practical point of view.

It is relevant to note that in the cases here analysed non-verbal requests to be assigned the right to speak are made only by the parties themselves, and not by legal professionals, as the latter are more acquainted with the procedures and therefore are more aware of what the most appropriate moment to intervene is: they generally wait for the arbitrator to ask if they have anything to add, or intervene verbally during the conversation if they believe it is absolutely necessary at that point.

5.3. Interactional sequence

The adjacency pair can be defined as the basic unit of sequence construction, which in its minimal form is composed of two turns adjacently placed, taken by different speakers (Schegloff 2007: 13). In this case the First Pair Part is usually followed directly by a Second Pair Part. For most parts of the examinations analysed, the pattern seems to correspond to the typical sequence of court examinations and assumes quite a schematic structure in which the question-answer sequence is generally followed. In particular, in most of the situations analysed the First Pair Part is represented by the arbitrator or by the President of the panel (A) and the Second Pair Part is represented by one of the parties, either the claimant or the respondent (C1 or R1). For example, in observing a section of one hearing it emerges that the order followed is extremely precise and could be schematised in the following way:

A - R1 - A - R1 - A - R1 - A - R1 - A - C1 - A - C1 - A - C1 - A - C1 - A - R1 - A - C1 - A - C1 - A - C1

At this point, though, the sequence is interrupted by lawyer RL1:

(18) RL1: Io avevo solo da fare dei quesiti per precisare l'oggetto delle prime domande. Li facciamo adesso o dopo?
A: Assolutamente sì, io direi di seguito, se voi siete d'accordo.
[RL1: I wanted to ask some questions regarding the subject-matter of the first questions. Shall we ask them now or later?
A: Absolutely. I would say now, if you agree.]

In this case the President poses a question to both lawyers, who answer one after the other:

(19) RL1: Come avevamo detto, di seguito.
CL1: Confermo, va benissimo, possiamo andare di seguito alle domande.
[RL1: As we had said, now.
CL1: I agree, it's fine. We can ask the questions now.]

At this point once it has been established that further questions may be asked by the lawyers, what takes place is a series of questions addressed to one of the parties, according to the following sequence:

RL1- C1- RL1- C1- RL1- C1- RL1- C1- RL1- C1- RL1

Such approach is intuitively similar to the typical structure of witness examinations in litigative contexts. The arbitrators do not interrupt this series of questions until the lawyer concludes this phase with the expression *thank you* and it is therefore clear that all questions have been asked. At this point the President intervenes and asks if anyone has any further questions to pose, so that the other lawyer may also enjoy the right to examine the parties. In certain cases the question-answer sequence can be interrupted, for example by the lawyers assisting their clients in order to modify (or to guide, to complete, to correct etc.) the clients' answers.

(20) A: [...] Renda in modo specifico le sue pretese per poi essere, così, oggetto del
CL1: Rammostro solo al mo cliente i conteggi, perché non li sa a memoria
A: Prego
C1: […] i costi che
CL1: Interrompo solo per ricordare che […].
[A: […] please specify your requests that will be the object of
CL1: I'll show my client the calculations, because he doesn't know them by heart
A: Ok
C1: […] the costs that
CL1: I'd like to interrupt just to point out that […]].

In other cases the sequential organisation is structured in a more complex way. The President of the arbitration panel can address one of the parties and ask them to report directly to the panel and not to the other party. In the following example, the parties are interacting directly without the mediation of the arbitrator, who immediately points out that this is not the procedure to be followed:

(21) A: Bene, qualcuno ha qualche domanda a chiarimento da chiedere?
RL2: Se può chiedere se * disponeva di una propria rete di agenti.
C2: No, non disponeva di una propria rete di agenti.
RL2. di agenti per la vendita […]?
C2: No,[…]
A: Ecco, io chiedo ai colleghi però, per il buon andamento, che le domande le rivolgete al collegio, dopodiché il collegio valuta se darvi corso oppure no, e dopo la persona risponde. Quindi prego, collega, se ha delle altre domande a chiarimento da chiedere su questo fatto dell'attività.
RL2: Grazie Presidente. Se può chiedere qual era la forma contrattuale […].

[A: Well, does anybody have any questions or clarifications to ask for?
RL2: If you could ask if * had their own network of agents.
C2: No, they didn't have their own network of agents.
RL2: Sales agents […]?
C2: No, […]
A: Well, for the good running of the proceedings I'll ask the colleagues, though, to pose your questions to the panel, then the panel will decide whether to accept them or not, and then the person will answer. So, please, my colleagues, if you have any more questions about this point?
RL2: Thank you President. If you can ask what the contractual form was […]].

In this case the role of the President of the panel as a regulator of the right to speak is quite evident. The lawyer has to ask the arbitrator to formulate a certain question to the other party or to his/her client. That means that questions must be asked to the President, who will then pose the question (if it is considered appropriate) to the party. The sequence will therefore tend to assume this form:

X → arbitrator → (reformulation) → (consensus to answer) → Y

X usually represents one of the parties (and questions are usually asked by their lawyers) and Y may represent the other party. Alternatively, in certain exchanges a lawyer (X) poses a question to his/her client (Y). This pattern is clearly followed in example 22:

(22) A: Bene, qualche chiarimento?
RL2: Sì, Presidente. Vogliamo chiedere al dott. R2 se in questa sua attività ha utilizzato materiale o qualsiasi altro elemento proveniente da o comunque appartenente a *.
A: Prego, il dott. R2 risponda.
R2: Allora, […].
[A: Good, any questions?
RL2: Yes, President. We would like to ask Mr. R2 if he has used any material or other element coming from or belonging to * for his business.
A: Mr R2, please answer.
R2: Well,[…]].

This excerpt represents the typical sequence in which the question is clearly addressed to the President, who then addresses the question to the other party, without repeating the question but simply asking the party to answer the question. In this context self-selection of speaker is clearly not common because of the need to respect the standard procedure according to which the arbitrator constantly selects the speakers.

5.4. Is turn transition 'locally managed' in arbitration?

Unlike in ordinary conversation, in legal contexts turn transitions are not generally 'locally managed' (Atkinson/Drew 1979: 65) but tend to be pre-established. Nevertheless, turn size and timing of speaker transitions cannot be precisely pre-established and usually derive from the current communicative situation. This also happens in informal party examination. The turn size is particularly variable, because most questions are asked by the arbitrator, who tends to ask open questions, as the main aim of this phase is to better understand the issues and clarify certain points. Answers, therefore, have a very flexible length. These answers are not often interrupted (excluding certain cases, such as objections, corrections, etc.), because the participants are aware of the fact that at the end of the turn they will have the right to intervene. This procedure is explicitly pointed out by the arbitrator in the following example:

(23) A: Io invito innanzitutto C1 a terminare la propria esposizione, poi, proprio perché siamo qui nel confronto, vedo già il sig. R1 che mi chiede la parola e quindi gliela cederemo sicuramente.
[A: First of all, I'd like to ask C1 to finish his explanation, then, as we are here to have clarifications, I can see Mr. R1 would like to speak so he will certainly be allowed to speak.]

In this case it is clear that it is not necessary for R1 to interrupt the other speaker, as he has been guaranteed that he will have his turn at the end of C1's. Such an approach stresses the fact that both parties have the right to intervene, as that is the procedure to be followed. The arbitrator also reminds the parties about the crucial principle on which a hearing is based, i.e. the *principio del contraddittorio*[3], according to which every party is allowed an equal and reasonable possibility of speaking:

(24) A: Allora adesso, per diritto di contraddittorio, chiederei a * di riproporre la domanda di prima.
[A: Now, as for the *principio di contraddittorio (Audi alteram partem)*, I would ask * to pose the previous question again.]

This is typical also of court examinations. Atkinson and Drew suggest (1979: 66) that "Whereas in conversation the competition among possible next speakers to self-select can inhibit long turns, in examination that pressure is relaxed, given that each speaker is assured of a next turn". In particular, in a legal setting where the official transcripts constitute a legally valid document, it is of crucial importance to guarantee that all declarations are clearly comprehensible. This is emphasized in one case by the President:

(25) A: Allora, io prego tutti di non sovrapporre le voci, proprio perché lo scopo dell'interrogatorio libero di oggi è quello di chiarire i fatti e di avere un verbale odierno che rappresenti il più possibile quello che stiamo dicendo.
[A: Well, please do not overlap your voices, just because the aim of the informal party examination is to clarify the facts and have some minutes that represent as well as possible what we are saying today.]

In certain types of institutional talk, such as the one in question, unlike in ordinary conversation, overlaps rarely occur because turns are clearly structured.

---

3 For a discussion of the *principio del contraddittorio* and its application to arbitration procedures see Magnone/Cavatorta (2008: 59-70).

6. Concluding remarks

This analysis shows how fruitful it may be to apply some of the concepts and principles related to Conversation Analysis to arbitral language in order to achieve a better understanding of the linguistic and communicative choices that characterise the language of arbitration. As has been shown, CA was not systematically applied, because the aim of this analysis differed from the intrinsic aims of the discipline. In particular, if we assume that the essence of CA lies "in questioning *how* conversational actions are accomplished as the systematic products of sequentially ordered interaction rather than *why* they are performed" (Benwell/Stokoe 2006: 63, original emphasis), it is clear that the approach here adopted was considerably different, as I tried to combine descriptive and explanatory elements.

With this in mind, it is possible to affirm that spoken interaction in arbitration proceedings is characterized by a sort of tension between litigative interaction on the one hand and less specialised types of oral interaction on the other, to the extent that it even presents certain features that could be associated with ordinary conversation. In fact, it is important to point out that the relationship with other forms of spoken legal interaction is particularly strong, but it is nonetheless undeniable that significant differences in the communicative interaction remain.

More specifically, this chapter has offered insights into the way spoken interaction develops and is organised in arbitration, and has pointed out some of the legal and practical reasons underlying certain communicative and linguistic choices, thanks to the valuable contribution of professionals in the field. Drawing on authentic instances of arbitration proceedings, I have attempted to describe some features of talk-in-interaction in arbitration. In particular, I have provided examples showing the importance of speaker selection processes in arbitration, the relative standardisation of turn-taking dynamics and the fundamental role played by the arbitrator in establishing specific interactional sequences. Thus, analyses of this kind can be very helpful in the exploration of a rather complex and relatively unexplored area, such as spoken arbitration language in arbitration and in its different phases.

References

Atkinson, J. Maxwell 1992. Displaying Neutrality: Formal Aspects of Informal Court Proceedings. In Drew, Paul / Heritage, John (eds) *Talk at Work*. Cambridge: Cambridge University Press, 199-211.

Atkinson, J. Maxwell / Drew, Paul 1979. *Order in Court: The Organisation of Verbal Interaction in Judicial Settings*. London: Macmillan.

Benwell, Bethan / Stokoe, Elisabeth 2006. Discourse and Identity. Edinburgh: Edinburgh University Press.

Bhatia, Vijay / Candlin, Christopher N. 2004. Analysing Arbitration Laws across Legal Systems. *Hermes* 32, 13-44.

Bhatia, Vijay / Candlin, Christopher N. / Gotti, Maurizio (eds) 2003. *Arbitration in Europe: Legal Discourse in Multilingual and Multicultural Contexts*. Bern: Peter Lang.

Biber, Douglas 1993. Representativeness in Corpus Design. *Literary and Linguistic Computing* 8/4, 243-257.

Boden, Deidre / Zimmerman, Donald H. (eds) 1991. *Talk and Social Structure*. Cambridge: Polity.

Bowles, Hugo / Seedhouse, Paul (eds) 2007. *Conversation Analysis and Language for Specific Purposes*. Bern: Peter Lang.

Cicourel, Aaron 2003. On Contextualising Applied Linguistic Research in the Workplace. *Applied Linguistics* 24/3, 360-373.

Cicourel, Aaron 2007. A Personal, Retrospective View of Ecological Validity. *Text & Talk – An Interdisciplinary Journal of Language, Discourse Communication Studies* 27/5-6, 735-752.

Drew, Paul 1985. Analysing the Use of Language in Courtroom Interaction. In van Dijk, Teun A. (ed.) *Handbook of Discourse Analysis* (vol. 3). London: Academic Press, 133-148.

Drew, Paul / Heritage, John 1992. *Talk at Work*. New York: Cambridge University Press.

Have, Paul ten 1990. Methodological Issues in Conversation Analysis. Electronic version available at: <http://icar.univ-lyon2.fr/ecole_thematique/contaci/documents/bonu/MethodologicalIssues.pdf>,

Originally published in *Bulletin de Méthodologie Sociologique* 23, 23-51.

Have, Paul ten 1999. *Doing Conversation Analysis: A Practical Guide*. London: Sage.

Heath, Christian, / Hindmarsh, Jon 2002. Analysing Interaction: Video, Ethnography and Situated Conduct. In May, Tim (ed.) *Qualitative Research in Action*. London: Sage, 99-122.

Heffer, Chris 2005. *The Language of Jury Trial: A Corpus-aided Analysis of Legal-Lay Discourse*. Basingstoke: Palgrave Macmillan.

Heritage, John 1998. Conversation Analysis and Institutional Talk: Analyzing Distinctive Turn-Taking Systems. In Cmejrková, Svetla / Hoffmannová, Jana / Müllerová, Olga / Svetlá, Jindra (eds) *Proceedings of the 6th International Congress of IADA (International Association for Dialog Analysis)*. Tubingen: Niemeyer, 3-17.

Hutchby, Ian / Woofitt, Robin 1998. *Conversation Analysis. Principles, Practices and Applications*. Cambridge: Polity.

Jefferson, Gail 1983. Issues in the Transcription of Naturally-Occurring Talk: Caricature versus Capturing Pronunciational Particulars. *Tilburg Papers in Language and Literature* 34, 1-12. Tilburg: Tilburg University.

Jefferson, Gail 2004. Glossary of Transcript Symbols with an Introduction. In Lerner (ed.), 13-31.

Labov, William 1972. *Sociolinguistic Patterns*. Philadelphia: Philadelphia University Press.

Lerner, Gene H. (ed.) 2004. *Conversation Analysis: Studies from the First Generation*. Amsterdam: John Benjamins.

Magnone Cavatorta, Stefania 2008. *Prova documentale e arbitrato*. [Documentary Evidence and Arbitration]. Padova: Cedam.

Pallotti, Gabriele 2007. Methodology, Machinery and Application to Specific Settings. In Bowles/Seedhouse (eds), 37-67.

Peräkylä, Anssi 1997. Reliability and Validity in Research Based on Transcripts. In Silverman, David (ed.) *Qualitative Research. Theory, Method and Practice*. London: Sage, 201-220.

Richards, Keith / Seedhouse, Paul (eds) 2005. *Applying Conversation Analysis*. New York: Palgrave Macmillan.

Sacks, Havery / Schegloff, Emanuel A. / Jefferson, Gail 1974. A Simplest Systematics for the Organisation of Turn-taking for Conversation. *Language* 50, 696-735.

Schegloff, Emanuel A. 2007. *Sequence Organisation in Interaction.* Cambridge: Cambridge University Press.

GIROLAMO TESSUTO

US Commercial Arbitration Rules and Mediation Procedures: Linguistic and Discoursal Features of a Genre in Action

1. Introduction

It is widely recognised that mediation and arbitration, as non-judicial processes, are the traditional methods of dispute settlement of controversies arising between individuals, businesses and countries. In the United States, commercial mediation and arbitration are often used to assist in the resolution of disputes, arising, for example, in the construction, labour and shareholder industry, and may operate voluntarily on an ad hoc or institutional basis or by governmental institution or organisation.

Although, in the past, the US government intervened in the resolution of commercial arbitration by statute (Interstate Commerce Act 1887; Federal Arbitration Act 1925), today's practice is for self-regulatory institutions and organisations to intervene in the parties' decision to mediate or arbitrate in a variety of disputes. This is the case of US reputable organisations, such as the National Arbitration Forum (commercial and civil disputes), FINRA (security industry) and the American Arbitration Association (AAA), providing independent arbitration and mediation services. While such institutions play an important role in US law, their operation of arbitration and mediation processes and procedures is certainly prompted by the major commercial developments in the world economy.

The present analysis investigates Commercial Arbitration Rules and Mediation Procedures (CARMP), as coded by the AAA, which operates under minimised statutory intervention. As a professional genre resulting from the increasing bureaucratisation of written disciplinary discourse practices on the web, CARMP represent a useful analytical site in which a wide audience can be in contact with an organisation that regulates commercial arbitration and mediation. This analysis focuses on the macro and micro-level linguistic realizations of the US rules and procedures, and provides insights into the degree to which generic integrity is maintained in the expression of such rules and procedures in English.

2. CARMP as a professional genre in action: defining issues

An understanding of CARMP (hereinafter referred to as 'the text') as a genre in action initially brings into focus the ways in which the text is constructed and used to achieve professional goals. Following Bhatia's (2004) discussion of generic integrity, this notion can be evidenced in the text under examination in terms of 'text-external factors', connecting to "the wider context of the disciplinary community and culture in which the text is used and interpreted" (Bhatia 2004: 123). As a result of these factors, 'discursive procedures', as claimed by Bhatia, come to describe in the text under scrutiny "the procedural aspects of genre construction, such as *'who' contributes 'what'* to the construction and interpretation of specific generic actions; 'participatory mechanisms' which indicate *'at what stage'* and *'by which means'* does one participate in the genre", which also account for "'interdiscursivity' in genre construction" (Bhatia 2004: 128, italics in the original).

To illustrate such procedural aspects in the construction and use of the text, it should be noted that CARMP are not part of a legislative genre in the narrow sense in that they do not evolve from the US legislative action. CARMP emanate strictly from the American Arbitration Association itself, as the largest and most reputable US arbitration forum, although there is a broad federal statute entitled the Federal

Arbitration Act[1] and, more recently, the Uniform Arbitration Act 2000 and the Uniform Mediation Act 2001.[2] Of these, the Federal Act provides the most influential source for the AAA for judicial facilitation of private dispute resolution through commercial arbitration. The relevant point about this statute is that it does not authorise or require any specific rules for conducting arbitrations; rather, it implicitly gives discretion to the AAA, as a private organisation, to design its own rules and procedures.[3]

2.1. Mechanisms in CARMP as an administrative-regulatory genre in action

Consequent on this focus on procedure, we may identify the *who* and *what* mechanisms theorised by Bhatia. Reasonably, these mechanisms emphasise CARMP being mandated to the AAA, as a "not-for-profit, public service organization" (CARMP: Introduction), to handle the resolution of disputes in the United States in the form of administrative support provided to arbitration proceedings and mediations across a wide range of industries and case types. By coding two separate discursive practices in ADR, the task of the AAA, as a community of practice, is therefore to establish a versatile goal-specific genre in professional practice, with the relevant law playing a facilitative role in private or judicial commercial arrangements.

---

1 The Federal Act was first enacted in 1925 and later codified by various amendments until 1990. This Act is found at Title 9, US Code, Sections 1-14, and sets out contractually-based binding arbitration resulting in an arbitration award.

2 Although recommended for all US states, these acts have been enacted only in some of them. Unike the Federal Act, however, the Mediation Act, for instance, seeks to broker an agreement between the two sides by providing a strong evidentiary privilege that permits the parties, mediator, and non-party participants to make statements made in mediation inadmissible as evidence in later legal proceedings.

3 I am grateful to Patricia McCoy, Professor of Law, University of Connecticut, School of Law, for informing me about this particular point.

Given these *who/what* mechanisms, the genre may typically be characterised as an instance of administrative-regulatory writing, deriving its source from the authority and powers vested in the AAA. The latter participates in the construction and production of the genre under the guidelines established notably by the Federal Arbitration Act, as the *means* mechanisms in Bhatia's terms.

In a context where 'helping' laws and rules are established in many countries for the enforcement of arbitration clauses, and where most national courts acknowledge the validity of international commercial arbitration awards, the AAA responds through its regulatory genre by competitively inviting those across the globe to travel to New York and elsewhere in the USA to resolve their disputes by arbitration, mediation, or through other ADR forms. As a code, in fact, this genre becomes an important tool for the International Centre for Dispute Resolution to administer international arbitration commenced under the AAA's rules, and as such becomes a critical site where national/international discourse practices in ADR come into play.

3. Material and method

3.1. CARMP: rationale and function

The defining issues above provide the procedural mechanisms by which to understand the administrative-regulatory genre material for analysis. This material was obtained from the AAA's institutional website, which brings the genre into the world of a digital document (Yates/Sumner 1997) allowing reference by a global audience, whether lay or expert, seeking information on all forms of ADRs. Accordingly, the material, as amended and effective of September 1, 2007, allows the AAA to detail the steps in the resolution process between individual consumers and businesses in lieu of going to court, thus ensuring that all parties to a case are treated fairly and equitably, as they would be when going to a public court. By providing the relevant generic information to achieve these goals, the material may be qualified as 'prescriptive' in function (Šarčević 2000: 9), bearing close similarity to the wider notion of 'legislative or statutory writing' (Bhatia 1983: 2), based on its own communicative purpose.

This function or purpose is evidenced by the nature of the *rules* (in arbitration) and *procedures* (in mediation) under scrutiny. Both terms, in fact, are used to prescribe that in given circumstances a specific behaviour is expected of legal subjects to engage in. Therefore, the *rules* and *procedures* as used in the current material imply a general norm mandating conduct in a given type of situation, and provide the justifying reason for the internal operating prescriptions of the AAA. As will be shown, the contours of this writing system attempt to be not only specific in their prescriptions, but also all-encompassing in their operation.

3.2. Methodological procedure

In an attempt to combine material-based data with recently emerging views on arbitration discourse, this methodological analysis follows the argument made by Bhatia, Candlin and Engberg (2008) in regard to the distinctive rules in this type of discourse. They provide a neat dichotomy between "two major genres: *statutes and executive orders* that function as the national or international statutory authority for international commercial arbitration, and *arbitration rules* of individual chambers of commerce, which govern the arbitration procedures. The second genre may be seen as concrete instantiations of procedural rules within the framework set up by the first genre" (2008: 13, italics in the original). As a result of the emphasis on *rules*, therefore, the 'regulatory' label attached to the current material would reasonably fall within the second genre as identified by Bhatia, Candlin and Engberg by assuming that the chambers of commerce share similarities to the AAA in regard to the writing systems of rules and procedures in arbitration/mediation.

Following the theoretical perspectives of genre and discourse studies (Gustafsson 1975, 1984; Bhatia 1993, 2004; Tiersma 1999; Hiltunen 2001; Gotti 2003), and modality (Garzone 2001; Gotti/

Dossena 2001; Williams 2005), the analysis in this chapter targets the main linguistic features emerging from the genre – namely, the organisation and layout of the text; the structure of sentences and other syntactic realisations, such as binomials and multinomials, embedded clauses; modal auxiliaries, and lexicon. In relation to the wider construct of legislative writing, the ultimate aim of the analysis is to discuss the issue of integrity of the genre in professional discourse, by relating it to the degree of shared generic features with statutes on similar or other topics.

Quantitative data were obtained via ordinary computer scanning and were then manually analysed for specific linguistic items and their percentages. The aim was to contribute, by drawing on comparable data, to the outcomes of previous investigations of arbitration rules as documented in the publications of the international research project entitled *International Commercial Arbitration Practices: A Discourse Analytical Study* (<http://www.english.cityu.edu.hk/arbitration/>).

4. Results and discussion

4.1. Overall textual organisation: similarities to legislative drafting standards

As as result of the wider tradition of legislative or statutory writing as established within the framework of statutes in arbitration writing, the general layout of the text bears similarities to the traditional legislative drafting standards found in other statutes on similar topics, such as the English Arbitration Act 1996 (Tessuto 2003) or the US Uniform Mediation Act 2001 in English-speaking countries.

As Table 1 shows, these standards are based on the method of legislative division of the text into sections, grouping together, with a letter reference, Commercial Mediation Procedures (M), Commercial Arbitration Rules (R), Expedited Procedures (E), Procedures for Large, Complex Commercial Disputes (L), Optional Rules for Emergency Measures of Protection (O), as well as Administrative Fees, with no letter reference. The latter are given considerable emphasis in the text since the issue of costs is clearly of great importance in commercial mediation and arbitration. The layout makes use of short headings that usually arrange the material on the subject matter in single clauses and, where clauses are considerably lengthy, their contents are divided into sub-clauses as (a), (b), (i), (ii) to identify semantic units and enable the information to be easily referred to.

CARMPs	
Commercial Mediation Procedures	M: 17
Commercial Arbitration Rules	R: 54
Expedited Procedures	E: 10
Procedures for Large, Complex Commercial Disputes	L: 4
Optional Rules for Emergency Measures of Protection	O: 8
Administrative Fees	Unnumbered
	Total: 93

Table 1. Overall textual organisation based on the legislative drafting division.

4.1.1. Regulatory versus legislative drafting format

Unlike statutes on similar topics, the regulatory format of this text is evidenced by its opening sections that are labelled as IMPORTANT NOTICE, INTRODUCTION, standard ARBITRATION and MEDIATION CLAUSE, these being immediately followed by the contents of the Rules and Procedures themselves. Where IMPORTANT NOTICE and INTRODUCTION are concerned, their function is to provide some form of a preamble, setting out the scope, content, and purposes of the rules in explanatory user-friendly format. The contents of these sections emphasise the role of the AAA as an international institution providing a forum for dispute resolution proceedings for the parties. Thus, we read:

(1) IMPORTANT NOTICE
These rules and any amendment of them shall apply in the form in effect at the time the administrative filing requirements are met for a demand for arbitration or submission agreement received by the AAA. To ensure that *you* have the most current information, see our Web Site at www.adr.org.

In the example above, the assumption of a range of audiences is clear from the INTRODUCTION by its reference to *business executives*, *trade associations*, *families*, etc., collectively addressed to as *you* (used 3 times) and *your* (3 times) throughout the text. Although the direct addressing of the audience/reader as *you* is not by any means the traditional, legislative approach, where the provision style is highly impersonal (Bhatia 1993: 102),[4] its use not only emphasises the primacy, and hence the needs, of the audience/reader over the writer (or drafter) in the 'expert' text but, most importantly, enables the language used in the text to become inherently *dialogic* in nature, in Bakhtin's (1981) terms.

Nonetheless, it is a feature of the professional practice and conventions of the AAA to include in the text a reference to a standard ARBITRATION or MEDIATION clause, naming itself as the organisation that will provide administrative support to (but not arbitrate) disputes between the parties. The aim behind such clauses, to be later included in commercial contracts, is to create a dispute resolution process that provides, in a structured manner, a viable negotiated solution before a formal adjudicatory process such as arbitration can commence. The rhetorical picture of a standard Arbitration clause for future disputes is as follows:

(2) Standard Arbitration clause
Any controversy or claim arising out of or relating to this contract, or the breach thereof, shall be settled by arbitration administered by the American Arbitration Association under its Commercial Arbitration Rules, and judgment on the award rendered by the arbitrator(s) may be entered in any court having jurisdiction thereof.

The case in (2) provides a taste of the lexical and syntactic features of the rules and procedures to be dealt with under separate headings in the later linguistic analysis. The case is one in which the 'all-inclu-

---

4 In English-speaking countries, however, it is not difficult to find civil law (private) documents, such as contracts, being drafted in *you* gender-neutral pronoun. Common examples are those in which the terms of specific clauses (such as breach of contract) to a party are set out by reference to *you* neutral orientation.

sive' function of the clause (Bhatia 1993: 108) is observable by the use of a multinomial structure linked by the *or* inclusive conjunction and initialised by the determiner *any*. The multinomial clause also illustrates some degree of syntactic discontinuity arising from the present participle (*arising out*), placed after the noun (which has the same 'identifying' function as a relative clause), and the second and third use of *or* conjunction (*or relating ..., or the breach thereof*), both of them separating the binomial subject (*Any controversy or claim*) from the *shall* verbal phrase. As part of referential devices, the arbitration clause includes archaic, formal *There* + adverbial words, avoiding repetition of the textual element in the clause. The example clearly highlights the standard deontic *shall* and *may* in the verbal group. In the case of existing disputes, the clause in (2) becomes operational by using the following statements:

(3) We, the undersigned parties, hereby agree to submit to arbitration administered by the American Arbitration Association under its Commercial Arbitration Rules the following controversy: (describe briefly). We further agree that the above controversy be submitted to (one) (three) arbitrator(s). We further agree that we will faithfully observe this agreement and the rules, that we will abide by and perform any award rendered by the arbitrator(s), and that a judgment of any court having jurisdiction may be entered on the award.

Here, the emphasis is on the arbitrators who are chosen in compliance with the parties' agreement or, failing that, in compliance with the AAA rules. While the use of the first person plural *We* in the opening statement is explanatory of a private agreement,[5] the resulting drafting of the clause reflects similar standards of writing national and international arbitration/mediation clauses. In terms of specific speech acts, accompanied by normally appropriate contextual conditions, the pronoun co-occurs with the legal adverbial of explicit performativity *hereby*, expressed in the active present simple tense of the performative (commissive) verb *agree* (Searle 1979: 12-29). The latter performs the illocutionary act of agreeing to the terms of the AAA which,

5 However, the use of *we* orientation reflects other contextually different contexts of legal drafting, such as constitutional preambles, where the *we* pronoun is usually found.

as noted, does not itself arbitrate but administers disputes.[6] The *we*-explicit performative utterance appears in a sequence of sentences, in which several noun clauses introduced by *that* function either as a complement after a verb or equally as a complement, listing a series of ideas as a means of presenting complex information in the sentences.

(4) Standard Mediation clause
If a dispute arises out of or relates to this contract, or the breach thereof, and *if* the dispute cannot be settled through negotiation, the parties agree first to try in good faith to settle the dispute by mediation administered by the American Arbitration Association under its Commercial Mediation Procedures before resorting to *arbitration, litigation, or some other dispute resolution procedure*.

By emphasising the US convention of highlighting 'client-directed' solutions in a variety of processes and procedures (*negotiation, mediation, arbitration, litigation, other dispute resolution procedures*), this clause presents hypothetical discourse in *if*-clauses, in which the use of nominalised forms are combined with *or*-multinomial structures, thus allowing the reader to gain the information needed in all-inclusive sentences. Given the voluntary, informal and non-binding process of mediation, as opposed to the formal and binding nature of arbitration, choice is given to the parties to use a mediator to resolve an existing dispute by *agreeing* to the following submission:

(5) The parties hereby submit the following dispute to mediation administered by the American Arbitration Association under its Commercial Mediation Procedures.

4.2. Text length

In a context where, as we have seen, the regulatory drafting format characteristically deviates in some structural aspects from the legisla-

6 In the realm of ADR, however, explicit performative acts are also common to the discourse system of English arbitration awards in collocation with the first person singular (*I*) used in the 'find/hold' + *that*-clause and 'I hereby award and direct' performative formulae (Tessuto 2008: 181-197).

tive format, the topics provide the essential content of the genre. Table 1 above, in fact, has shown that these topics are determined by the number of individual sets of mediation (17), arbitration (54) and other procedural rules, totalling a number of 93 procedural rules.

However, as Table 2 shows, these macro-structural features result in the total length of the text (12,311) justifying a drafting system which favours the expansive and detailed expression of the rules and procedures by exploring every possible scenario, as advocated by Common Law legal academics (e.g. Twining/Miers 1999: 245-253), a feature similarly found in other comparable national or international statutes or arbitration rules (Bhatia/Candlin/Gotti 2003). In the current text, this preference for details places an emphasis on the need to strike the right balance between legal certainty, flexibility, and the requirements of a diverse range of potential readers who need to know how the rules or procedures apply in differing circumstances.

CARMP	
Word length (tokens)	12,311
Sentences	406 (including disclaimer sections)
Word length per sentence	Minimum: 7 / Maximum: 163
Average sentence length	30.32

Table 2. Text length per total number of words, total sentences, and sentence length.

The effect of this is realised in two main ways. Firstly, by sentence length, which is determined by the presentation of contents, as a consequence of whether consideration is given to divisions of the rules and procedures by clauses or paragraphing. Secondly, in quantitative terms, by considering the striking variation in sentence length, ranging from an astonishing minimum of seven to a maximum of 163 words, and resulting in an average sentence length of 30.32 words. This average figure is neither less nor more than that reported by other scholars (e.g. Belotti 2003; Garzone 2003), investigating corpus-based arbitration rules in the medium of English.

Sentence length and contents are reflected in the communicative purpose of the rules and procedures. As a result of the text acting as an administrative-regulatory instrument, its purpose is to impose obligations, confer rights, benefits and privileges to arbitrators, mediators, and the parties who are subject to them. These become evident in the textual development of the variously headed rules and procedures, such as those spelling out the Appointment of the Mediator (M-4) being immediately followed by Mediator's Impartiality and Duty to Disclose (M-5). Clearly, these precepts are communicated within 'less stringently' configured rhetorical contexts of the law than would otherwise be the case of communicating in the legislative genre, where rule-breaking sanctions arising from a high-ranking legislative source are involved. Nonetheless, it is not unusual to find such precepts sharing similarities with the latter discourse, and giving rise to the resulting macro-structure of the writing under scrutiny.

As a consequence, the writing implies that the function of ensuring generic integrity is primarily performed by qualifications, "consisting of the main *provisionary clause* and the attendant *quailfications* of various kinds" (Bhatia 1993: 115, emphasis in the original), including the nominal character of the genre (Bhatia 1993: 148). By functioning as basic textual devices for arbitrators, mediators, and ultimately judges to argue over and interpret the particular rule or procedure in question, qualifications therefore spell out the case, conditions, exceptions or contingencies to be satisfied in the discourse at hand. Thus, by covering every possibile scenario by the use of qualifications, the current system of textualisation leads the genre to be "precise, clear, unambiguous and all-inclusive" (Bhatia 1993: 117).

4.3. Sentence structure

As a result of this cognitive structuring, it is not surprising that the text consists of the highest percentage number of complex sentences (0.39%), followed by compound sentences (0.17%), down to simple sentences (0.14%) and, finally, to the lowest percentage number of compound-complex sentences (0.09%), as shown in Table 3.

Simple	Compound	Complex	Complex-compound
0.14%	0.17%	0.39 %	0.09%

Table 3. Distribution of sentence types.

These figures suggest that the length and the complexity of sentence structure continue to be a prominent feature in the text under scrutiny, as frequently described by scholars dealing with English legal discourse and genre (Gustafsson 1975; Bhatia 1993; Tiersma 1999; Hiltunen 2001; Gotti 2003). Where intricate patterns of coordination and subordination leading to rule specification are avoided in favour of simple sentences, the latter bring their own benefit by expressing only one idea, thus facilitating the understanding of the rule or procedure in a single reading. However, simplicity of expression holds only as a principle when the general content of the rule/procedure requires.

In an attempt to visualise the four types of sentences combined by clauses of different types, reference is made to the basic building blocks of English sentence structure rules as identified in traditional grammars (e.g. Yule 2006). Although these blocks generally occur in ordinary English discourse, they appear to accommodate the sentence structure and inherent intricacy of current legal discourse. To illustrate, simple sentences intrude into the text with a single clause which contains only one predicate about the subject, as in:

(6) The claimant shall present evidence to support its claim.

Compound sentences also occur, such as:

(7) *In Mediation, the neutral mediator assists the parties in reaching a settlement* but does not have the authority to make a binding decision or award.

Complex sentences are also common. In this context of rule structure, the different frequencies of *if* (101), *unless* (35), *when* (13), *where* (11), and *whenever* (2) subordinating conjunctions, explaining the adverbial meaning of the clause, add to those of other adverbial or prepositional clauses, such as *subject to* (6), and *prior to* (11), thus totalling a high number of occurrences (173). Although *if*-adverbial clauses rank high in the frequency list, and are occasionally rephrased by the conventionally legal conjunction *provided that* (3) in final position, the list of adverbial clauses is found primarily in initial pre-main clause position to provide 'initial case descriptions' (Bhatia 1994: 144-146) of the relevant rule or procedure. As part of qualifications, such clause patterns are used to set out conditions, case, or exceptions (*unless*) to be satisfied there. Thus we read:

(8) If the agreement of the parties names an arbitrator or specifies a method of appointing an arbitrator, *that designation or method shall be followed.*

In a context where pre-positioned clause patterns (qualifications) also tend naturally to develop the information encoded in the previous text of the rule or procedure, their predominant structural placing accounts for their main function (in grammatical terms) as initial focus of the whole sentence (Quirk *et al.* 1985: 491), or in a similar way as setting the framework for the proposition of the sentence (Chafe 1976: 50-51). In general, this semantic function is accompanied by the tendency of drafters to avoid too much by way of adverbial clause (case/ condition), possibly because excessive initial case descriptions would be detrimental to the imposition of duties and acquisition of rights among public users in the current text. After all, this text is based on the overall mission of ADR which strives to ensure that the AAA's services are fair, expedient and cost-effective. However, as we discuss the drafters' tendency towards exploiting initial case descriptions within which the rules and procedures are confined, the semantic role of the initial adverbials would also imply a particular reader's perception and interpretation of the message, as it helps the reader in arriving at the conclusion as to whether the rules/procedures are applicable in scope. Conversely, case descriptions placed at the end of the rule/procedure would only seem to make the focus on adverbial qualifications less prominent. As such, as we argued earlier, they are intended to restrict the scope of the rule/procedure immediately preceding, as an introduction to any other part of the sentence. However, the exploiting of other initial case descriptions, such as *Before proceedings are ... / At the request of ... / Upon receipt of ... / Immediately after ...*, which equally explain the adverbial meaning of the clause (such as with an adverbial of time), only plays a marginal role. The same holds for the single instance of the literary inversion structure of the modal *should*, with contingency value (i.e. referring to a more remote possible future event), which deviates from the specificity of case descriptors realised in the form 'If there is' or 'Where there is':

(9) *Should there be* a failure to confirm in writing any such oral notice, the proceeding shall nevertheless be valid [...].

Finally, compound-complex sentences intrude into the text with "three or more clauses joined by both coordinating and subordinating conjunctions" (Yule 2006: 12), as in:

(10) *The parties shall be deemed to have made these rules a part of their arbitration agreement* whenever they have provided for arbitration by the American Arbitration Association (hereinafter AAA) under its Commercial Arbitration Rules or for arbitration by the AAA of a domestic commercial dispute without specifying particular rules.

Although the majority of sentence types, as described, indicate that consideration is given to divisions of the rules/procedures by clauses or paragraphing, there is only one instance which provides an exception to the conventionalised use of division. This instance, astonishingly consisting of 110 words, illustrates the difficulty in reading the single rule expressed in a single paragraph:

(11) No party and no one acting on behalf of any party shall communicate ex parte with an arbitrator or a candidate for arbitrator concerning the arbitration, except that a party, or someone acting on behalf of a party, may communicate ex parte with a candidate for direct appointment pursuant to Section R-12 in order to advise the candidate of the general nature of the controversy and of the anticipated proceedings and to discuss the candidate's qualifications, availability, or independence in relation to the parties or to discuss the suitability of candidates for selection as a third arbitrator where the parties or party-designated arbitrators are to participate in that selection.

The density of information encoded in this highly compound-complex type of sentence presents difficulties for the reader, whether lay or expert, principally by the use of conjoined or disjoined propositions and avoiding paragraphing which might act to make the rule clearer and enable its content to be more easily accessed. Here Bhatia's (1993) claim for 'easified' sentences might have made the rule above more accessible to such readers, while at the same time ensuring the integrity of rule specification.[7] In the realm of complex sentence structure, the frequency of the word *that*, occurring in a total number of 69 elements, is used to introduce a noun clause or a relative clause. In the former case (noun clause), accounting for 45 instances, most representative examples include *that* as described below:

(a) after a verb or noun: *To ensure that you have the most current information, ... / ... the presumption that hearing will proceed ...;*
(b) as an object after a verb: *We agree that ...;*
(c) in a list for a series of linked ideas or alternatives to present complex information: *We further agree that we ..., that we ..., and that ..;*
(d) as a subject or object: *The fact that a party had or had not ...;*
(e) in phrases: *In the event that a party disagrees ... .*

In relative clauses, *which* (31 times) and *who* (11 times) are used instead, including *where* and *when* after nouns for places or time. In this context, drafters occasionally provide a neat dichotomy between restrictive and non-restrictive clauses. Restrictive modifiers are used three times in *that*-clause form:

(12) Information *that a party wishes to keep confidential* may be sent to the mediator [...].

Non-restrictive *which*-clauses are introduced in two instances, where they occur in the middle of the sentence and separated by commas. Although these clauses are not essential to understanding the sentence, since they provide additional information about the subject or object by serving a parenthetical function, their use leads to a further outcome when they are measured against the genre-based view of writing. This result is easy to perceive by the clauses which allow for some degree of syntactic discontinuity to arise between the subject

7 Any such effort would have also brought into focus the arguments for plain language drafting (by the Plain English Movement), now being almost universal among legal practitioners, including US drafters.

and the verbal form. However, the focus on all-inclusiveness will justify such a discontinuity as will (from a different analytical perspective) the parenthetical function served by such clauses.

However, there are occasions when drafters tend to be rather obsolete in the use of the *which+noun* relative clauses, used three times in the text, as in:

(13) The initiating party (the 'claimant') shall, within the time period, if any, specified in the contract(s), give to the other party (the 'respondent') written notice of its intention to arbitrate (the 'demand'), *which demand* shall contain a statement setting forth the nature of the dispute, the names and addresses.

However, drafters convert the *which+noun* relative clause into separate sentences on specific occasions. The result is that they produce shorter sentences within single rules or procedures, as shown in (14) and (15). Here, drafters develop the sequence of thematic and rhematic items of the information (Halliday 1985: 38), so that the Rheme in one sentence usually becomes the (developed) Theme in the following sentence by repeating the rhematic item, as in (14), or by using spatial deixis realised exclusively in the form of determiners, such as *this* and *that*, as in (15):

(14) The mediator shall conduct the mediation based on the principle of *party self-determination. Self-determination* is the act of coming to a voluntary, uncoerced decision in which each party makes free and informed choices as to process and outcome.

(15) The cost of mediation is based on the *hourly mediation rate* published on the mediator's AAA profile. *This* rate covers both mediator compensation and an allocated portion for the AAA's services.

In regard to the eleven instances of restrictive *who*-clauses, five of them reveal a different degree of syntactic discontinuity arising when the clause does not immediately follow its grammatical subject but is embedded. To illustrate, example (16) is one in which the short quailficational insertion (i.e. the subordinating conjunction being very slightly distanced from the verbal form) is easy to absorb in terms of content. By contrast, the case in (17) shows that two conjoined relative clauses have been inserted between the subject and the verbal form, thus being separated by 29 words. As a result, the complex-compound sentence structure, including the binomial device (*any provision or requirement of these rules*), ostensibly creates more problems in processing the text.

(16) Section R-18(a) does not apply to arbitrators directly appointed by the parties who, *pursuant to Section R-17(a)*, have agreed in writing are non-neutral.

(17) *Any party* who proceeds with the arbitration after knowledge that any provision or requirement of these rules has not been complied with and who fails to state an objection in writing *shall be deemed to have waived the right to object.*

However, some rules are not relativised with the *who* pronoun, which is omitted in place of the gerund, as in the following:

(18) The parties shall ensure that appropriate representatives of each party, *having authority to consummate a settlement*, attend the mediation conference.

This strategy of not marking a relative clause within a complex sentence is recorded in three other instances using the present participle (*A party intending to be represented ...*).

4.4. Embedded clauses

The section above has already given an indication of 'qualificational insertions within their syntactic boundaries' (Bhatia 1994: 146) which, as we have seen, arise from the legal requirement of making the discoursal structure of sentences generally intricate. The following are the most observable cases of syntactic discontinuities recorded in the text:

(a) within the main verbal phrase (10): *The parties may, upon receiving disclosure of actual or potential conflicts of interest of the mediator, waive such conflicts ... / The initiating party (the "claimant") shall, within the time period, if any, specified in the contract(s), give to the other party (the "respondent") written notice ... / ... the AAA shall, unless the parties agree otherwise, conduct ... /... the party may, if it so desires, make the appointment*. Here, a different cognitive processing of information is presented by the number of inserted words, ranging from a minimum of three to 13;

(b) within the binomial or multinomial structure, including *if*-conditional clauses (6): *The award shall be made promptly by the arbitrator and, unless otherwise agreed by the parties or specified by law, no later that 30 days from the date of closing the hearing, or, if oral hearings have been waived, from the date* ...; including cases where discontinuity arises from the present participle (*arising out*), placed after the noun (which has the same 'identifying' function as a relative clause), and the second and third use of *or* inclusive conjunction in multinomial structure (*or relating ..., or the breach thereof*), both of them separating the binomial styled subject (*Any controversy or claim*) from the *shall* verbal phrase (*Any controversy or claim arising out of or relating to this contract, or the breach thereof, shall be settled by arbitration ...*);

(c) within non-restrictive clauses (2) and *who*-relative clauses (5), as already noted.

4.5. Binomials and multinomials

This all-inclusive effect is also conventionally achieved in the form of the use of bi- and multinomials (Gustafsson 1975, 1984; Quirk *et al.* 1985; Bhatia 1993; Hiltunen 2001), realised in syntactic structures with *and* parallel coordination (95) and *or* alternative coordination (118). Such figures reflect the favour for alternative coordination in the current genre, as also found in previously investigated legal texts on similar topics (Garzone 2003: 202-203; Giannoni 2003: 231-234).

The difference in frequency can be seen in the use of bi- and multinomials connecting a string of words placed in a semantic relationship of (near) synonymy, antonomy, or complementarity, the latter semantic relation holding only when the expression is intended to cover maximum ground with the whole meaning conveyed by the binomial (Gustafsson 1975: 102-103). The most common examples include: *actual and potential conflicts*; *final and binding determination; impartial and independent arbitrator; claim and counterclaim; admissibility, relevance and materiality of the evidence; immediate and irreparable loss or damage; The AAA shall establish and maintain a National Roster of Commercial Arbitrators; Any award shall be in writing and signed by; Large, Complex Commercial cases shall be heard and determined by; necessary or proper party; any remedy or relief that the arbitrator deems just and equitable; necessary or desirable; null and void; any error, act or omission; including interim, interlocutory or partial rulings, orders and awards; with respect to the existence, scope or validity of the arbitration agreement; person or persons; terms, conditions, features or choices; any new or different claim; such steps as they may deem necessary or desirable to avoid delay; Any party may be represented by counsel or other authorized representative*.

In addition, the difference can be seen in the use of *or*-bi/multinomials connecting several clauses in a sentence, as in (19), where the constituents of simple coordination can be *if*-clauses rather than two words which are syntactically coordinated and semantically related. As a result of this use, *or*-bi/multinomials show the effect of setting out all-inclusively two alternative cases and conditions that must be fulfilled in order for the rule to become operative:

(19) If the parties fail to agree on any of the mediators listed, *or* if acceptable mediators are unable to serve, *or* if for any other reason the appointment cannot be made from the submitted list, the AAA shall have the authority to make the appointment from among other members of the Panel of Mediators without the submission of additional lists.

Where the fulfillment is one of three alternative cases or conditions, the latter are set out in an enumerative sequence of multiple coordination of clauses and noun phrases in *or*-multinomial type, using the paragraphing format. This format reveals the logical structure of the sentence at a glance:

(20) The mediation shall be terminated:
i. By the execution of a settlement agreement by the parties; *or*

ii. By a written or verbal declaration of the mediator to the effect that further efforts at mediation would not contribute to a resolution of the parties' dispute; *or*
iii. By a written or verbal declaration of all parties to the effect that the mediation proceedings are terminated; *or*
iv. When there has been no communication between the mediator and any party or party's representative for 21 days following the conclusion of the mediation conference.

Although *or*-multinomials are used only marginally (2 instances) in paragraphing format, as is *and*-multinomial type (2 instances), setting out cumulative conditions/cases in a similar format, the general tendency of drafters is to provide *and/or* bi- and multinomials outside the paragraphing system. However, further opportunies do arise from the genre, as shown in (21):

(21) By agreement of the parties *and/or* order of the arbitrator(s), the pre-hearing activities and the hearing procedures that will govern the arbitration will be memorialized in a Scheduling and Procedure Order.

Here the expression *and/or*, found in eight instances in the text, is suggestive of a contradictory effect arising from the rule. This effect can be perceived in the use of *and*, which normally implies a conjunctive reading, combined with *or*, which normally implies a disjunctive reading. Despite the danger of ambiguity arising from such readings, it is more likely than not that drafters were guided by the need to cover all possible scenarios, so that the expression becomes one of a complementarity relationship within the *and/or*-binomial clause, as mentioned.

4.6. The use of modal auxiliaries

As shown in Table 4, central modal verbs intrude into the text to express the legal effect of the rules and procedures under scrutiny. The quantitative data reveal that there are mainly two levels of deontic/ prescriptive force, ranging from the most frequently used modal auxiliary *shall* (211 – 50.47%) followed by the second most frequent modal *may* (124 – 29.66%). While the incidence of *shall* alone reflects similar data reported by Gotti (2008: 238), in regard to "the frequent employment of this auxiliary in the UNCITRAL texts", the heavy incidence of deontic *shall* and *may* taken together (335 – 80.14%) also reflects the frequency data reported by other scholars (e.g. Belotti 2003: 26-28; Dossena 2003: 104-107; Garzone 2003: 203-208), investigating arbitration statutes and rules, and by this author (Tessuto 2003: 347-348) reporting modals in qualitative terms.

CAN	10	2.39%
COULD	2	0.48%
MAY	124	29.66%
MIGHT	3	0.72%
MUST	11	2.63%
SHALL	211	50.47%
SHOULD	5	1.20%
WILL	49	11.72%
WOULD	3	0.72%

Table 4. Occurrences and percentages of central modal verbs in the text.

As part of the deonticity analysis, however, attention will also be given to the use of *must* (11 – 2.63%), as well as *will* (49 – 11.72%), which provides food for thought on account of its incidence and specificity of use in the current text. Other central modals will be left out of the current analysis in that they are the least frequent in the text and are not relevant to the thrust of this analysis.

4.6.1. Shall

Considering that only two instances of 'definition rules' (Gunnarsson 1984: 84) are recorded in the text, where present simple is used, it is often the case that the modal *shall* is found in 'action rules' and 'stipulation rules' (Gunnarsson 1984: 84), where it occurs more in active than passive constructions, in third persons singular and plural. As shown in the example below, the 'core' semantic function of this modal, in positive and negative contexts, is that of imposing or negating a duty/obligation in an imperative sense, and has deontic force (e.g.

Coates 1983; Quirk *et al.* 1985; Leech 1987; Palmer 1990, 2001; Bybee/Fleischman 1995; Gotti/Dossena 2001; Huddleston/Pullum 2002):

(22) All expenses of the mediation, including required traveling and other expenses or charges of the mediator, *shall* be borne equally by the parties unless they agree otherwise. The expenses of participants for either side *shall* be paid by the party requesting the attendance of such participants.

Given its distinctive value of conveying both obligation and futurity (Gotti 2001: 93), often in 'agent-oriented modality' (Bybee/ Fleischman 1995: 5), it is hardly surprising that the modal is used in many rules and procedures in which there is a manifest intent to detail the procedural steps in the private resolution process, by directing counsels to parties and the parties themselves to perform in the specified manner. As a consequence, this intent allows for the rules and procedures often to acquire a 'directory' function, "requiring a certain course to be taken but imposing no sanction for breach" (Butt/Castle 2001: 150).[8] We are aware of the difficulties involved when seeking to identify whether *shall* is intended to be imperative or directory in function, because of the generality and attendant confusion arising from the imperative-directory dichotomy of the law which, in sociological terms, always reflects the pervasiveness of 'rules' in constantly setting requirements and standards in human conduct. Despite this difficulty, the regulatory nature of the genre will determine that instances of directory *shall* are the result of the role played by the

8 In the current analysis, the label attached to 'directory' reflects the discussions made by linguists (Šarčevic 2000: 138; Williams 2005: 46-48) and legal experts (Butt/Castle 2001: 150), who provide a neat dichotomy between 'mandatory' and 'directory' *shall* provisions. Although it should be admitted that the difference in terminology is purely legalistic, deriving from English law, the argument made by this author for 'directory' rather than 'mandatory' (i.e. leading to sanctions) *shall* also arises from the word 'sanction' and others with similar meanings being completely absent from the text. This means that, when sanctions are specified (e.g. by payment of fees and costs related to mediation, empowering the mediator to suspend mediation, preclusion of court hearing in arbitration, etc.), they are to be found in state or federal laws – most notably the Federal Arbitration Act (which the AAA most notably refers to).

AAA in providing administrative support from filing to closing disputes, where logically the deontic meaning is also implied.

In the text analysed here, the *shall* modal intrudes in the conventionalised drafting system of inserting qualifications within the main verb phrase, where the modal is used to qualify the legal action (*within the time period, if any, specified in the contract(s) / at the time of any such filing*). Equally, the modal intrudes in conjunction with the conventional 'deeming' device (i.e. 'consider', 'determine'), occurring 25 times in the text in modalised as well as indicative constructions with prescriptive value. As a legal fiction created by the law, the device serves a useful function of allowing a US public court to dispose of an arbitration matter. Quite surprisingly, however, the text is indicative of only one instance shown below in which the use of the *shall* modal in the conditional clause would seem to be the verbal equivalent of the present simple construction:

(23) If any mediator *shall* become unwilling or unable to serve, the AAA <u>will</u> appoint another mediator, unless the parties agree otherwise, in accordance with section M-4.

In terms of its semantic function, the modal *shall* seems to add no deonticity to the proposition since it is used to mark a futurity, as *will* does in ordinary English language, so that the *shall* construction sounds somewhat dysfunctional allowing confusion and ambiguity to creep into the procedural rule. As will be discussed below concerning the *will* form, this rule would seem to be the equivalent of 'If any mediator becomes unwilling or unable to serve, the AAA shall appoint another mediator ...' . Apart from subordination, however, a similar dysfunctional *shall* can be found occasionally in instances where it is used twice in passive constructions in the same sentence:

(24) Parties to an arbitration under these rules <u>shall</u> be deemed to have consented that *neither the AAA nor any arbitrator* <u>*shall*</u> *be liable to* any party in any action for damages or injunctive relief for any act or omission in connection with any arbitration under these rules.

Here, considering that the meaning of 'responsible by law' conveyed by the adjective *liable* reiterates the idea of an obligation implied in *shall*, the latter verbal phrase may perhaps have been avoided in this context. Here, the use of *shall* with negative subjects would reasonably be the plain alternative drafting of *will be liable* or *is liable* clauses.

4.6.2. *Must*

The large majority of finite verb forms in the text are modalised by *shall*, which is certainly more characteristic of a formal, conventionalised legal English than, for example, the indicative form (Garzone 2001: 169). The latter accounts only for a total of 13 occurrences with performative value, in both present and present perfect simple, outside subordinating clauses. Where *must* is concerned, this modal is still a notable marker of deonticity with regard to the source imposing the obligation, but has gained little ground in the current rules and procedures, on account of its low incidence (11). To illustrate this use, we consider the example in (25), in which the modal *must* does not appear to imply any distinction from *shall* in terms of obligation, and presumably indicates drafters wishing to use it as a result of the overuse of *shall* in the text:[9]

(25) The product or service *must* be for personal or household use.

In other instances, however, the deontic effect of the rule or procedure revolves around different modal forms, as in:

(26) The application <u>shall</u> also set forth the reasons why the party is entitled to such relief. Such notice may be given by facsimile transmission, or other reliable means, but *must* include a statement certifying that all other parties have been notified or an explanation of the steps taken in good faith to notify other parties.

---

9 Outside arbitration statutes and rules, however, it may be useful to note some of the recent developments reported by Williams (2007: 114) in regard to "a reduced use of *shall* and an increase in *must*" in UK recently re-drafted laws".

In this context, the use of *must* would seem to reinforce, still in a directory future sense, the idea of obligation already conveyed by directory *shall* form.

4.6.3. May

The modal *may* is used only in positive contexts of action or stipulation rules, and confers a deontic discretionary power, privilege, or a right, as in:

(27) A claim or counterclaim *may* be increased in amount, or a new or different claim or counterclaim added, upon the agreement of the other party, or the consent of the arbitrator.

Apart from the modal often alternating with other modal forms in the same sentence, it is useful to point out that there are marginal cases (5) in which different language choices appear in present simple passive constructions to denote discretionary meanings. In example (28), the context of what is being said in the first sentence using *may* suggests that the verb phrase *is not empowered* negates a discretionary act (prohibition), and is a clearer, more definite paraphrase of the alternative *may not* deontically constructed sentence:

(28) Within 20 days after the transmittal of an award, any party, upon notice to the other parties, may request the arbitrator, through the AAA, to correct any clerical, typographical, or computational errors in the award. The arbitrator *is not empowered* to redetermine the merits of any claim already decided. The other parties shall be given 10 days to respond to the request. The arbitrator shall dispose of the request within 20 days after transmittal by the AAA to the arbitrator of the request and any response thereto.

Similarly, the context of the procedural rule in (29), suggests that the phrase *is authorised* is a clearer, more definite paraphrase of the alternative *may* deontic sentence, also for discretionary acts.

(29) The mediator *is authorized* to conduct separate or ex parte meetings and other communications with the parties and/or their representatives, before, during, and after any scheduled mediation conference. Such communications may be conducted via telephone, in writing, via email, online, in person or otherwise.

As a result of the modal meanings of 'power' and 'authorisation' being made more explicit by the expressions used, the latter at least may have the advantage of reducing the problem of semantic indeterminacy intensified by an epistemic reading of the *may* rule ('possibly will').

4.6.4. Will

To illustrate the distinctive value of *will* in the text, we begin with example (37), examined earlier, which encodes the formal statements intended to become operational in a Standard Arbitration clause for later inclusion in commercial contracts.

(30) We, the undersigned parties, hereby agree to submit to arbitration administered by the American Arbitration Association under its Commercial Arbitration Rules the following controversy: (describe briefly) We further agree that the above controversy be submitted to (one) (three) arbitrator(s). We further agree that we will faithfully observe this agreement and the rules, that we will abide by and perform any award rendered by the arbitrator(s), and that a judgment of any court having jurisdiction may be entered on the award.

In a context where the clause illustrates explicit performativity with formal *hereby* in present simple first plural active form, and carries over the next two sentences, the repeated use of *will* (2) in the first plural person retains, as a marker of futurity, the modal meanings of firm volition or intention. Nonetheless, by denoting the free will of the parties to abide by their contractual 'promises', the meaning of willingness expressed by the modal comes to imply duties and obligations being laid down externally on the parties by law.

In the remaining instances of *will* (47), the modal seems to go beyond the mere concept of willingness or prediction. Drawing on Leech's (1987: 86) notion of 'authority over addressee' conveyed by *will*, this notion is enhanced by the nature of the genre we are dealing with, in which the nature of the prescription involves a duty, permission, power or other authority, so that the modal provides no exception to the idea of a deontic prediction about future actions or events. As a result, and particularly when the modal co-occurs with other modality expressions, such as in example (31), predictive *will* would seem to instantiate the modal phrase *may apply*, as a deontic alternative, though more indeterminate than the original, and *shall/must state* in (32), in which the co-occurence with the verb 'require', meaning 'specifying as compulsory', would arguably imply more or less the same deontic strength as *shall/must*:

(31) The AAA *will* have the discretion to apply or not to apply the Supplementary Procedures and the parties ... .

(32) Where a monetary claim amount is not known, parties *will* be required to state a range of claims or be subject to the highest possible filing fee.

Where these variants are admitted, and despite the extremely persuasive arguments that "resort to *will* is quite unusual in legal English" (Garzone 2003: 208) or, similarly, that obligatory *will* is "relatively rare in prescriptive texts" where "*shall* is normally used" (Williams 2005: 133), the frequency of the modal (47) in the current text cannot be ignored, and would seem to open up two different hypotheses. Firstly, American drafters tend to categorise predictive *will* with deontic meanings in less formal terms than their British counterparts, using more *shall*, *may* or *must* specialised forms. Secondly, the context of the rule/procedure requires drafters to disregard specialised forms (possibly because of the resulting indeterminacy), by means of the care they take to avoid a strong, less-transparent effect on the disputing parties and their needs. This may be accounted for by the notion of fair and expedient ADR processes and the 'private' issue of costs and fees, with the latter assuming prominence in private, informal ADRs in common law jurisdictions.[10] Although both hypotheses may be controversial, my interpretation leans towards the former hypothesis, a position also justified by the differences related to the

---

10 The important issue of lower costs and fees in 'private'-based ADR is at the heart of mediation, which is inexpensive, and arbitration, which is cost-effective. Issacharoff, an American professor of procedural jurisprudence, reports that "ADR procedures are typically much more informal than litigation under the Federal Rules. [...] Moreover, the procedures *can be tailored to the needs of the litigants*, and range from mediation to more formalized arbitration" (2005: 168, my italics).

cultural values of the two English-speaking communities. American English uses *will* in many situations with a sense of strong determination, thus tending to be more direct and vivid, as in the current text, whereas British English has a tendency to a more disciplined, consistent use of modals.

In any case, the extent to which American *will* in the current genre shifts to a less visible deontic strength than specialised forms, does not seem to compromise the efficacy and equity of the commercial rules and procedures as far as their US audience is concerned. Where, however, such rules and procedures are geared towards an international audience, as is precisely the case of the Centre for Dispute Resolution, then the American use of the modal form may have the effect of compromising the efficacy and equity of ADR processes and procedures as perceived by a global audience from different backgrounds.

4.7. Lexicon: vague and ambiguous words

From a lexical point of view, we may note problems with ambiguous and vague words leading to uncertainty in the text. Whether defined under the two separate concepts of ambiguity and vagueness, characterising the comprehensive notion of semantic indeterminacy (Bhatia *et al.* 2005: 12), or as traditionally linked to hedging (e.g. Lakoff 1973; Channell 1994; Hyland 1998), instances of vague and ambiguous lexical items are usually found to occur in adjectival, adverbial, or phrasal form, including evaluative standards (such as, *as soon as practicable, award is appropriate, fair opportunity, the award shall be made promptly, necessary measures, as promptly as practicable, on proof satisfactory to it, good cause, good faith, reasonable costs, reasonable inquiry, any circumstance likely to give rise to justifiable doubt*). Of these, it is telling that the abstract and broad concept of *good faith* has become part of different legal discourses and genres in which they have no technical meaning or statutory definition either, whether or not in the US law.

In a context where nominalisations, understood as a requirement for all-inclusiveness (Bhatia 1993: 148), also intrude by the use of nominal items, few opportunities arise from the text in which lexical verbs with modal meaning are also used (such as, *the arbitrator determines as appropriate, the AAA shall as an administrative practice suggest to the parties, that the arbitrator considers that*). The lexical types so observed occur, on average, in every three or four rules/procedures, and are used invariably to refer to AAA, arbitrators, mediators and the parties for whom they provide a degree of choice so that defensible behaviour may proceed in the mediation and arbitration processes and the courts. Whatever the degree of the choice conferred by the regulatory genre, in pragmatic terms, the exploration and attribution of purposes to vague and ambiguous words remain vital for the integrity of the rules and procedures. As is typical of a variety of legal texts, including the legislative, the text is not exempt from the vague, legalistic use of the word *such ... as* occurring in 16 instances, as in:

(33) The arbitrator shall require the party who is present to submit *such* evidence *as* the arbitrator may require for the making of an award.

Here, it seems reasonable that the use of the word in this and other examples detracts from the clarity of the rule or procedure, and therefore creates potential ambiguity. This use adds to the many instances (48 times) in which *such* is mostly used anaphorically to refer to its nearest antecedent. It therefore lessens the danger of ambiguity arising from such rule/procedure.

4.8. Technical terms

As part of the nature and purpose of the text, we note the use of keywords as technical terms which are intended to prevail over any ordinary meaning they may otherwise have. In fact, efforts are made by the AAA to provide a list of such terms in the form of an Arbitration Glossary annexed to the text: *claimant, respondent, ADR process, arbitration, desk arbitration, telephone hearing, in person hearing, mediation, neutral, case manager, ADR agreement, ADR program, independent ADR institution*. Unlike the proper legislative drafting format, where definition sections are used, this glossary is meant to substitute for such sections, except when the current regulatory format provides intra-clause definition of the term *arbitrator* (referring to the arbitration panel composed of one or more arbitrators: R-3) to leave no doubt in the mind of the reader.

By defining, for instance, the terms *claimant* and *respondent* as the disputing parties, the text is explicit about the parties who are identified as either the *consumer* or the *business*. Indeed, as a result of the claimant filing the *claim* and the respondent stating a *counterclaim* in arbitration proceedings, these procedural terms intrude into the text with variable frequency (*claim*: 54 – *counterclaim*: 32), where they are left undefined because they are terms of international use intruding in a variety of written legal genres. Apart from linguistic features, the difference in the frequency between the two terms can be said to lie in *counterclaim* occurring less in ADR process and procedure, since a respondent is given a choice whether or not to reply against the other party with a *counterclaim*.

4.8.1. Technical terms versus ordinary language words

In a context where ordinary language choices alternate with technical terms, the text reveals that the lion's share in such a frequency is occupied by the ordinary English word *dispute*, occurring 65 times, including one instance in which it co-occurs synonymously with *claim* (*dispute or claim*). The ordinary word *controversy*, occurring only six times, is also found to be used as a synonym of *dispute*, whether or not in collocation with *claim*. The ordinary words *demand* (9 times) and *answer* (10) are used as lexical variants of *claim* and *counterclaim*, respectively, with the latter (*answer*) also occurring in *answering statement* modifying structure (9 times). Where neither *claimant* nor *respondent* is mentioned, the verb choice referred to both parties becomes *assert*, used three times in indicative forms (*If a counterclaim is asserted / The party asserting such a claim or counterclaim / a statement of issues asserted by each party*) in neutral collocations with *claim* or *counterclaim*.

4.8.2. Latin terms

As a result of legal tradition, Latin terms are still but only marginally to be found in the text. Of these terms, the adjective *interim* (provisional, temporary) occurs in first place (14) to qualify various nouns (*relief, measures, awards, orders, rulings*). This is followed by the much lower frequency of the term *ex parte* (3), used as an adjective and adverb to refer to the interests of one side in arbitration, or with respect to their interests; and the term *subpoena* (in its extended form *subpoena ad testificandum*), used two times either as a plural noun (*issuance of subpoenas*) or as a verb (*to subpoena witnesses*), in relation to an arbitrator compelling the appearance and testimony of witnesses in a public court.

While it is true that the virtue of legal latinity – which has endured through time in English language – is to give pleasing resonances towards conservative legal writing, it has the effect of meeting the integrity requirement of writing in terms of generic conventions. Further, this point leads to its closest relative in the analysis of lexical conventions: archaic terms.

4.8.3. Archaic terms

Although often criticised by Plain Language proponents, who favour modern English equivalents, antiquated words formed by adverb and preposition slip naturally into the text where they only play a marginal role. Of the terms listed in Table 5, the relatively higher incidence of *thereof* (6) occurs three times in the annexed Arbitration and Mediation clauses and three times in the rules and procedures, where it is dotted across the text.

Hereby	3
Hereinafter	1
Thereby	1
Therefore	1
Therein	1
Thereof	6
Thereto	3

Table 5. Type and number of occurrences of archaic words.

Thus, for example:

(34) the arbitration award may be entered in any federal or state court having jurisdiction *thereof.*

As part of referential devices, the function of these legalistic terms is easy to perceive by the specific reference to a piece of information in the rule or procedure (for example: 'jurisdiction *thereof*' = 'jurisdiction over the arbitration award'), which therefore results in it being shorthand for presenting information. However, further opportunities arise from the text in which drafters tend to occasionally use spatial deixis in the form of the determiner *this*, which locates the terms of the relation of reference unambiguously in the discourse situation (*as provided in Section O-1 of this article*). Indeed, an exception to legalistic terms with referential value is provided by *therefore*, used rather as a rhetorical device expressing 'for that reason, consequently':

(35) and that such party is entitled to such relief, the emergency arbitrator may enter an interim award granting the relief and stating the reasons *therefore.*

4.8.4. Internal textual authority: complex prepositional phrases

To conclude this analysis of lexical features, the text is not imbued with complex prepositional phrases, which have long characterised legal discourse. The only such occurrences are represented by *with respect to* (5 instances) and *in accordance with* (7 instances). Although the reason for keeping these phrases is to avoid ambiguity (Bhatia 1993: 107) in favour of some legal flavouring, drafters are serious about replacing them by the simple preposition *under* (36 times), followed by the very low frequency of the preposition *by* (4). As textual-mapping devices (Bhatia 1998), these phrases and prepositions however only provide internal references to the matters being dealt with in the text (such as: Commercial Mediation Procedures, sections, arbitration agreement, disputes) rather than to other external references of any sort.

5. Conclusion

From the perspective of discourse and genre analysis, this chapter has sought to identify *US Commercial Arbitration Rules and Mediation Procedures* as an example of an administrative-regulatory genre in action, viewed as a *secondary genre* which fulfils the same prescriptive function as legislation. The chapter has focused on the discursive practices and tasks of the AAA, as an authoritative community originating the genre, and which provides the response to its own professional objectives, by codifying rules and procedures for the arrangement of mediation and arbitration to serve the interests of a national and international audience. The AAA's professional discourse practices have been examined in terms of the essential integrity of the genre as a consequence of the use of most common lexico-grammatical and discoursal features. The quantitative and qualitative analyses of the data have shown that the genre maintains, in both macro and micro-level features, its required integrity and identity in the US law. Such features are not dissimilar to those reported in previously investigated texts on national/international arbitration rules and statutes influenced by the Common Law drafting system.

In relation to legislative writing, an attempt has been made to identify a recognisable standard for the regulatory genre in terms of textual structure and level of shared generic integrity with legislative writing. Despite some noticeable differences in textual organisation between the legislative and regulatory genres, similarities between the two have been found to work significantly at various textual levels involving the 'scope' of the rules (the case/conditions under which the rule applies). These include the complex range of qualifications, in mainly initial positions (embedded clauses), and the use of bi/multinomials, all of which act within the dominant structure of sentences created by various intricate patterns of coordination and subordination. Although the meaning of the rules and procedures may sometimes become even more complex by a failure to arrange sentences in a paragraph format, as a means of fine tuning legal drafting to aid readability of the detailed contents, the genre-based function performed by such textual realisations achieves, both conventionally and pragmatically, all-inclusiveness in terms of the information provided. The effect is that they become advantageous and therefore, with no contradiction in terms, 'transparent' for counsels to parties and judges when arguing and determining parties' claims via the rules or procedures.

The 'scope' of the rules/procedures (cognitive-structural aspect) has been examined in regard to the micro-level 'character' (level of prescription) involved in their verbal formulation. Here, the analysis has shown that *shall* and *may* forms operate as the two main modal auxiliaries with deontic value that shape the integrity of the rule/procedure, in regard primarily to the directive function of *shall*. Although the dominant character of *shall/may* rules points to a similar level of shared generic integrity with normative discourse, we cannot disregard the fact that deontic prediction created by *will* also has a bearing on the prescriptive character of the rules/procedures examined. Thus, the assumption is that the incidence of formal *shall*, rather than *must* alternative, is preferred by US conservative drafters who consider the conventionalised use of the modal as having an enduring place in English legal drafting, despite the finer shades of meaning the modal may have.

Other (micro) lexical-level features have been shown to contribute, although to varying degrees, to maintaining the essential stability of the regulatory genre in the Common Law drafting philosophy. Of these, the frequency of Latin and archaic terms can be said to act only as a residual tradition of drafting in the textual conventions of such a philosophy. These items, still act as a common denominator in the philosophy of the genre, and therefore constantly maintain integrity in the expression of rules/procedures. Of course, stability in the genre is also achieved by the proportion of technical terms, the quantity and distribution of which depend upon the nature and purpose of the text. Ordinary words are unlikely to maintain the essential integrity of the genre since they result from the drafters' own choices in terms of alternating between varying ordinary lexical options in communicating the rules or procedures.

References

Bakhtin, Mikhail M. 1981. Discourse in the Novel. In Holquist, M. (ed.) *The Dialogic Imagination.* Austin. University of Texas Press, 259-435.

Belotti, Ulisse 2003. Generic Integrity in Italian Arbitration Rules. In Bhatia/Candlin/Gotti (eds), 19-40.

Bhatia, Vijay K. 1983. *An Applied Discourse Analysis of English Legislative Writing*. PhD thesis (unpublished) Birmingham: University of Aston.

Bhatia, Vijay, K. 1993. *Analysing Genre: Language Use in Professional Settings*. London: Longman.

Bhatia, Vijay K. 1994. Cognitive Structuring in Legislative Provisions. In Gibbons J. (ed.) *Language and the Law*. London: Longman, 136-155.

Bhatia, Vijay K. 1998. Intertexuality in Legal Discourse. *The Language Teacher* 22/11, 13-39.

Bhatia, Vijay K. 2004. *Worlds of Written Discourse. A Genre-based View*. London: Continuum.

Bhatia, Vijay K. / Candlin, Christopher / Engberg, Jan (eds) 2008. *Legal Discourse Across Cultures and Systems*. Hong Kong: Hong Kong University Press.

Bhatia, Vijay K. / Candlin, Christopher, N. / Gotti, Maurizio (eds) 2003. *Legal Discourse in Multilingual and Multicultural Contexts: Arbitration Texts in Europe.* Bern: Peter Lang.

Bhatia, Vijay K. / Engberg, Jan / Gotti, Maurizio / Heller, Dorothee (eds) 2005. *Vagueness in Normative Texts*. Bern: Peter Lang.

Butt, Peter / Castle, Richard 2001. *Modern Legal Drafting. A Guide to Using Clearer Language.* Cambridge: Cambridge University Press.

Bybee, Joan / Fleischman, Suzanne (eds) 1995. *Modality in Grammar and Discourse*. Amsterdam: John Benjamins.

CARMP = *Commercial Arbitration Rules and Mediation Procedures 2007*. At <http://www.adr.org/consumerarbitration>.

Chafe, Wallace L. 1976. Giveness, Contrastiveness, Definiteness, Subjects, Topics, and Point of View. In Li, Charles N. (ed.) *Subject and Topic*. New York: Academic Press, 27-55.
Channell, Joanna 1994. *Vague Language*. Oxford: Oxford University Press.
Coates, Jennifer 1983. *The Semantics of Modal Auxiliaries*. London: Croom Helm.
Dossena, Marina 2003. Arbitration in Scotland: Local Specificity and International Homegeneity. In Bhatia/Candlin/Gotti (eds), 87-109.
Garzone, Giuliana 2001. Deontic Modality and Performativity in English Legal Texts. In Gotti/Dossena (eds), 153-173.
Garzone, Giuliana 2003. Arbitration Rules across Legal Cultures: An Intercultural Approach. In Bhatia/Candlin/Gotti (eds), 177-220.
Giannoni, Davide S. 2003. The UNCITRAL Model and Italian Statute Law: A Linguistic and Topical Description. In Bhatia/Candlin/Gotti (eds), 221-246.
Gotti, Maurizio 2001. Semantic and Pragmatic Values of *Shall* and *Will* in Early Modern English Statutes. In Gotti/Dossena (eds), 89-112.
Gotti, Maurizio 2003. *Specialized Discourse. Linguistic Features and Changing Conventions*. Bern: Peter Lang.
Gotti, Maurizio 2008. Cultural Constraints on Arbitration Discourse. In Bhatia/Candlin/Engberg (eds), 221-252.
Gotti, Maurizio / Dossena, Marina (eds) 2001. *Modality in Specialized Texts*. Bern: Peter Lang.
Gunnarsson, Britt-Louise 1984. Functional Comprehensibility of Legislative Texts: Experiments with a Swedish Act of Parliament. *Text* 4/1-3, 71-105.
Gustafsson, Marita 1975. Some Syntactic Properties of English Law Language. *Publications of the Department of English* 4. Turku: University of Turku.
Gustafsson, Marita 1984. Syntactic Features of Binomial Expressions in Legal English. *Text* 4/1-3, 123-141.
Halliday, Michael A. K. 1985. *Introduction to Functional Grammar*. London: Edward Arnold.

Hiltunen, Risto 2001. Some Syntactic Properties of English Law Language. In Hiltunen, Risto / Battarbee, Keith / Peikola, Matti / Tanskanen, Sanna-Kaisa (eds) *English in Zigs and Zags: A Festscrift for Maita Gustafsson*. Anglicana Turkuensia, 23 Turku: University of Turku, 53-66.

Huddleston, Rodney / Pullum, Geoffrey K. 2002. *The Cambridge Grammar of the English Language*. Cambridge: Cambridge University Press.

Hyland, Ken 1998. *Hedging in Scientific Research Articles*. Amsterdam: John Benjamins.

Issacharoff, Samuel 2005. *Civil Procedure*. New York: The Foundation Press.

Lakoff, George 1973. Hedges: A Study in Meaning Criteria and the Logic of Fuzzy Concepts. *Journal of Philosophical Logic* 2, 458-508.

Leech, Geoffrey 1987. *Meaning and the English Verb*. London: Longman.

Palmer, Frank R. 1990. *Modality and the English Modals*. London: Longman.

Palmer, Frank R. 2001. *Mood and Modality*. Cambridge: Cambridge University Press.

Quirk, Randolph / Greenbaum, Sidney / Leech, Geoffrey / Svartvik, Jan 1985. *A Comprehensive Grammar of the English Language*. London: Longman.

Šarčević, Susan 2000. *New Approach to Legal Translation*. The Hague: Kluwer Law International.

Searle, John R. 1979. *Expression and Meaning*. Cambridge: Cambridge University Press.

Tessuto, Girolamo 2003. Legislative Discourse in Arbitration Language: The English 1996 Arbitration Act and the UNCITRAL Model Law. In Bhatia/Candlin/Gotti (eds), 337-379.

Tessuto, Girolamo 2008. Discourse Systems in English Arbitration Awards. In Bhatia/Candlin/Engberg (eds), 181-197.

Tiersma, Peter 1999. *Legal Language*. Chicago: The University of Chicago Press.

Twining, William / Miers, David 1999. *How To Do Things with Rules*. London: Butterworths.

Williams, Christopher 2005. *Tradition and Change in Legal English*. Bern: Peter Lang.

Williams, Christopher 2007. Crossovers in Legal Cultures in Westminster and Edinburgh: Some Recent Changes in the Language of the Law. *ESP Across Cultures* 4, 101-118.

Yates, Simeon J. / Sumner, Tamara R. 1997. Digital Genres and the New Burden of Fixity. In *Proceedings of the 30th Hawaii International Conference on System Sciences (HICSS 97)*, VI, 3-12.

Yule, George 2006. *Oxford Practice Grammar*. Oxford: Oxford University Press.

ALESSANDRA FAZIO*

Variation in the Juridical Language of Sports Arbitration

1. Introduction

The aim of this study is to verify whether the use of English as a lingua franca (vehicular language) in sports arbitration is different from the formal use of the specific legal terminology which, it is assumed, has already been standardized and harmonised. Italian sports arbitrators who are obliged to use English in an international setting were observed in a preliminary study. Reiterated language patterns were noticed which differed from those used by their mother-language counterparts (see for example the role of 'conciliation' procedure). Taking the language used by Italian sports arbitrators in international settings as a starting point, similar language patterns will be sought and analysed with particular emphasis on socio-cultural factors. The hypothesis is that a specific linguistic code (even an informal one) may be outlined which can affect formal patterns already in use. This analysis will be carried out not only on complex strings and terms but also on additional linguistic occurrences, in an attempt to trace underlying connections or conflicts that may influence their use.

* The research on which this chapter is based is part of an international research project entitled *International Commercial Arbitration Practices: A Discourse Analytical Study* (http://www.english.cityu.edu.hk/arbitration/), headed by prof. Vijay Bhatia of the City University of Hong Kong. It also contributes to the National Research Programme *Tension and Change in Domain-specific Genres* directed by prof. Maurizio Gotti of the University of Bergamo, funded by the Italian Ministry of University (COFIN Grant No. 2007JCY9Y9).

2. Phraseological representation of key concepts

Variation in the expression of key concepts in juridical language of sports arbitration will be carried out through corpus analysis. Two corpora were examined and compared: Court of Arbitration for Sport (CAS) awards and European Court of Justice (ECJ) judgements. Starting from CAS awards, the main area of this investigation, the objective was to study key concepts in sports arbitration and identify whether variations in comparable concepts in the ECJ could be found. In so doing, we considered the CAS awards corpus as a sort of *sub-language* which in Biber's words is "a language that operates within specific domains of use with restricted subject matter" (1995: 15). The analysis of terminology variation has been carried out considering terms and formulaic sequences (FS). By 'terms' we refer to concepts whereas by 'FS' we mean occurrences of word/term strings according to the phraseological representation of key concepts. Formulaic sequences refer to a wide range of subtypes of multi-word strings that, in Wray's words (2002: 9) are defined as

> a sequence, continuous or discontinuous, of words or other elements, which is, or appears to be, prefabricated: that is stored and retrieved whole from memory at the time of use, rather than being subject to generation or analysis by the language grammar [...].

Here the emphasis is on sequences of lexis or sequences as representation of whole logical units. However, Schmitt stresses the difficulty of defining FS due to their diversity resulting in a great variety of terminology. According to Schmitt, "formulaic sequences result in a variety of terminology to express them: chunks, collocations, multi-word units, etc. [...]" (2004: 3).

In this chapter, the interest is on concepts and underlying concepts, no matter how they are represented, and strings are examined only when they define key concepts or variations in the expression of key concepts (see examples in Section 3.1).

3. Methodology

In order to establish and analyse the phraseological representation of key concepts, two corpora (CAS awards and ECJ judgements) were collected, processed and compared. The CAS awards corpus (1994-2009) consists of 197 files (1,321,215 tokens; 19,579 types) while the ECJ corpus (2005-2009) consists of 951 files (2,620,501 tokens; 21,976 types). The quantitative analysis applied is in line with forensic linguistic research trends outlined by Mortara Garavelli (2001: 34-54). CAS awards relate to sports disputes in general. They deal mainly with the contractual and disciplinary nature of these disputes which are merely occasional and probably worth further socio-cultural insight. ECJ judgements uphold the rule of European law. The various types of proceedings are: references for preliminary rulings, actions for failure to fulfil obligations, actions for annulment, actions for failure to act, appeals and reviews.

According to Hunston (2002: 131), in forensic linguistics "corpus techniques are used particularly in comparing documents with each other, or parts of a document with other parts [...]". We collected and processed the original documents with one another, and considered the two classes – CAS awards and ECJ judgements – as comparable.

This investigation sets out to establish and highlight key concepts as they are represented in FS in the CAS corpus. In so doing, we will start from empirical investigation into data collected in the CAS index. We will successively compare key concepts from the CAS corpus to the ECJ corpus (used as a reference corpus). Statistical analysis of key concept distribution (wordlists) and key concept distribution in terms of 'keyness' (keyword list) will be carried out to avoid comparison between items without statistical significance. Formulaic sequences linked to key concepts will also be identified and retrieved. Some examples of phraseological representation of key concepts and related variation will be reported in Section 3.1.

3.1. Observations on the CAS corpus: a dual path

At first, the CAS awards corpus was compared to the CAS index established and published in the CAS Digest. The CAS index provides the periodically updated general jurisdictional terminology. The CAS Digest is a compilation of judicial activity from 1986 to 2003 entitled *Digest of CAS Awards* and published in three volumes (1986-1998: vol.I; 1998-2000: vol.II; and 2000-2003: vol.III). From an empirical observation of the CAS corpus as well as the comparison with the CAS index found in the CAS Digest, what emerges are mainly terms or term-strings[1] referred to the various different sports (i.e. duathlon), sports equipment (i.e. bodysuits), facilities (i.e. photo finish); and concepts linked to the various sports disputes.

Two main types of sports disputes emerge (respectively of a contractual and of a disciplinary nature) as shown in Figure 1.

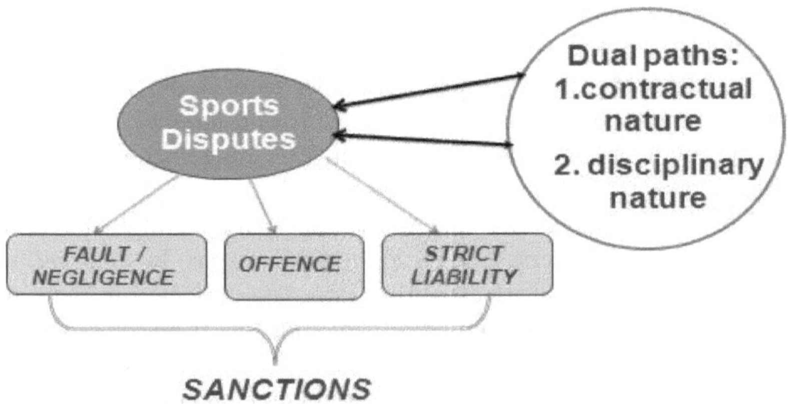

Figure 1. CAS awards dual paths.

1 Strings are often used to represent concepts that are not yet completely defined, for which simple terms are still unavailable. For example, "threshold of/ for endogenous substances", "unannounced doping control", "liability of clubs for the behaviour of their supporters", "refusal of team to play in a match".

The statistical analysis of the relevant terminological data highlighted that sports disputes concern mainly three major conceptual classes of legal principles: FAULT, OFFENCE, STRICT LIABILITY. These concepts are included in the CAS index and are, therefore, comparable.

Every CAS award includes a conceptual development leading to a final decision which, in the case of a judgment of responsibility, becomes a specific sanction. A sanction in particular is an indicator of a great difference in terms of keyness. In CAS awards the concept of SANCTION is strictly linked to a wide terminology related to different types of sanctions. This terminology is particularly interesting because it has nothing to do with juridical language of international award codes (for example, it includes concepts such as SUSPENSION, LIFE-BAN, DISQUALIFICATION, TWO-YEAR DISQUALIFICATION etc.). Figure 2 shows how CAS award dual paths become articulated.

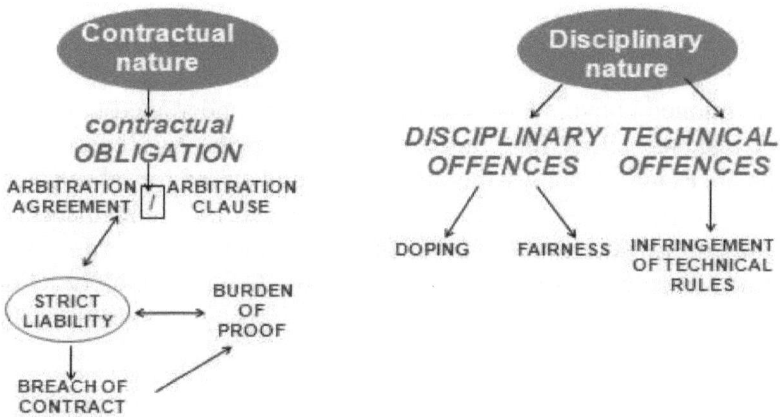

Figure 2. CAS awards dichotomy.

The different type styles in this diagram are used to indicate different functions: italics indicate juridical standardised and accepted concepts, while bold indicates recurring expressions used to identify different concepts (i.e. concept representations). Both frames reflect fundamental key concepts typical of juridical structure in the awards.

The dichotomy represented in these types of disputes is reflected in the relevant specific terminology. The contractual section is connected to the concept of OBLIGATION while the terminology expressing the concept of DISCIPLINARY INFRINGEMENT is linked to the concept of OFFENCE. In the case of OBLIGATION, the terms expressing this relationship are centered around ARBITRATION AGREEMENT / ARBITRATION CLAUSE. The frequency count of co-occurrences and the mention of keyness concur to signal this sector as highly significant (terms such as STRICT LIABILITY, BURDEN OF PROOF, BREACH OF CONTRACT are mutually interrelated). An Arbitration agreement always involves STRICT LIABILITY.

In the case of OFFENCES, terms like DOPING, FAIRNESS, TECHNICAL INFRINGEMENT emerge as highly inter-related (they are interdependent) even though the concept of DOPING statistically prevails, possibly due to contemporary sociological and historical factors (for example, that it is a global phenomenon).

3.2. Statistical analysis of the key concept distribution

As mentioned above, a statistical analysis was undertaken to establish top frequency terms for comparison between the two corpora. The graph in Figure 3 shows the statistical analysis of top absolute frequency profile in CAS awards in comparison to ECJ judgements. The results confirm the occurrence of the above mentioned terms and reveal a difference in frequency in the two lists with a clearly evident peak in the case of DOPING. The issue of frequency, as Hunston (2008: 272) points out, is not simple. In fact,

> a sequence of words that is claimed to represent something that is 'frequent' may not itself be frequent in absolute terms. This may be because the frequency is a feature of meaning elements in the sequence rather than a feature of the words themselves.

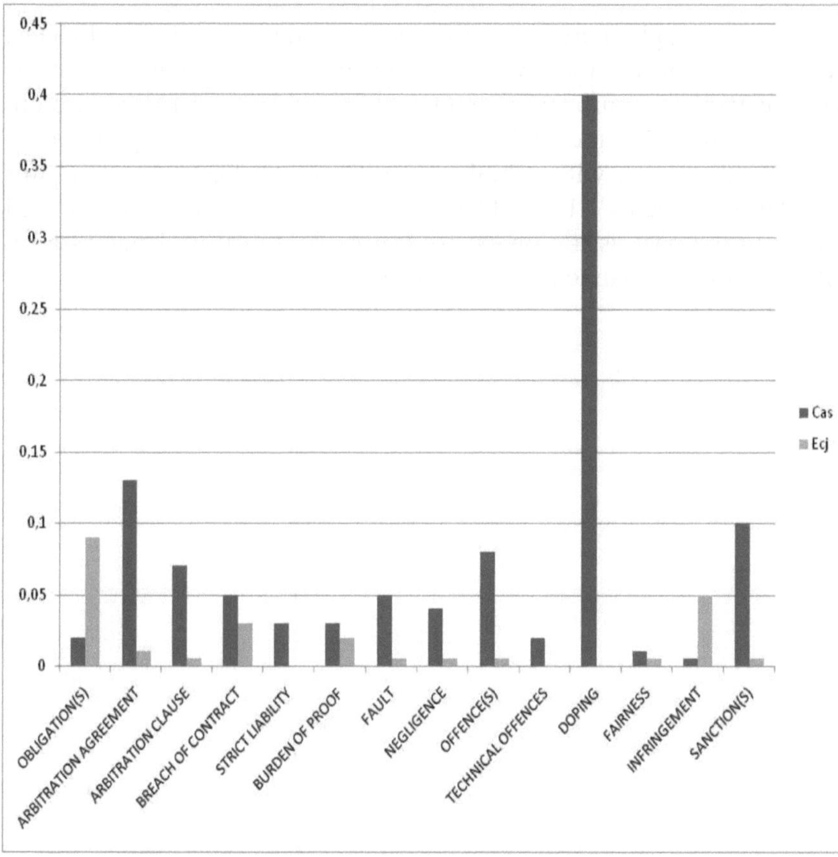

Figure 3. Comparison of key concept distribution frequency (CAS vs ECJ).

Consequently, in the graph in Figure 4, key concepts distribution is shown in terms of keyness. In the keyness analysis a substantial difference in meaning emerged. Some terms appear significant in only one corpus while others are significant in the other corpus only, thus confirming a substantial difference in the conceptual trend between the two corpora. The concepts of ARBITRATION CLAUSE, BREACH OF CONTRACT, STRICT LIABILITY, FAULT, NEGLIGENCE, OFFENCE, DOPING, FAIRNESS, SANCTIONS are representative of the CAS corpus in terms of importance and significance. The keyness distribution of ARBITRATION AGREEMENT and BURDEN OF PROOF are representative of both corpora, although there is a difference in degrees of significance. These two concepts may be compared in terms of numerical occurrence as well as significance. OBLIGATION and INFRINGEMENT are only representative of the ECJ corpus. STRICT LIABILITY is quoted only in the CAS corpus with a highly significant quotient. Actually, this term, in de Franchis' (1984: 1402) definition, once present in the ECJ corpus in the past, is no longer used in present jurisprudence as a result of a gradual change occurred throughout time.

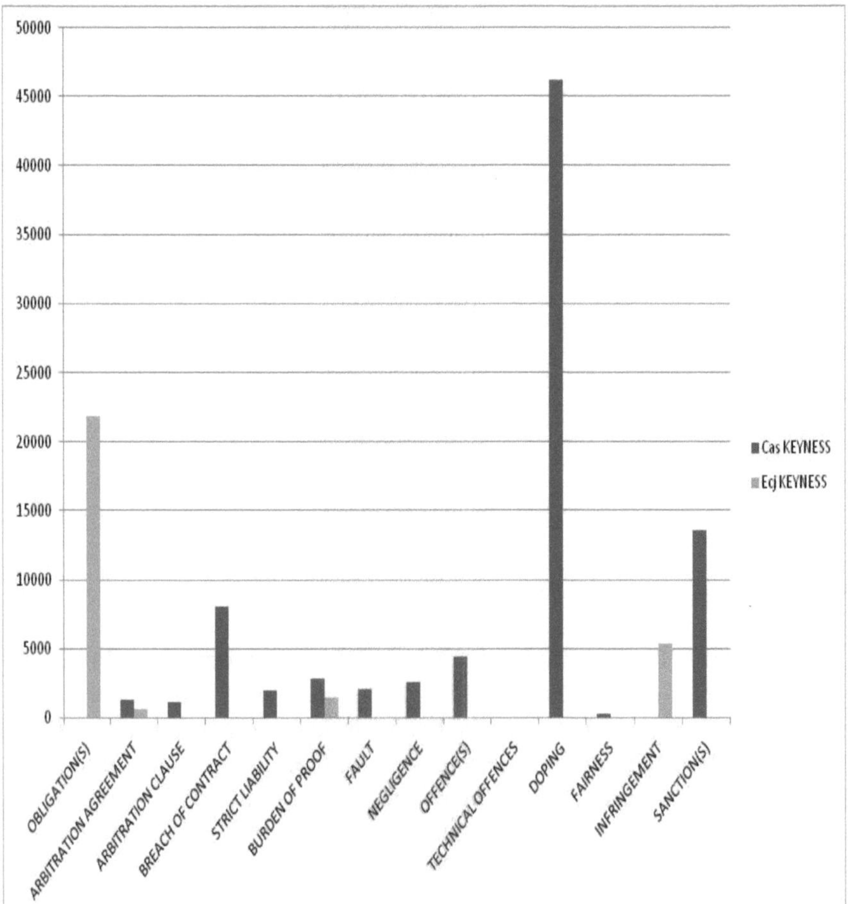

Figure 4. Comparison of key concept distribution in terms of keyness (CAS vs ECJ).

These results seem to confirm the initial hypothesis of expected variation. Not only did we expect these results to display a trend of a general difference in their conceptual specificity but also the expected deviances/diversity examined identified the differences between the two standardised legal text genres. The two peaks, OBLIGATION and DOPING, representing respectively ECJ and CAS top conceptual significance, are outstandingly relevant each for its own setting and range of influence. This relevance may be explained in terms of a trend recurrence due to prevailing sociological factors, especially DOPING.

3.3. Pros & cons of quantitative analysis

The 'pros & cons' of quantitative analysis and analysis in terms of keyness must at this point be mentioned briefly. According to Oakey 2002: 116), "corpus analysis can speed the identification of word strings in a large corpus, but traditional intuitive judgment must still play a large part in deciding whether a particular string performs a particular function". In fact, frequency gives us a global picture of concept occurrences while keyness allows the specificity of the concepts to be identified and analysed. Therefore keyness is crucial to the interpretation of the results and the identification of the formulaic sequences. Keyness may be defined as a quality that words can have in a given text, or at a given time in history, rather than in a given language, while specificity is directly related to a specific setting.

4. Examples of phraseological representation of CAS key concepts and related variation in ECJ

With regard to the concept of ARBITRATION AGREEMENT or ARBITRATION CLAUSE, it is to be noted that the variation ARBITRATION CLAUSE, although frequently occurring in the CAS, never occurs in the ECJ list, thus proving that only one of the strings is necessary for a term which is rarely used (see Table 1). In addition to this, the number of different verbal occurrences accompanying the key term is drastically reduced in the ECJ list (see Table 2).

CAS
CAS ARBITRATION
SPORTS ARBITRATION CAS
SPORTS RELATED ARBITRATION
APPEALS ARBITRATION DIVISION
THE ARBITRATION AGREEMENT
THE ARBITRATION CLAUSE
SPECIFIC ARBITRATION AGREEMENT
THE CAS APPEALS
THE PRESENT ARBITRATION
THE APPEALS ARBITRATION
THE ARBITRATION PROCEEDINGS

Table 1. Lexical variation around the concept of ARBITRATION AGREEMENT/ CLAUSE.

CAS corpus	*ECJ corpus*
WOULD APPLY/ENTAIL	IS VOID
SHALL BE GOVERNED	IS NULL
VALID	TO BE RAISED
SIGN	MUST BE RAISED
PROVIDES	IN THE COURSE
REACHED	CONTAINS
ENTERED	
CONTAINED	
INCLUDED	
BINDING	
RELATED	
ENTERED	
PRESENTS	
SET FORTH	
CONTAINED	

Table 2. Example of verbal variation related to ARBITRATION AGREEMENT.

Nevertheless, a significant observation here is that keyness helps to understand that the defining part of the noun-string (ARBITRATION AGREEMENT, ARBITRATION CLAUSE) lies in the word ARBITRATION in an adjectival position (see Table 1). The concept of BURDEN OF PROOF, instead, is a simpler example of a multi-word string linked to a well-established and recognised legal concept. As anticipated, we find here a lower degree of variation and the prepositional aspect adds a defining value. Both lists propose prepositional and verbal variations of the central core lemma *burden of proof* (see Table 3).

CAS corpus	*ECJ corpus*
THE BURDEN OF	THE BURDEN OF
BURDEN OF PROOF	BURDEN OF PROOF
HAVE THE BURDEN	OF THE BURDEN
SHALL HAVE THE	BURDEN ON THE
THE BURDEN TO	TO THE BURDEN
BURDEN OF PROVING	BURDEN OF PROVING
BURDEN TO ESTABLISH	*AN UNREASONABLE BURDEN*
BURDEN OF ESTABLISHING	OF PROVING THAT
TO *ESTABLISH* THAT	BURDEN BORNE BY
OF ESTABLISHING THAT	*THE BURDEN BORNE*
HIS BURDEN OF	THAT THE BURDEN
BEARS THE BURDEN	BORNE BY THE
OF PROOF UPON	OF PROOF IN
OF PROVING THAT	OF PROOF UPON

Table 3. Variations of *burden of proof*.

It should be added that in ECJ the adjective specification *unreasonable* is the only negative connotation expressed. This kind of negative connotation, as Tiersma (1999: 66), points out is very frequent in traditional legal language use but it never occurs in the CAS corpus.

5. Conclusions

The quantitative analysis has signalled a difference in the frequency of some keywords when the two corpora are compared. The keyness comparison highlighted and confirmed the importance of certain crucial concepts. However, in terms of significance this analysis has highlighted extreme no-occurrence values such as no-occurrences of DOPING or OFFENCES in ECJ corpus; no OBLIGATION in the CAS corpus.

From this analysis the variation of key concepts in the juridical language of sports arbitration compared with the ECJ corpus seems to show a trend featuring a radical conceptual diversity in the two standardised legal texts. Consequently, we found limited terminological and conceptual analogies. Whereas the prototypical structure of CAS awards closely reflect ECJ judgements, there is a great degree of terminological variation.

In the future, it may be well worth developing the analysis using the ConcGram software. ConcGram carries out the automatic identification of phraseological variation (i.e. a phraseological search engine) specifically designed to find all word co-occurences (concgrams) in a text (cfr. Milizia/Spinzi 2008: 326-345), thus leaving the evaluation to the researcher to determine whether those co-occurrences constitute meaningful word associations. Phraseological representation of key concepts or occurrences of adjacent terms and related variations may be pursued further in an in-depth study of ConcGrams, i.e. co-occurrences both contiguous and non-contiguous.

References

Biber, Douglas, 1995. *Dimensions of Register Variation*, Cambridge: Cambridge University Press.

De Franchis, Francesco, 1984. *Dizionario Giuridico/Law Dictionary*, Milano: Giuffrè.

Digest of CAS Awards (1986-1998), edited by M. Reeb, Staempfli, Bern, 1998.

Digest of CAS Awards (1998-2000), II, edited by M. Reeb, Kluwer, The Hague, 2002.

Digest of CAS Awards (2000-2003), III, edited by M. Reeb, Kluwer, The Hague, 2005.

Hunston, Susan 2002. *Corpora in Applied Linguistics*. Cambridge: Cambridge University Press.

Hunston Susan 2008. Starting with the Small Words: Patterns, Lexis and Semantic Sequences. *International Journal of Corpus Linguistics* 13/3, 271-295.

Milizia Denise, Spinzi Cinzia, 2008. The 'Terroridiom' Principle between Spoken and Written Discourse. *International Journal of Corpus Linguistics* 13/3, 323-350.

Mortara Garavelli, Bice 2001. *Le parole e la giustizia*, Torino: Einaudi.

Oakey, David 2002. Formulaic Language in English Academic Writing: A Corpus-based Study of the Formal and Functional Variation of a Lexical Phrase in Different Academic Disciplines. In Reppen, Randi / Fitzmaurice, Susan M. / Biber, Douglas (eds) *Using Corpora to Explore Linguistic Variation*. Amsterdam: John Benjamins., 111-129.

Tiersma, Peter M. 1999. *Legal Language*, Chicago: The University of Chicago Press.

Schmitt, Norbert 2004. *Formulaic Sequences, Acquisition, Processing and Use*, Amsterdam: John Benjamins.

Wray, Alison 2002. *Formulaic Language and the Lexicon.* Cambridge: Cambridge University Press.

Internet addresses

Court of Arbitration for Sport <http://www.tas-cas.org/>.

European Court of Justice <http://www.curia.europa.eu>.

Notes on Contributors

PATRIZIA ANESA is a doctoral student at the Department of English Studies, University of Verona, Italy. Her research interests lie mostly in the area of specialised discourse, with particular reference to legal language and courtroom communication. She is currently focusing on the exploration of spoken interaction in jury trials as well as in arbitration practices. She is also particularly interested in the applications of Critical Discourse Analysis and Conversation Analysis to LSP.

VIJAY BHATIA is a Visiting Professor in the Department of English at the City University of Hong Kong. Some of his recent research projects include *Analyzing Genre-bending in Corporate Disclosure Documents*, and *International Arbitration Practice: A Discourse Analytical Study*, in which he leads research teams from more than 20 countries. His research interests are: Genre Analysis of academic and professional discourses, including, legal, business, newspaper, advertising, genres; ESP and Professional Communication; simplification of legal and other public documents; cross-cultural and cross-disciplinary variations in professional genres. His publications include international journal articles, edited books, individually written books, two of which, *Analysing Genre: Language Use in Professional Settings* and *Worlds of Written Discourse: A Genre-based View,* are widely used in genre theory and practice.

CHRISTOPHER N. CANDLIN is Senior Research Professor in the Department of Linguistics at Macquarie University, Sydney. His research interests encompass discourse analysis and pragmatics, and their application to workplace and professional-client communication in the fields of law, dispute resolution, medicine and healthcare, and in disciplinary variation in academic discourse. Recent research has been in the field of HIV/AIDS healthcare, lawyer-client conferencing, psychotherapeutic discourse, arbitral discourse and the discursive bases of professional expertise. His publications include international journal articles and edited books, the most recent of which is *Discourses of Deficit* (with Jonathan Crichton) with Palgrave Macmillan. He edits several international book series, sits on the Editorial Board of key international journals and co-edits the *Journal of Applied Linguistics and Professional Practice* (with Srikant Sarangi).

PAOLA CATENACCIO is a Tenured Researcher at Università degli Studi di Milano. Her research interests span from second language acquisition to translation and discourse analysis, especially in the context of LSP research and with special regard for linguistic aspects of corporate communication. Some of her latest publications are: *Corporate Press Releases: An Overview* (2008); 'De-humanising the Alien: The Construction of Migrants' Rights in EU Legislation' (2007); 'Press Releases as a Hybrid Genre: Addressing the Informative/Promotional Conundrum' (2008). She has also co-edited, with Giuliana Garzone and Gina Poncini, *Multimodality in Corporate Communication. Web Genres and Discursive Identity* (2007) and, with Giuliana Garzone, *Language and Bias in Specialised Discourse* (2008) and *Identities Across Media and Modes: Discursive Perspectives* (2009).

LARISSA D'ANGELO is a research fellow at the Department of Languages, Literatures and Cultures of the University of Bergamo. After graduating in Foreign Languages and Literatures, she specialized in English Language in the USA (Youngstown State University), obtaining an MA, a TESOL Certificate and a Certificate in Children's and Young Adult Literature. Her main research interests deal with the analysis of gender and cultural identity variation in academic discourse. She has been involved in national and international research projects on academic language and legal discourse.

CHIARA DEGANO is a Tenured Researcher in English Linguistics and Translation at Università degli Studi di Milano, Department of Contemporary Languages and Cultures. Her research focuses mainly on Discourse Studies, which she integrates with corpus linguistics and argumentation theory. Within this frame, her interests concentrate on two main strands of research: representation of conflict in the media, and language for special purposes with particular regard for corporate communication. She is the author of a monograph (*Discorsi di guerra. Il prologo del conflitto iracheno nella stampa britannica e italiana* [War discourses. The prologue of the Iraqi conflict in the British and Italian press] 2008), and of several articles published in international journals and in edited volumes.

OLGA DENTI is a researcher and lecturer of English Language and Translation at the Faculty of Economics, University of Cagliari, Italy. Her research interests include Sociolinguistics, Discourse Analysis, Gender and ESP. She is currently focusing her research on Legal English and the Language of Tourism.

ALESSANDRA FAZIO specialised in Terminology at the Ecole de Traduction et d'Interpretation at the University of Geneva. She is a researcher in English Studies at the Università degli Studi di Roma 'Foro Italico'. Her research interests lie in terminology and in the creation of terminological tools, applied linguistics and cognitive linguistics. She is mainly involved in the analysis of the specific language of sport and sports sciences. Recently she has addressed the problem of sports related arbitration discourse analysis. She has participated in several national and international research projects. Currently, she is a member of the Advisory Committee of the European Association for Terminology AET-EAFT and of the International Society for Knowledge Organization (ISKO).

CELINA FRADE has a PhD in Linguistics from Universidade Federal do Rio de Janeiro and is currently a lecturer in English for Specific Purposes at the Multidisciplinary Institute of Universidade Federal Rural do Rio de Janeiro, Brazil. As an ESP researcher, mainly in legal English, she designs and develops legal materials for Brazilian professionals and has published various articles and chapters in related journals and books, such as *International Journal for the Semiotics of Law* and Peter Lang's *Linguistic Insights* series. Since 2002, she has been investigating the discourse of international arbitration and its implications in Brazil as part of international projects conducted by a group of linguists and legal practitioners.

GIULIANA GARZONE is Full Professor of English Linguistics and Translation at Università degli Studi di Milano, Italy. Her main field of investigation is specialized discourse in its different domains, which she has explored in a discourse analytical perspective, integrating it whenever necessary with computerized interrogation routines, also in light of her work on the theoretical issues involved in combining Critical Discourse Analysis with Corpus Linguistics. She has co-ordinated several research projects and published extensively on legal language, on scientific discourse, and on business communication. In the latter domain, she has recently devoted specific attention to multimodality and to the analysis of text types and genres embedded in the web-mediated environment, an issue she has also investigated with reference to other types of communication, e.g. political communication. She has also (co-)edited several volumes (most recently, *Discourse, Ideology and Specialized Communication*, with S. Sarangi, 2007; *The Use of English in Institutional and Business Settings,* with C. Ilie, 2007; *Language and Bias,*2008, and *Identities Across Media and Modes: Discursive Perspectives*, 2009, with P. Catenaccio). Her other research interests are in translation and interpreting studies, on which she has also published extensively. She is general editor (with A. Cardinaletti e F. Frasnedi) of the book series *Lingua, traduzione, didattica.*

MICHELA GIORDANO is a researcher and lecturer of English Language and Translation in the Faculty of Political Science, University of Cagliari, Italy. Her research interests include Language Teaching and Methodology, Sociolinguistics, Psycholinguistics, Gender, and ESP. She is currently focusing her research on the Language of Politics and Legal English.

MAURIZIO GOTTI is Professor of English Language and Translation and Director of the Research Centre on Specialized Languages (CERLIS) at the University of Bergamo. He has been President of the Italian Association of University Language Centres (1997-2000; 2004-2007), of the Italian Association of English Studies (1999-2001) and of the European Confederation of University Language Centres (2000-2004). His main research areas are English syntax (*English*

Diachronic Syntax (ed.), 1993; *Variation in Central Modals* (co-author), 2002), English lexicology and lexicography (*The Language of Thieves and Vagabonds*, 1999) and the features and origins of specialized discourse, both in a synchronic and diachronic perspective (*Robert Boyle and the Language of Science*, 1996; *Investigating Specialized Discourse*, ^{2}2008). He is a member of the Editorial Board of national and international journals, and edits the *Linguistic Insights* series for Peter Lang.

STEFANIA M. MACI is Researcher of English Language at the University of Bergamo. She is currently involved in international research projects on academic English and legal discourse. She has recently coedited with D.S. Giannoni, *Identity Traits in English Academic Discourse*. Special issue of *Linguistica e Filologia* 27 (2008) and published 'The Research Letter: an emerging medical genre', in Di Martino/Polese/Solly (eds) *Identity and Culture in English Domain-specific Discourse* (2008); 'Litigation Procedures in Arbitral Practice: A case of Arbitral Litigation?', in S. Sarčevič, *Legal Language in Action*. Zagreb (2009).

MICHELE SALA, PhD (University of Bergamo), MA (Youngstown State University, Ohio), is a researcher in English Language and Translation at the University of Bergamo (Faculty of Foreign Languages and Literatures). His research activity and major publications deal with language for specific purposes and, more specifically, the analysis of the linguistic, textual and pragmatic aspects of legal translation, and the application of genre and discourse analytical methods to a corpus-based study of legal discourse ('Argumentative styles as cultural identity traits in legal studies', 2008). He has also published in the field of academic discourse (*Persuasion and politeness in academic discourse*, 2008), pragmatics and cognitive linguistics.

GIROLAMO TESSUTO is Associate Professor of English Language and Translation at the Faculty of Law of Seconda Università degli Studi di Napoli. His research interests are mainly in the field of English legal discourse and genre analysis in academic and professional settings. Besides a monograph on discourse, language and terminology applied to English criminal law, he has published several research papers in English legal language in a variety of applications. His most recent publications are 'Discourse Systems in English Arbitration Awards' (2008), 'Drafting Laws in UK Settings: Implementing Plain Language and Discourse?' (2008), 'Legal Concepts and Terminography: Analysis and Application' (2008), 'Writer Identity in the Introduction Section of Academic Law Research Articles' (2008).

ANNE WAGNER (Ph.D.) is Senior Lecturer at the Université du Littoral Côte d'Opale (France) and Research Professor in Legal Semiotics and Legal Discourse Analysis at China University of Political Science and Law (Beijing). She is a member of the *Hong Kong SAR Competitive Earmarked Research Grant* project on 'International Commercial Arbitration Practices: A Discourse Analytical Study'. She is the Editor-in-Chief of the *International Journal for the Semiotics of Law* (Springer). She is the President of the *International Roundtables for the Semiotics of Law*. She is an editorial board member of *SemiotiX* and one of the three international advisors of the *Translated Series on Law and Language* (China University of Political Science and Law Press). She has extensively published research papers in the area of law and semiotics, legal discourse, law and culture, and legal translation. Her books include *La Langue de la Common Law* (2002), *Contemporary Issues in the Semiotics of Law: Cultural and Symbolic Analyses in a Global Context* (2005), *Images in Law* (2006), *Legal Language and the Search for Clarity* (2006), *Interpretation, Law and the Construction of Meaning* (2006), *Obscurity and Clarity in the Law* (2008), *Diversity and Tolerance in Socio-Legal Context* (2009).

Linguistic Insights

Studies in Language and Communication

This series aims to promote specialist language studies in the fields of linguistic theory and applied linguistics, by publishing volumes that focus on specific aspects of language use in one or several languages and provide valuable insights into language and communication research. A cross-disciplinary approach is favoured and most European languages are accepted.

The series includes two types of books:

- **Monographs** – featuring in-depth studies on special aspects of language theory, language analysis or language teaching.
- **Collected papers** – assembling papers from workshops, conferences or symposia.

Each volume of the series is subjected to a double peer-reviewing process.

Vol. 1 Maurizio Gotti & Marina Dossena (eds)
Modality in Specialized Texts. Selected Papers of the 1st CERLIS Conference.
421 pages. 2001. ISBN 3-906767-10-8. US-ISBN 0-8204-5340-4

Vol. 2 Giuseppina Cortese & Philip Riley (eds)
Domain-specific English. Textual Practices across Communities and Classrooms.
420 pages. 2002. ISBN 3-906768-98-8. US-ISBN 0-8204-5884-8

Vol. 3 Maurizio Gotti, Dorothee Heller & Marina Dossena (eds)
Conflict and Negotiation in Specialized Texts. Selected Papers of the 2nd CERLIS Conference.
470 pages. 2002. ISBN 3-906769-12-7. US-ISBN 0-8204-5887-2

Editorial address:

Prof. Maurizio Gotti
Università di Bergamo, Facoltà di Lingue e Letterature Straniere,
Via Salvecchio 19, 24129 Bergamo, Italy
Fax: 0039 035 2052789, E-Mail: m.gotti@unibg.it

Vol. 4 Maurizio Gotti, Marina Dossena, Richard Dury, Roberta Facchinetti & Maria Lima
Variation in Central Modals. A Repertoire of Forms and Types of Usage in Middle English and Early Modern English.
364 pages. 2002. ISBN 3-906769-84-4. US-ISBN 0-8204-5898-8

Vol. 5 Stefania Nuccorini (ed.)
Phrases and Phraseology. Data and Descriptions.
187 pages. 2002. ISBN 3-906770-08-7. US-ISBN 0-8204-5933-X

Vol. 6 Vijay Bhatia, Christopher N. Candlin & Maurizio Gotti (eds)
Legal Discourse in Multilingual and Multicultural Contexts. Arbitration Texts in Europe.
385 pages. 2003. ISBN 3-906770-85-0. US-ISBN 0-8204-6254-3

Vol. 7 Marina Dossena & Charles Jones (eds)
Insights into Late Modern English. 2nd edition.
378 pages. 2003, 2007.
ISBN 978-3-03911-257-9. US-ISBN 978-0-8204-8927-8

Vol. 8 Maurizio Gotti
Specialized Discourse. Linguistic Features and Changing Conventions.
351 pages. 2003, 2005.
ISBN 3-03910-606-6. US-ISBN 0-8204-7000-7

Vol. 9 Alan Partington, John Morley & Louann Haarman (eds)
Corpora and Discourse.
420 pages. 2004. ISBN 3-03910-026-2. US-ISBN 0-8204-6262-4

Vol. 10 Martina Möllering
The Acquisition of German Modal Particles. A Corpus-Based Approach.
290 pages. 2004. ISBN 3-03910-043-2. US-ISBN 0-8204-6273-X

Vol. 11 David Hart (ed.)
English Modality in Context. Diachronic Perspectives.
261 pages. 2003. ISBN 3-03910-046-7. US-ISBN 0-8204-6852-5

Vol. 12 Wendy Swanson
Modes of Co-reference as an Indicator of Genre.
430 pages. 2003. ISBN 3-03910-052-1. US-ISBN 0-8204-6855-X

Vol. 13 Gina Poncini
Discursive Strategies in Multicultural Business Meetings.
2nd edition. 338 pages. 2004, 2007.
ISBN 978-3-03911-296-8. US-ISBN 978-0-8204-8937-7

Vol. 14 Christopher N. Candlin & Maurizio Gotti (eds)
Intercultural Aspects of Specialized Communication.
2nd edition. 369 pages. 2004, 2007.
ISBN 978-3-03911-258-6. US-ISBN 978-0-8204-8926-1

Vol. 15 Gabriella Del Lungo Camiciotti & Elena Tognini Bonelli (eds)
Academic Discourse. New Insights into Evaluation.
234 pages. 2004. ISBN 3-03910-353-9. US-ISBN 0-8204-7016-3

Vol. 16 Marina Dossena & Roger Lass (eds)
Methods and Data in English Historical Dialectology.
405 pages. 2004. ISBN 3-03910-362-8. US-ISBN 0-8204-7018-X

Vol. 17 Judy Noguchi
The Science Review Article. An Opportune Genre in the Construction of Science.
274 pages. 2006. ISBN 3-03910-426-8. US-ISBN 0-8204-7034-1

Vol. 18 Giuseppina Cortese & Anna Duszak (eds)
Identity, Community, Discourse. English in Intercultural Settings.
495 pages. 2005. ISBN 3-03910-632-5. US-ISBN 0-8204-7163-1

Vol. 19 Anna Trosborg & Poul Erik Flyvholm Jørgensen (eds)
Business Discourse. Texts and Contexts.
250 pages. 2005. ISBN 3-03910-606-6. US-ISBN 0-8204-7000-7

Vol. 20 Christopher Williams
Tradition and Change in Legal English. Verbal Constructions in Prescriptive Texts.
2nd revised edition. 216 pages. 2005, 2007. ISBN 978-3-03911-444-3.

Vol. 21 Katarzyna Dziubalska-Kolaczyk & Joanna Przedlacka (eds)
English Pronunciation Models: A Changing Scene.
2nd edition. 476 pages. 2005, 2008. ISBN 978-3-03911-682-9.

Vol. 22 Christián Abello-Contesse, Rubén Chacón-Beltrán, M. Dolores López-Jiménez & M. Mar Torreblanca-López (eds)
Age in L2 Acquisition and Teaching.
214 pages. 2006. ISBN 3-03910-668-6. US-ISBN 0-8204-7174-7

Vol. 23 Vijay K. Bhatia, Maurizio Gotti, Jan Engberg & Dorothee Heller (eds)
Vagueness in Normative Texts.
474 pages. 2005. ISBN 3-03910-653-8. US-ISBN 0-8204-7169-0

Vol. 24 Paul Gillaerts & Maurizio Gotti (eds)
Genre Variation in Business Letters. 2nd printing.
407 pages. 2008. ISBN 978-3-03911-681-2.

Vol. 25 Ana María Hornero, María José Luzón & Silvia Murillo (eds)
Corpus Linguistics. Applications for the Study of English.
2nd printing. 526 pages. 2006, 2008. ISBN 978-3-03911-726-0

Vol. 26 J. Lachlan Mackenzie & María de los Ángeles Gómez-González (eds)
Studies in Functional Discourse Grammar.
259 pages. 2005. ISBN 3-03910-696-1 / US-ISBN 0-8204-7558-0

Vol. 27 Debbie G. E. Ho
Classroom Talk. Exploring the Sociocultural Structure of Formal ESL Learning.
2nd edition. 254 pages. 2006, 2007. ISBN 978-3-03911-434-4

Vol. 28 Javier Pérez-Guerra, Dolores González-Álvarez, Jorge L. Bueno-Alonso & Esperanza Rama-Martínez (eds)
'Of Varying Language and Opposing Creed': New Insights into Late Modern English.
455 pages. 2007. ISBN 978-3-03910-788-9

Vol. 29 Francesca Bargiela-Chiappini & Maurizio Gotti (eds)
Asian Business Discourse(s).
350 pages. 2005. ISBN 3-03910-804-2 / US-ISBN 0-8204-7574-2

Vol. 30 Nicholas Brownlees (ed.)
News Discourse in Early Modern Britain. Selected Papers of CHINED 2004.
300 pages. 2006. ISBN 3-03910-805-0 / US-ISBN 0-8204-8025-8

Vol. 31 Roberta Facchinetti & Matti Rissanen (eds)
Corpus-based Studies of Diachronic English.
300 pages. 2006. ISBN 3-03910-851-4 / US-ISBN 0-8204-8040-1

Vol. 32 Marina Dossena & Susan M. Fitzmaurice (eds)
Business and Official Correspondence: Historical Investigations.
209 pages. 2006. ISBN 3-03910-880-8 / US-ISBN 0-8204-8352-4

Vol. 33 Giuliana Garzone & Srikant Sarangi (eds)
Discourse, Ideology and Specialized Communication.
494 pages. 2007. ISBN 978-3-03910-888-6

Vol. 34 Giuliana Garzone & Cornelia Ilie (eds)
The Use of English in Institutional and Business Settings.
An Intercultural Perspective.
372 pages. 2007. ISBN 978-3-03910-889-3

Vol. 35 Vijay K. Bhatia & Maurizio Gotti (eds)
Explorations in Specialized Genres.
316 pages. 2006. ISBN 3-03910-995-2 / US-ISBN 0-8204-8372-9

Vol. 36 Heribert Picht (ed.)
Modern Approaches to Terminological Theories and Applications.
432 pages. 2006. ISBN 3-03911-156-6 / US-ISBN 0-8204-8380-X

Vol. 37 Anne Wagner & Sophie Cacciaguidi-Fahy (eds)
Legal Language and the Search for Clarity / Le langage juridique et la quête de clarté.
Practice and Tools / Pratiques et instruments.
487 pages. 2006. ISBN 3-03911-169-8 / US-ISBN 0-8388-5

Vol. 38 Juan Carlos Palmer-Silveira, Miguel F. Ruiz-Garrido &
Inmaculada Fortanet-Gómez (eds)
Intercultural and International Business Communication:
Theory, Research and Teaching.
2nd edition. 343 pages. 2006, 2008. ISBN 978-3-03911-680-5

Vol. 39 Christiane Dalton-Puffer, Dieter Kastovsky, Nikolaus Ritt &
Herbert Schendl (eds)
Syntax, Style and Grammatical Norms: English from 1500–2000.
250 pages. 2006. ISBN 3-03911-181-7 / US-ISBN 0-8204-8394-X

Vol. 40 Marina Dossena & Irma Taavitsainen (eds)
Diachronic Perspectives on Domain-Specific English.
280 pages. 2006. ISBN 3-03910-176-0 / US-ISBN 0-8204-8391-5

Vol. 41 John Flowerdew & Maurizio Gotti (eds)
Studies in Specialized Discourse.
293 pages. 2006. ISBN 3-03911-178-7

Vol. 42 Ken Hyland & Marina Bondi (eds)
Academic Discourse Across Disciplines.
320 pages. 2006. ISBN 3-03911-183-3 / US-ISBN 0-8204-8396-6

Vol. 43 Paul Gillaerts & Philip Shaw (eds)
The Map and the Landscape: Norms and Practices in Genre.
256 pages. 2006. ISBN 3-03911-182-5 / US-ISBN 0-8204-8395-4

Vol. 44 Maurizio Gotti & Davide Giannoni (eds)
New Trends in Specialized Discourse Analysis.
301 pages. 2006. ISBN 3-03911-184-1 / US-ISBN 0-8204-8381-8

Vol. 45 Maurizio Gotti & Françoise Salager-Meyer (eds)
Advances in Medical Discourse Analysis: Oral and Written Contexts.
492 pages. 2006. ISBN 3-03911-185-X / US-ISBN 0-8204-8382-6

Vol. 46 Maurizio Gotti & Susan Šarcević (eds)
Insights into Specialized Translation.
396 pages. 2006. ISBN 3-03911-186-8 / US-ISBN 0-8204-8383-4

Vol. 47 Khurshid Ahmad & Margaret Rogers (eds)
Evidence-based LSP: Translation, Text and Terminology.
584 pages. 2007. ISBN 978-3-03911-187-9

Vol. 48 Hao Sun & Dániel Z. Kádár (eds)
It's the Dragon's Turn: Chinese Institutional Discourses.
262 pages. 2008. ISBN 978-3-03911-175-6

Vol. 49 Cristina Suárez-Gómez
Relativization in Early English (950-1250): the Position of Relative Clauses.
149 pages. 2006. ISBN 3-03911-203-1 / US-ISBN 0-8204-8904-2

Vol. 50 Maria Vittoria Calvi & Luisa Chierichetti (eds)
Nuevas tendencias en el discurso de especialidad.
319 pages. 2006. ISBN 978-3-03911-261-6

Vol. 51 Mari Carmen Campoy & María José Luzón (eds)
Spoken Corpora in Applied Linguistics.
274 pages. 2008. ISBN 978-3-03911-275-3

Vol. 52 Konrad Ehlich & Dorothee Heller (Hrsg.)
Die Wissenschaft und ihre Sprachen.
323 pages. 2006. ISBN 978-3-03911-272-2

Vol. 53 Jingyu Zhang
The Semantic Salience Hierarchy Model: The L2 Acquisition of Psych Predicates
273 pages. 2007. ISBN 978-3-03911-300-2

Vol. 54 Norman Fairclough, Giuseppina Cortese & Patrizia Ardizzone (eds)
Discourse and Contemporary Social Change.
555 pages. 2007. ISBN 978-3-03911-276-0

Vol. 55 Jan Engberg, Marianne Grove Ditlevsen, Peter Kastberg & Martin Stegu (eds)
New Directions in LSP Teaching.
331 pages. 2007. ISBN 978-3-03911-433-7

Vol. 56 Dorothee Heller & Konrad Ehlich (Hrsg.)
Studien zur Rechtskommunikation.
322 pages. 2007. ISBN 978-3-03911-436-8

Vol. 57 Forthcoming.

Vol. 58 Carmen Frehner
Email – SMS – MMS
294 pages. 2008. ISBN 978-3-03911-451-1

Vol. 59 Isabel Balteiro
The Directionality of Conversion in English: A Dia-Synchronic Study.
276 pages. 2007. ISBN 978-3-03911-241-8

Vol. 60 Maria Milagros Del Saz Rubio
English Discourse Markers of Reformulation.
237 pages. 2007. ISBN 978-3-03911-196-1

Vol. 61 Sally Burgess & Pedro Martín-Martín (eds)
English as an Additional Language in Research Publication and Communication.
259 pages. 2008. ISBN 978-3-03911-462-7

Vol. 62 Sandrine Onillon
Pratiques et représentations de l'écrit.
458 pages. 2008. ISBN 978-3-03911-464-1

Vol. 63 Hugo Bowles & Paul Seedhouse (eds)
Conversation Analysis and Language for Specific Purposes.
2nd edition. 337 pages. 2007, 2009. ISBN 978-3-0343-0045-2

Vol. 64 Vijay K. Bhatia, Christopher N. Candlin & Paola Evangelisti Allori (eds)
Language, Culture and the Law.
The Formulation of Legal Concepts across Systems and Cultures.
342 pages. 2008. ISBN 978-3-03911-470-2

Vol. 65 Jonathan Culpeper & Dániel Z. Kádár (eds)
Historical (Im)politeness.
300 pages. 2010. ISBN 978-3-03911-496-2

Vol. 66 Linda Lombardo (ed.)
Using Corpora to Learn about Language and Discourse.
237 pages. 2009. ISBN 978-3-03911-522-8

Vol. 67 Natsumi Wakamoto
Extroversion/Introversion in Foreign Language Learning.
Interactions with Learner Strategy Use.
159 pages. 2009. ISBN 978-3-03911-596-9

Vol. 68 Eva Alcón-Soler (ed.)
Learning How to Request in an Instructed Language Learning Context.
260 pages. 2008. ISBN 978-3-03911-601-0

Vol. 69 Domenico Pezzini
The Translation of Religious Texts in the Middle Ages.
428 pages. 2008. ISBN 978-3-03911-600-3

Vol. 70 Tomoko Tode
Effects of Frequency in Classroom Second Language Learning.
Quasi-experiment and stimulated-recall analysis.
195 pages. 2008. ISBN 978-3-03911-602-7

Vol. 71 Egor Tsedryk
Fusion symétrique et alternances ditransitives.
211 pages. 2009. ISBN 978-3-03911-609-6

Vol. 72 Cynthia J. Kellett Bidoli & Elana Ochse (eds)
English in International Deaf Communication.
444 pages. 2008. ISBN 978-3-03911-610-2

Vol. 73 Joan C. Beal, Carmela Nocera & Massimo Sturiale (eds)
Perspectives on Prescriptivism.
269 pages. 2008. ISBN 978-3-03911-632-4

Vol. 74 Carol Taylor Torsello, Katherine Ackerley & Erik Castello (eds)
Corpora for University Language Teachers.
308 pages. 2008. ISBN 978-3-03911-639-3

Vol. 75 María Luisa Pérez Cañado (ed.)
English Language Teaching in the European Credit Transfer System:
Facing the Challenge.
251 pages. 2009. ISBN 978-3-03911-654-6

Vol. 76 Marina Dossena & Ingrid Tieken-Boon van Ostade (eds)
Studies in Late Modern English Correspondence. Methodology and Data.
291 pages. 2008. ISBN 978-3-03911-658-4

Vol. 77 Ingrid Tieken-Boon van Ostade & Wim van der Wurff (eds)
Current Issues in Late Modern English.
436 pages. 2009. ISBN 978-3-03911-660-7

Vol. 78 Marta Navarro Coy (ed.)
Practical Approaches to Foreign Language Teaching and Learning.
297 pages. 2009. ISBN 978-3-03911-661-4

Vol. 79 Qing Ma
Second Language Vocabulary Acquisition.
333 pages. 2009. ISBN 978-3-03911-666-9

Vol. 80 Martin Solly, Michelangelo Conoscenti & Sandra Campagna (eds)
Verbal/Visual Narrative Texts in Higher Education.
384 pages. 2008. ISBN 978-3-03911-672-0

Vol. 81 Meiko Matsumoto
From Simple Verbs to Periphrastic Expressions:
The Historical Development of Composite Predicates, Phrasal Verbs,
and Related Constructions in English.
235 pages. 2008. ISBN 978-3-03911-675-1

Vol. 82 Melinda Dooly
Doing Diversity. Teachers' Construction of Their Classroom Reality.
180 pages. 2009. ISBN 978-3-03911-687-4

Vol. 83 Victoria Guillén-Nieto, Carmen Marimón-Llorca & Chelo Vargas-Sierra (eds)
Intercultural Business Communication and
Simulation and Gaming Methodology.
392 pages. 2009. ISBN 978-3-03911-688-1

Vol. 84 Maria Grazia Guido
English as a Lingua Franca in Cross-cultural Immigration Domains.
285 pages. 2008. ISBN 978-3-03911-689-8

Vol. 85 Erik Castello
Text Complexity and Reading Comprehension Tests.
352 pages. 2008. ISBN 978-3-03911-717-8

Vol. 86 Forthcoming.

Vol. 87 Carmen Navarro, Rosa Mª Rodríguez Abella, Francesca Dalle Pezze
& Renzo Miotti (eds)
La comunicación especializada.
355 pages. 2008. ISBN 978-3-03911-733-8

Vol. 88 Kiriko Sato
The Development from Case-Forms to Prepositional Constructions
in Old English Prose.
231 pages. 2009. ISBN 978-3-03911-763-5

Vol. 89 Dorothee Heller (Hrsg.)
Formulierungsmuster in deutscher und italienischer Fachkommunikation.
Intra- und interlinguale Perspektiven.
315 pages. 2008. ISBN 978-3-03911-778-9

Vol. 90 Henning Bergenholtz, Sandro Nielsen & Sven Tarp (eds)
Lexicography at a Crossroads. Dictionaries and Encyclopedias Today,
Lexicographical Tools Tomorrow.
372 pages. 2009. ISBN 978-3-03911-799-4

Vol. 91 Manouchehr Moshtagh Khorasani
The Development of Controversies: From the Early Modern Period
to Online Discussion Forums.
317 pages. 2009. ISBN 978-3-3911-711-6

Vol. 92 María Luisa Carrió-Pastor (ed.)
Content and Language Integrated Learning: Cultural Diversity.
178 pages. 2009. ISBN 978-3-3911-818-2

Vol. 93-94 Forthcoming.

Vol. 95 Facchinetti Roberta, Crystal David, Seidlhofer Barbara (eds)
From International to Local English – And Back Again.
268 pages. 2010. ISBN 978-3-0343-0011-7

Vol. 96 Forthcoming.

Vol. 97 Sylvie Hancil (ed.)
The Role of Prosody in Affective Speech.
403 pages. 2009. ISBN 978-3-03911-696-6

Vol. 98 Marina Dossena & Roger Lass (eds)
Studies in English and European Historical Dialectology.
257 pages. 2009. ISBN 978-3-0343-0024-7

Vol. 99 Christine Béal
Les interactions quotidiennes en français et en anglais.
De l'approche comparative à l'analyse des situations interculturelles
424 pages. 2010. ISBN 978-3-0343-0027-8

Vol. 100 Maurizio Gotti (ed.)
Commonality and Individuality in Academic Discourse.
398 pages. 2009. ISBN 978-3-0343-0023-0

Vol. 101 Javier E. Díaz Vera & Rosario Caballero (eds)
Textual Healing: Studies in Medieval English Medical,
Scientific and Technical Texts.
213 pages. 2009. ISBN 978-3-03911-822-9

Vol. 102 Nuria Edo Marzá
The Specialised Lexicographical Approach: A Step further in Dictionary-making.
316 pages. 2009. ISBN 978-3-0343-0043-8

Vol. 103 Carlos Prado-Alonso, Lidia Gómez-García, Iria Pastor-Gómez &
David Tizón-Couto (eds)
New Trends and Methodologies in Applied English Language Research.
Diachronic, Diatopic and Contrastive Studies.
348 pages. 2009. ISBN 978-3-0343-0046-9

Vol. 104-108 Forthcoming.

Vol. 109 Ángeles Linde López & Rosalía Crespo Jiménez (eds)
Professional English in the European context: The EHEA challenge.
374 pages. 2010. ISBN 978-3-0343-0088-9

Vol. 110 Rosalía Rodríguez-Vázquez
The Rhythm of Speech, Verse and Vocal Music: A New Theory.
394 pages. 2010. ISBN 978-3-0343-0309-5

Vol. 111 Anastasios Tsangalidis & Roberta Facchinetti (eds)
Studies on English Modality. In Honour of Frank Palmer.
392 pages. 2009. ISBN 978-3-0343-0310-1

Vol. 112-114 Forthcoming.

Vol. 115 Giuliana Garzone & Paola Catenaccio (eds)
Identities across Media and Modes: Discursive Perspectives.
379 pages. 2009. ISBN 978-3-0343-0386-6

Vol. 116 Elena Landone
Los marcadores del discurso y cortesía verbal en español.
390 pages. 2010. ISBN 978-3-0343-0413-9

Vol. 117 Forthcoming.

Vol. 118 David Hirsh
Academic Vocabulary in Context.
217 pages. 2010. ISBN 978-3-0343-0426-9

Vol. 119-122 Forthcoming.

Vol. 123 Vijay K. Bhatia, Christopher N. Candlin & Maurizio Gotti (eds)
The Discourses of Dispute Resolution.
290 pages. 2010. ISBN 978-3-0343-0476-4